THE WOMAN
IN JEWISH STUDIES

The Woman Question in Jewish Studies

SUSANNAH HESCHEL
AND SARAH IMHOFF

PRINCETON UNIVERSITY PRESS
PRINCETON & OXFORD

Published by Princeton University Press
41 William Street, Princeton, New Jersey 08540
99 Banbury Road, Oxford OX2 6JX

press.princeton.edu

Library of Congress Cataloging-in-Publication Data

Names: Heschel, Susannah, author. | Imhoff, Sarah, author.
Title: The woman question in Jewish studies / Susannah Heschel and Sarah Imhoff.
Description: Princeton : Princeton University Press, [2025] | Includes bibliographical references and index.
Identifiers: LCCN 2024023699 (print) | LCCN 2024023700 (ebook) | ISBN 9780691215433 | ISBN 9780691215440 (pbk.) | ISBN 9780691215426 (ebook)
Subjects: LCSH: Women in Judaism—Study and teaching. | BISAC: SOCIAL SCIENCE / Women's Studies | RELIGION / Judaism / General
Classification: LCC HQ1172 .H444 2025 (print) | LCC HQ1172 (ebook) | DDC 296.082—dc23/eng/20240730
LC record available at https://lccn.loc.gov/2024023699
LC ebook record available at https://lccn.loc.gov/2024023700

British Library Cataloging-in-Publication Data is available

Editorial: Fred Appel and James Collier
Production Editorial: Natalie Baan
Cover Design: Katie Osborne
Production: Lauren Reese
Publicity: William Pagdatoon
Copyeditor: Kathleen Kageff

This book has been composed in Arno

10 9 8 7 6 5 4 3 2 1

CONTENTS

ACKNOWLEDGMENTS

WE BEGIN BY EXPRESSING OUR GRATITUDE to all our colleagues who shared their stories with us. We're especially mindful that some stories of discrimination and harassment were painful to discuss. In including your voices in our book, we hope to bring radical change to the field.

We thank our colleagues, students, and friends: With your openness and willingness to think with us, you reminded us what a truly remarkable field Jewish studies can be. Thank you to Kecia Ali, Sarah Ifft Decker, Marianne Hirsch, Rachel Adler, Naomi Seidman, and Nancy Chi Cantalupo for being great conversation partners and colleagues. We appreciate colleagues and editors who took the time to read this work: Samira Mehta and Heather White each read and commented on sections, and Laura Holliday read the manuscript in its entirety. Our anonymous reviewers helped us improve the book in countless ways.

This book is a collaborative effort, but we also have individual people we'd like to thank.

Sarah: I would like to express my gratitude for the many brilliant graduate students who helped us think about the book, and whose presence reminded us of why the future of the field matters so much. I want to offer special thanks to Sabina Ali for her immaculate attention to the manuscript in its final stages; to Esra Onal and Deepthi Murali, who worked tirelessly to wrangle data from pdfs to csvs; to Admiral Weiland, who helped imagine what data we could collect; to Alex Tran, who helped with data visualization; and to all the graduate students in the Borns Jewish Studies Program and Religious Studies Department at Indiana University, who inspire me to think boldly about the future of academic life. I also want to offer special thanks to Kathryn Cooper, who read through textbooks and compiled all the mentions of women and gender in each. And then there is the gratitude I do not express enough, to the family I was born with and the families we made along the way: Michael Dodson, Eva Mroczek, my parents, Moses the dog, and Mr. Meowgi the cat.

Susannah: I started thinking about this book while staying in the home of Irene Kacandes and began writing it in the beautiful summer garden of Klaus Milich: two warm and generous Dartmouth colleagues and friends whom I thank for their extraordinary hospitality over many years. I also would like to thank several colleagues for their guidance, including Kristi Clemens, Courtney Irby, Giavanna Munafo, Jennifer Brooke Sargent, Sonu Bedi, Carrie Pelzel, and Kate Norton. Our fantastic Dartmouth students make our classrooms exciting sites of intellectual collaboration, and several of my students were especially helpful with research for this book, particularly Juliann Li, Katelyn Zeser, and Morgan Pak. To Deans Elizabeth Smith and Matthew Delmont: my gratitude for your support over the years. I also thank Constance Buchanan and Alison Bernstein, both now deceased, who gave me two generous personal grants from the Ford Foundation that launched my engagement with feminist issues in Islamic and Jewish studies. Most of all, thanks to the family and friends who keep me happy, wined, and dined: Jim, Gittel, Avigael, Elda, Dierre, Julie, Annette, Rick, Joe, Siegfried, Thomas, Harry, Mark, Cathy, Shaul, Veronika, Jonathan, Ezzedine, Sean, and Tarek.

We both wish to thank our respective academic institutions, Indiana University and Dartmouth College, for their generous financial support for our scholarship and for giving us the time we need for our research and writing. Sarah extends special gratitude to Kalani Craig, Michelle Dalmau, and everyone at Indiana

University's Institute for Digital Humanities for both funding and intellectual support as she ventured into bibliometrics.

Our special thanks to Fred Appel for his helpful and encouraging editorship and to all those at Princeton University Press, who produce important and beautiful books.

Introduction

WHEN SUSANNAH WAS AN UNDERGRADUATE, she had no women professors in any subject. When she entered graduate school in the 1980s, there were women on the faculty at the university, but none in Jewish studies and very few women graduate students. In class, when she raised a question about women in Jewish history or brought a feminist analysis to a text, she was met with dismissiveness ("that's not relevant" or "let's move on"), and male professors and graduate students would go off for lunch or coffee together without including her. As a graduate student, she developed a course, "The Feminist Critique of Judaism." After she graduated, a male adjunct took over the course and changed its title to "The Jewish Woman." No women served on her dissertation committee because there were no tenured women professors in her subfield.

When Sarah was a graduate student in the early 2000s, she had several women professors, including one on her dissertation committee. In her day, more and more women were entering the field as graduate students, but she still saw both the canonical works of Jewish studies and the towering scholars in the field as overwhelmingly male. Trans and nonbinary scholars were rarely included at all. Now she is a tenured full professor in a Jewish studies program that had few women faculty in the mid-1990s but whose core faculty is now made of five women and seven men.

In our careers, both of us have had wonderful male mentors and colleagues. We have also witnessed sexism and harassment.

When we look back, we see a field that has not always welcomed people who are not white, Jewish, cisgender, or straight men, or people who want to study gender or use feminist methods. But we also recognize how much has changed.

From the outset, we have struggled with how to talk about women and gender without essentializing or suggesting that a man-woman gender binary is an objective truth. Much of our struggle stems from the fact that in both the historical moments we discuss and our present moment, many people believe and act as if the categories of men and women are fixed and unchangeable. We understand gender to be constructed by historical and cultural forces, but we also recognize that those cultural and historical forces have created a normative male-female binary in most of the contexts within which Jewish studies has operated. By describing worlds in which many people assume that there are men and there are women, we do not mean to endorse this view of the world, but we equally do not want to deny that these binarisms strongly shape the academic and professional worlds of Jewish studies scholars. In this book, we focus largely on people who identify (or identified) as women because we believe that we can demonstrate many of the gendered issues the field faces through their stories.

Our decision to write this book together arose from our frustration over recent scholarship in Jewish studies that excludes, ignores, or tokenizes women. We began collecting evidence: We counted the anthologies, conferences, and editorial boards of journals that had no women, or had just one or two. We noted scholarship that ignores gender in inexcusable ways, such as studies of pogroms that glossed over rape with a passing phrase, and studies that think about gender only in relation to women, as if femaleness is the only gender.

Speaking to scholars in the field, we were very disturbed to find that so many people, from graduate students to full professors, have been targets of gendered exclusion, denigration, harassment, or even assault. We present their accounts anonymously and ask our readers to give them careful attention. We know women in nearly every workplace have had similar experiences; here, we ask what is specific to Jewish studies. Drawing a connection between our quantitative data on citation of women with the discrimination and harassment reported to us leads us to question the culture of the field. We look at the field's history as it first took shape during the nineteenth century, and we look at specific subfields to understand examples of the institutional structures and ethos that work against women. Women's experiences point to a culture of sexism within the field that requires repair.

Today the field of Jewish studies has expanded enormously in the United States and around the world and enjoys interest from scholars in adjacent fields. As growing numbers of women and nonbinary scholars have entered Jewish studies in the last decades, they have expanded the study of women, gender, and sexuality. While we celebrate the professional opportunities that have grown, we also present serious problems that require attention. Our book takes stock: Where do we stand today, and how did we get here?

What obstacles face us? We begin by presenting quantitative data regarding percentage of women as professors of Jewish studies, citations of women scholars in academic journals in the field, and women as journal editors and board members, and we examine how gender is presented in major textbooks. We tell the history of the field: the nineteenth-century Wissenschaft movement (chapter 4), its connections to traditional religious study (chapter 5), and the growth of Jewish studies in US institutions (chapter 6). We connect those histories to our contemporary moment, where we focus on silencing. Manels, manthologies, mansplaining, and harassment: there are crucial links between the exclusion of women from public academic forums and the harassment that so many women have experienced.

Let us be clear: our book is not an ethnography, nor have we undertaken formally constructed surveys. We have participated for years in this field, witnessed the treatment of women and their scholarship, listened to the difficulties faced by women and nonbinary students and colleagues, and talked at length with more than eighty colleagues. We present their voices anonymously, analyze their experiences, and consider both the causes and the solutions. Like our interlocutors, we love our work in the field of Jewish studies, our research and teaching, and the interesting ways Jewish studies complicates disciplines and methods. Our book focuses on a problem and how to fix it. We recognize that not all women have been harassed, and many men have been supportive allies, and we hope our book will convince more of our colleagues to help improve the culture of the field.

Jewish studies exhibits the gender problems we see throughout universities. Within the academy, scholars have long known that student evaluations of teaching show bias with respect to race and gender.[1] Hiring practices have involved explicit discrimination as well as implicit bias, despite legal and professional efforts to avoid both.[2] Women's careers are affected by entering a world geared to men, in which childbearing years coincide with graduate school and efforts to obtain tenure, paid parental leave is not guaranteed, care for elderly relatives falls unevenly on women, and the glass ceiling has yet to be shattered.[3]

1. John A. Centra and Noreen B. Gaubatz, "Is There Gender Bias in Student Evaluations of Teaching?," *Journal of Higher Education* 71, no. 1 (2000): 17–33; Therese A. Huston, *Empirical Research on the Impact of Race and Gender in the Evaluation of Teaching*, Center for Excellence in Teaching and Learning (Seattle, WA: Seattle University Press, 2005); Therese A. Huston, *Research Report: Race and Gender Bias in Student Evaluations of Teaching*, Center for Excellence in Teaching and Learning (Seattle, WA: Seattle University Press, 2005); Jane Sojka, Ashok K. Gupta, and Dawn R. Deeter-Schmelz, "Student and Faculty Perceptions of Student Evaluations of Teaching: A Study of Similarities and Differences," *College Teaching* 50, no. 2 (2002): 44–49; and Joey Sprague and Kelley Massoni, "Student Evaluations and Gendered Expectations: What We Can't Count Can Hurt Us," *Sex Roles* 53, nos. 11–12 (2005): 779–93.

2. Laura Hirschfield, "Not the Ideal Professor: Gender in the Academy," in *Disrupting the Culture of Silence: Confronting Gender Inequality and Making Change in Higher Education*, ed. Kristine De Welde and Andi Stepnick (New York: Routledge, 2014), 205–14.

3. There is evidence that when it is available to all, parental leave often benefits men professionally (who may take the time off from teaching to advance research)

Universities, like many businesses and professions, have instituted DEI (diversity, equity, and inclusion) mandates with obligatory training for all faculty and staff. However, these alone will not fix bias or discrimination. The problems are too complex, often too subtle, and rooted in social systems that extend far beyond the university. Nor are projects for different kinds of inclusion always aligned. For example, we mention in chapter 6 the tensions between some second-wave feminists and some Jewish Zionists. Colleagues in Jewish studies have also expressed concern that their work is marginalized within some progressive academic agendas in which they want to participate.[4]

The issues raised by second-wave feminists frequently focused on the difficulties faced by white, middle-class women, marginalizing women of color, women of lower socioeconomic status, queer women, and trans and nonbinary people. Today, concerns about women's statuses in society may seem dated to some of our readers, but our research has taught us that the problems faced by people who identify as women within the field of Jewish studies remain serious. We also see connections between the issues that face women and those experienced by queer, trans, and nonbinary people as well as by non-Jews in our field. While we recognize that different strategies will be important for each group, we also see solidarity. In his oft-quoted "Letter from a Birmingham Jail," Rev. Dr. Martin Luther King Jr. wrote, "Injustice anywhere is a threat to justice everywhere. We are caught in an inescapable network of mutuality, tied in a single garment of destiny. Whatever affects one

---

more than it does women. Gretal Leibnitz and Briana Keafer Morrison, "The Eldercare Crisis and Implications for Women Faculty," in De Welde and Stepnick, *Disrupting the Culture of Silence*, 137–45.

4. Marla Brettschneider has been a pioneer in feminist and multicultural academic communities; see Brettschneider, *Jewish Feminism and Intersectionality* (Albany: State University of New York Press, 2016); and Brettschneider, *The Narrow Bridge: Jewish Views on Multiculturalism* (New Brunswick, NJ: Rutgers University Press, 1996).

directly, affects all indirectly."[5] While our focus is primarily on women, we have also examined the situation of LGBTQ+ members of our profession, and we believe that improving the situation for each will improve the situation for the field as a whole.

All of us face gendered cultural problems beyond the university. A 2018 study undertaken by economists argues that the sexism young girls experience in childhood affects their lifelong earnings and accomplishments; growing up in a sexist culture brings a lifetime of consequences. It also found that sexism in a woman's workplace had additional negative effects on her socioeconomic outcomes.[6] The study was limited to white adults and did not include factors of religious belief or practice, but the findings urge us to recognize the role of cultural attitudes imbued in childhood when we try to understand why some women do not actively seek promotions, salary raises, and positions of leadership, let alone why they fail to report incidents of assault or actively support men who admit they commit harassment. In other words, sexism functions very broadly: as institutional structures and cultural attitudes held by people who then transmit those same ideas to others. The economists conclude that "sexism in a woman's state of birth and in her current state of residence . . . lower her wages and likelihood of labor force participation." This includes the sexism where a woman works, where "labor market outcomes seem to operate chiefly through the mechanism of market discrimination by sexist men. . . . Prejudice-based discrimination, undergirded by prevailing sexist beliefs . . . may be an important driver of women's

5. Martin Luther King Jr., "Letter from a Birmingham City Jail," in *A Testament of Hope: The Essential Writings and Speeches of Martin Luther King, Jr.*, ed. James Melvin Washington (San Francisco: Harper, 1968), 289–302; 290.

6. Kerwin Kofi Charles, Jonathan Guryan, and Jessica Pan, "The Effects of Sexism on American Women: The Role of Norms vs. Discrimination," *Journal of Human Resources* (published online before print: November 10, 2022), https://doi.org/10.3368/jhr.0920-11209R3.

outcomes in the US."[7] Sexist culture, in other words, limits women's ability to achieve parity with men in the labor market, as it prevents them from receiving offers for high-ranking positions and earning commensurate salaries. In the university, sexism also affects everyone's careers, hindering them from engaging with the scholarship of women and genderqueer scholars that often presents new ideas.

In addition to sharing the same gendered issues within and beyond the university, scholars in Jewish studies also face some distinctive issues. In this book, we describe what is distinctive about Jewish studies—that is, how the history and culture of the field have created particular assumptions about gender. We also find it worthwhile to think about the dynamics of Jewish studies and gender as a case study for related fields. Studies like ours have been undertaken in a variety of academic fields, from STEM to philosophy, and our study allows us to put Jewish studies' gender issues into focus and context.[8] Is Jewish studies worse than some other fields with respect to gender issues? Yes. Is it also better than some? Yes. Beyond a simplistic better/worse comparison, we explore how particular dynamics came to be, how they may differ among subfields, and what we can do to change the status quo.

To take an example of what this field questioning looks like, we might look to philosophy. The field of philosophy has long had a

7. Kerwin Kofi Charles, "Research Brief: The Effects of Sexism on American Women: The Role of Norms vs. Discrimination," University of Chicago Becker Friedman Institute for Economics website, August 1, 2018, https://bfi.uchicago.edu /insight/research-summary/the-effects-of-sexism-on-american-women-the-role-of -norms-vs-discrimination/.

8. Among the many studies of women in the academy in recent decades, we note Eileen Pollack, *The Only Woman in the Room: Why Science Is Still a Boys' Club* (Boston: Beacon, 2015); Paula J. Caplan, *Lifting a Ton of Feathers: A Woman's Guide to Surviving in the Academic World* (Toronto: University of Toronto Press, 1993); and Evelyn Fox Keller, *Reflections on Gender and Science* (New Haven, CT: Yale University Press, 1985).

very small percentage of women at the highest academic ranks.[9] Recently, scholars have brought to the fore long-neglected women philosophers, while others have questioned the gendered nature of foundational methods of philosophy.[10] Catherine Gardner's examination led her to ask "how and why certain forms [of philosophical arguments] become excluded."[11] She transformed her own question from a search for women's philosophical writings to a critique of philosophical practice: Just what gets counted as "philosophical"? Has the field of philosophy defined itself in such a way that it has become a tool for excluding women? We might ask the same questions of Jewish studies when we hear that over the course of Jewish history, women wrote no texts until recently, so that women's history cannot be included in the field. Yet that rationale rests on three assumptions: texts serve as the best and most important evidence (though much may be learned from material evidence and ethnography); stated authorship reflects reality (though women's contributions may have been unacknowledged or women may have used male pseudonyms); texts provide information rather than puzzles to be deciphered (though contrary evidence may be apparent if different tools of interpretation are used). One problem is the archives that construct future scholarship: If these archives limit themselves to documents and

9. For example, Sally Haslanger, "Changing the Ideology and Culture of Philosophy: Not by Reason (Alone)," *Hypatia* 23, no. 2 (Spring 2008): 210–23; Sally Haslanger, "Gender and Race: (What) Are They? (What) Do We Want Them to Be?," *Nous* 34, no. 1 (2000): 31–55.

10. Mary Ellen Waithe, *A History of Women Philosophers*, 4 vols. (Boston: M. Nijhoff, 1987–95); see also Eva Feder Kittay and Linda Martin Alcoff, *The Blackwell Guides to Feminist Philosophy* (Hoboken, NJ: Wiley-Blackwell, 2008); Karen J. Warren, *An Unconventional History of Western Philosophy: Conversations between Men and Women Philosophers* (Lanham, MD: Scarecrow, 2006); Mary Warnock, *Women Philosophers* (London: Orion, 1996); Sarah Tyson, *Where Are the Women? Why Expanding the Archive Makes Philosophy Better* (New York: Columbia University Press, 2019).

11. Catherine Villanueva Gardner, *Rediscovering Women Philosophers: Philosophical Genre and the Boundaries of Philosophy* (Boulder, CO: Westview, 2000), 1.

materiality, how will we learn about the private lives of women and their subjectivity?[12]

Throughout our study, we understand sexism and gender inequality as issues of institutions, structures, and cultures. This means that our story has no easy villains. We neither blame individual men for the overarching problem nor suggest that the solution will come when we root out sexism from the hearts and minds of a few bad apples. In examining sexism's wide range of manifestations, from the omission of scholarship by women and genderqueer people to harassment and sexual assault, we see it as stemming from a large cultural framework that requires repair. Ultimately, we are calling for widespread transformations in structures, academic cultures, and shared expectations.

One of the prominent ways we see issues of sexism framed is as a problem of bad apples, especially concerning the issue of sexual harassment or assault, an issue that forms the core of chapters 2 and 3. While it is certainly true that some individuals are guilty of harassment and assault, it is also true that a culture characterized by uneven power dynamics, assumptions, and willingness to look the other way, among other things, facilitates those actions. The underlying culture and structures reproduce sexism and exclusion in Jewish studies scholarly spaces. We see some similarities in the reactions to harassment and sexism: some people acknowledge the issue but see it as an individual problem (the bad apple theory, in which the solution is identifying and excluding the perpetrator); others will dismiss the issue as an essential feature of gender, about which there is little to be done ("boys will be boys" or "women just don't write about that topic"). We are interested in those dynamics because we see changing them as the key to changing the culture.

Thinking about sexism as an individual problem might at first seem appealing. If we can rid our organizations of the offenders,

---

12. There are now archives, such as the Jewish Women's Archive, that dedicate their collections to the goal of making Jewish women's history visible.

then our problem will be solved. However, history has shown us that this approach does not work. Something in the structures or the cultures allows the issues to continue—sometimes even when everyone involved means well. The bad apple theory also has a very difficult time accounting for why well-meaning people might still slip up. If sexism is just about someone's internal motivations and ethics, what do we make of the man who intentionally champions female graduate students but still discusses women only in the "gender week" near the end of his syllabus? How is it that even avowed feminists can find themselves writing a paper that cites few women? The answers cannot fully be found in individual hearts or minds, and so the solutions cannot take place only there.

We also do not think the gendered problems with academic culture can be boiled down to consent. Ensuring that people engaged in sexual activity are consenting adults is crucial, but this is insufficient as a model to cover all personal and professional relationships. In professional settings, power differences can so strongly color interactions and requests that we should not see all responses as fully freely chosen. For example, if a senior colleague asks a junior colleague to teach him how to use the university's teaching software program or take on additional service work, the junior colleague is very likely to say yes, even if they cannot afford the time. If they decline, there may be costs. A binary yes-or-no model of consent does not capture the dynamic here; we cannot simply say, "Well, she said yes to that service commitment, so it is her own doing." Exhorting women and underrepresented faculty to "learn to say no," as if the problem were that they took on additional tasks, will similarly not solve the problem.[13] Nor does consent address the exclusion of minoritized scholars from academic projects or conversations.

This book draws on private interviews we conducted with over eighty scholars, including nonbinary people, non-Jews, people of

---

13. Karen Pyke, "Faculty Gender Inequity and the 'Just Say No to Service' Fairy Tale," in De Welde and Stepnick, *Disrupting the Culture of Silence*, 83–95.

color, and people with disabilities; quotes from these interviews appear in italicized paragraphs throughout the book. The interviewees include graduate students, postdocs, junior professors, adjuncts, and senior full professors in Jewish studies. We heard their stories of discrimination, bias, harassment, and assault. Only three told us they never experienced or witnessed discrimination or bias in their careers. We heard multiple accounts of the same sorts of experiences, making it clear to us that such problems are widespread and affect people at all stages in their academic careers. In what follows we report the experiences they related to us, withholding their names (except where their accounts have already been published elsewhere), because their voices must be heard. Although academic societies, like universities, have established rules of behavior and committees to adjudicate complaints, almost none of the people we spoke to had filed complaints with the relevant authorities. Why not? We address the reasons in chapter 3 by presenting two cases discussed extensively in public media.

What we learned from our interviews led us to ponder why deep-seated biases remain so powerful, permitting some scholars to feel it is appropriate to exclude women from academic conferences and publications, or to think it is ethically permissible to harass or mock women, or that they can evade penalties when they assault women. For women, the consequences can be enduring and often devastating. Incidents that occurred years earlier can remain vivid and painful, leaving women feeling deeply unsure of their place in the academy, or even uncertain of their right to a scholarly voice.

We recognize that women are too often omitted from the image of the scholar. Most of us have seen the iconography at universities dominated by depictions of men: photographs, paintings, busts, and sculptures adorn countless scholarly libraries and meeting rooms. One of us took part in a Jewish studies tenure and promotion committee in an elegant room surrounded by walls holding large, framed paintings—all of them of men. The case under discussion regarded a candidate who would be only the second woman in her large department to receive tenure. Little wonder that women faculty on campus are so often misidentified as staff or students.

Despite all the problems we uncovered, we want to emphasize that a host of remarkable women and nonbinary scholars have entered the field of Jewish studies in the last fifty years and brought with them important changes. Scholarship about gender and interpretations drawing from feminist theory, sexuality studies, disability studies, studies of racism, postcolonial analysis, and many other theoretical modalities have grown during the past several decades. Some women now teach in doctoral programs, some hold endowed chairs, some have won awards for their publications, and some have served as presidents of academic associations.

Moreover, the field of Jewish studies in North America may now contain slightly more women than men. In 2022, the Association for Jewish Studies (AJS) reported that 47.6 percent of its members identify as women or female, 43.1 percent identify as men or male, and 1.4 percent as genderqueer or gender nonconforming; 7.7 percent preferred not to answer or left the question blank.[14] These numbers include people at all stages, from graduate students to emeritus faculty, from part-time adjuncts to full-time tenured professors, as well as people in related fields, such as library science. The proportion of nonmale-identified scholars in Jewish studies is higher than some academic fields, such as philosophy, computer science, economics, mathematics, and chemistry, and is similar to the overall gender balance in the humanities.[15]

14. Melinda Man, AJS staff, email correspondence with Sarah Imhoff, August 1, 2022. Rounding leads to totals that are not precisely 100 percent.

15. Kristen Monroe, Saba Ozyurt, Ted Wrigley, and Amy Alexander, "Gender Equality in Academia: Bad News from the Trenches, and Some Possible Solutions," *Perspectives on Politics* 6, no. 2 (2008): 221; Kristen Renwick Monroe, Jenny Choi, Emily Howell, Chloe Lampros-Monroe, Crystal Trejo, and Valentina Perez, "Gender Equality in the Ivory Tower, and How Best to Achieve It," *PS: Political Science and Politics* 47, no. 2 (2014): 418–26 and "Trends in the Demographics of Humanities

Yet Jewish studies continues to have a gender problem. Women and nonbinary scholars are clustered in certain areas of research while being woefully underrepresented in other areas; women are very much present at the junior levels but less so at the senior levels of academic institutions; women's scholarship is not cited as often as men's; trans and nonbinary scholars' work is often seen as marginal; scholarship about gender is too often missing from research projects, textbooks, and course syllabi. All too often, scholarship by men dominates conferences, journals, and anthologies, with others excluded from the very important conversations that propel scholarship forward. In short, women are qualified scholars who publish important work, yet they are not always included, and paths to seniority can be rocky and uncertain. This is a book about the enduring problem of bias in Jewish studies: why it happens, and what to do about it. As a colleague wrote to us, "the marginalization of women in the field itself has a history—and is in fact baked into the very formation of the field."

We examine the origins of Jewish studies in several ways. Chapter 4 looks at its formative years in nineteenth-century Germany, when men dominated the field and imagined their work as historians in eroticized metaphors. Chapter 5 traces those origins within several subdisciplines to focus on the different kinds of gendered problems and patterns in fields ranging from archeology to Holocaust studies. In chapter 6, we look at the economic and political origins of Jewish studies at contemporary US universities and the relationship of the field with other interdisciplinary programs. Demonstrating the origins, history, and contemporary manifestations of marginalization, discrimination, and harassment within Jewish studies is one purpose; our goal is to bring change

---

Faculty," American Academy of Arts and Sciences, accessed December 2, 2023, https://www.amacad.org/humanities-indicators/higher-education-surveys/trends -demographics-humanities-faculty. These data suggest that faculty gender ratios in the humanities as a whole have remained stable—at right about 50 percent—for more than a decade.

by articulating the problems, revealing their connections, and proposing some solutions.

We write together because we share convictions and some viewpoints. But we also draw on different strengths. We represent two academic generations, having received our doctorates about twenty years apart. Our research overlaps but also stretches into different fields: Susannah has worked on modern Jewish history and thought in Germany and North America, antisemitism, race and racism, and feminist theories and theologies. Sarah has written on masculinity, disability, Zionism, American Jews, and race in US contexts both past and present, as well as historical transnational subjects, including Israel/Palestine. Both of us are tenured, but Susannah teaches at a private, Ivy League, R1 university with an undergraduate program, and Sarah teaches at a large, R1 state university with a doctoral program. We have each learned from the other through our collaboration and shared concerns about the field and about the place of women and nonbinary scholars within it. We present this book not as an indictment but as an assessment of the field with an eye to its history and a concern for its future.

In writing about women, we include trans and cis women, and we think about gender as a social construct—that is, we do not see an essential maleness or femaleness, nor do we view binarism as fixed. In this way, we understand connections between women and other scholars who hold minoritized identities, such as nonbinary scholars in the field of Jewish studies, and scholars who are not white Ashkenazi Jews or who are not Jewish at all. We also give attention to biases toward scholars of color in the field, especially to Black and Asian scholars, and we hope that this attention will inspire additional research focused specifically on scholars of color. (Because some subfields in Jewish studies have a very small number of trans scholars or scholars of color, we often do not identify them as such when we are quoting them because that would compromise their anonymity.) We are not claiming to present a comprehensive study but one that calls attention to biases that will receive, we hope, further attention—and correction.

We note that sexism can be interpersonal or systemic, and we also draw attention to the ways that it is part of an academic culture. The problem is not only what is said or done to women; it is also the exclusion of women and nonbinary scholars, including from informal gatherings—for instance, meals at conferences—at which important conversations occur, collaborative projects begin, and people learn about one another's academic interests. When casual gatherings include only men, networking creates male-dominant systems that are unaware of women and nonbinary scholars and their scholarship and keep others from the intellectual exchanges that enhance our work. Funding for these scholars' studies may also suffer when they are excluded from informal conversations because these exclusions limit their professional networks. Gendered exclusion may be thoughtless, or it may be deliberate, such as with the "Mike Pence problem," in which men refuse to engage one on one with female colleagues, ostensibly for reasons of propriety. In some countries and in some subfields, men direct the major foundations that offer grants to scholars and to almost all the large institutes that employ numerous graduate students, postdocs, and junior faculty. Male networking assists in raising funds for such foundations and institutes, both from the government and from private sources.[16] When women's scholarship is not widely known and respected, women are less often asked to edit important volumes, invited to participate in conferences, and given grants for their projects.

We recognize that the field of Jewish studies is growing and now has an international footprint. Although our focus in this book is North America, we are well aware that many in our field spend time as students or researchers in Israel, Europe, North Africa, South and Central America, Asia, and elsewhere. Germany has more Jewish studies research programs than other European

16. For a larger discussion of how personal (gendered) networks affect philanthropy, see Amornrat Apinunmahakul and Rose Anne Devlin, "Social Networks and Private Philanthropy," *Journal of Public Economics* 92, no. 1–2 (2008): 309–28.

countries. Spain—which at the turn of the century established the first professorship in Jewish studies, held by Avraham Shalom Yahuda starting in 1915—today has a lively program of scholarship on Jewish history and philosophy, which flourished in Iberia prior to 1492.[17] China has several universities offering courses in Jewish studies;[18] the largest, an endowed program at the University of Nanjing, is directed by Xu Xin, a prolific scholar of Jewish literature and history. Israel is a central location for the libraries, archives, and universities in which many of us study, and archeologists work at specific locales in Israel and Palestine. Japan now has flourishing academic programs, and India has at least two Israel studies programs. Jewish studies is a field at Egyptian and Moroccan universities. While we have not systematically examined Jewish studies in other countries, many of the people we interviewed helped us see that the problems we address in this book have international resonance. Women scholars in Europe and Israel reported experiences that mirror those of women in the United States. For example, a woman who held a fellowship at a prestigious institute in Germany told us about a man who propositioned her in explicit sexual terms and then denigrated her scholarship when she rejected him. Across geographies, we heard similar stories describing dismissive attitudes and exclusion from conferences, anthologies, and conversations, as well as sexual harassment. No country has fully and successfully embraced gender parity and feminist scholarship. We believe the intellectual vibrancy of any academic field requires collegiality: politeness, responsiveness, and respect.[19]

17. Michal Rose Friedman, "Orientalism between Empires: Abraham Shalom Yahuda at the Intersection of Sepharad, Zionism, and Imperialism," *Jewish Quarterly Review* 109, no. 3 (Summer 2019): 438.

18. See Song Lihong, "Reflections on Chinese Jewish Studies: A Comparative Perspective," in *The Image of Jews in Contemporary China*, ed. James Ross and Song Lihong (Brighton, MA: Academic Studies, 2016), 206–33.

19. We take seriously the critiques of "collegiality" as a term rooted in the image of scholars as white and male. We use the term here to emphasize the frequent

Moreover, ours is an era of political polarization, rising anti-semitism and racism, and increasing authoritarianism, in which many of the great advances made in human rights and social justice are under threat or being eviscerated. Women's bodily autonomy, crucial for social and economic advancement, is threatened by governments that ban abortion, fail to fund day care, criminalize homosexuality, and do not provide affordable health insurance. In the United States, professorial tenure is under threat from some Republican governors and state legislatures, as is the freedom to teach certain topics, including racism, the Holocaust, gender, and sexuality.

We recognize that describing women's experiences will not be the same as describing all the marginalization within Jewish studies experienced in particular by scholars who are Asian, Black, Latine, trans, and nonbinary, and by those who are not Jewish, and we are indebted to researchers of intersectionality for their analyses of the ways race, gender, ability, and sexuality mutually inform one another.[20] In our study, we emphasize gender, but issues of sexuality, race, and Jewishness are never far from the surface.

In Jewish studies, these intersections can take on particular forms. Scholars of color are often marginalized or excluded from Jewish studies spaces and conversations. Sometimes that is because interlocutors assume that a scholar of color is not Jewish and that only Jews can be scholars of Jews, and sometimes it is because of a more generalized racism. Queer, trans, and nonbinary Jewish experiences are often treated as marginal topics that need

---

exclusion of women from the informal academic conversations that are crucial to intellectual stimulation and academic advancement. See Shawn Copeland, "Collegiality as a Moral and Ethical Practice," in *Practice What You Preach: Virtues, Ethics, and Power in the Lives of Pastoral Ministers and Their Congregations*, ed. James F. Keenan and Joseph Kotva (Franklin, WI: Sheed and Ward, 1999), 315–32; and Stacey Floyd-Thomas, "The Problem That 'Lies' Within: How 'Collegiality' Undermines the Academy," *Religious Studies News* 24, no. 4 (October 2009): 31.

20. For a collection of classic as well as newer essays, see Kimberlé W. Crenshaw, *On Intersectionality: Essential Writings* (New York: New Press, 2017).

not be addressed in mainstream Jewish studies scholarship, as we will demonstrate in our discussion of textbooks in chapter 1. In the past, when we have urged inclusion of women, some colleagues have countered that other issues are more pressing.[21] We acknowledge the existence of these other issues and see them as interconnected with gender-based exclusion. We have heard, loud and clear, the voices of Black, Asian, non-Jewish, trans, and nonbinary colleagues about the frequent discrimination they have experienced in the field.

One of us recently had an email exchange that helps illustrate the relationship of scholarly identity and diversity of viewpoints. After writing to a senior scholar who edited a volume that included few women writers, we received a sadly typical response: he had invited some women to contribute to his book, but none had said yes. While the invitation was a good first step, it indicates a deeper problem. We suggested to him that if he truly valued women's participation, perhaps next time he might begin a project by asking women scholars in his network what they consider to be important issues and then formulate the publication or conference with that in mind. His reply: "Now that gives me something to ponder." It is indeed time to ponder.

21. For example, Marcin Wodziński has argued that while women might be excluded, the more important issue is that non-Jews are excluded. "Where Are All the Others in Jewish Studies," *Forward*, January 16, 2020, https://forward.com/culture/438320/where-are-all-the-others-in-jewish-studies/.

Part I

1

Gender by the Numbers

THE CAMBRIDGE HISTORY OF JUDAISM series of books bills itself as "the fullest and most authoritative account of its subject" and promises it "will endure as an important scholarly resource."[1] At the time of this writing, eight books have been published in the series. Twelve men and no women have served as editors or coeditors. Oxford University Press's Very Short Introductions series includes seven hundred books.[2] Eight refer to Judaism and Jewish history, and all are written by men. Another major reference book series, Brandeis University Press's Library of Modern Jewish Thought, edited by two men, includes eleven books to date. Fourteen of the editors are men, and two are women.[3] The Yale Jewish Lives series, edited by a man and a woman, has published sixty-six biographies to date. Sixteen of its authors are women. Only seven

1. For this statement, see the homepage for the Cambridge History of Judaism series, accessed June 12, 2024, https://www.cambridge.org/core/series/cambridge -history-of-judaism/29093C42B02C8ECF05D2E9808123479C. The Cambridge History of Judaism series editors are W. D. Davies and Louis Finkelstein.

2. Information on the Very Short Introductions series published by Oxford University Press is from the press's website, accessed December 18, 2023, https://global .oup.com/academic/content/series/v/very-short-introductions-vsi/?lang=en&cc =us.

3. The Brandeis Library of Modern Jewish Thought series is edited by Eugene R. Sheppard and Samuel Moyn; see the Brandeis University Press website, accessed December 3, 2023, https://www.brandeis.edu/tauber/publications/blmjt.html.

books profile the lives of women.[4] The Jewish Publication Society's series Anthologies of Jewish Thought has published seven books thus far, and all are edited by men.[5] All these high-profile series remain active; the majority of these books have been published in the last twenty years.

One way to examine the gender problem in Jewish studies is by listening to the stories of women, trans, and nonbinary scholars. Another way is to analyze the history of the field and the content of its scholarship. We do both in this book. But this chapter begins by considering yet another source: quantitative data. What percentage of Jewish studies scholars are women? Are women cited in proportion to their presence in the field? How does Jewish studies compare to related fields when we look at gender and citations? Do the rates of citation differ among subfields or time periods in Jewish studies?

Quantitative data complement the other kinds of inquiry we pursue in this book: they can show us structural issues, trends, and generalizations, and they can quantify some aspects of inequality. We believe that sometimes data can provide a new way of seeing a complex picture. We also hope that carefully collected data can help convince those who might not otherwise recognize the scope of these issues. When we describe sexism in academic circles, colleagues sometimes respond by dismissing concerns as just about "hurt feelings," as a problem of one or two isolated old male scholars, as an issue that is just "your experience," or as merely anecdotal. We hope that colleagues who might have reacted in these ways will take a second look at this data-driven chapter—and maybe they will also then take more seriously the experiences,

---

4. The editors of the Jewish Lives series are Anita Shapira and Steven J. Zipperstein; see the Yale University Press website, accessed December 3, 2023, https://yalebooks.yale.edu/series/jewish-lives and https://www.jewishlives.org/.

5. See "JPS Anthologies of Jewish Thought," at the Jewish Publication Society website, accessed December 3, 2023, https://jps.org/product-category/collections/jps-anthologies-of-jewish-thought/.

anecdotes, historical inquiries, and philosophical arguments we offer in the rest of our analysis.

Data helped us test our hypotheses and impressions of women and women's scholarship in the field. It seemed to us that women make up a significant percentage of faculty members. Was that true, or was it just that our own networks included many women? It also seemed to us that, for quite a few years, at least half of graduate students interested in Jewish studies were women. Were those numbers reflected in numbers of PhD recipients? We also had the impression that men were cited more than women in Jewish studies journal articles. Was that actually the case? There were times in collecting and analyzing our data that we exhaled, deflated: this was worse than we thought. There were other times that we looked at the numbers and saw promising trends.

We analyze quantitative data not because we think that statistical analysis is somehow more "real" than people's experiences. It isn't. It can't tell us how change should happen or why things matter. Numerical data in isolation can flatten complex issues. Jewish studies scholars know this well: every time the Pew Forum publishes a survey of US Jews, scholars comment on how its categories are inadequate for describing how people really live, why its numbers don't tell us the whole story of American Judaism, how its methods might have undercounted some group, and a host of other issues. Our numerical data do not examine intersections of gender with other factors like race, disability, and Jewishness; nor do they describe gender diversity, such as the presence of genderqueer, nonbinary, or trans scholars in the field. We hope that they set the stage for others to do this research in the future.

This chapter's data focus on faculty positions, scholarly research, and textbooks in Jewish studies. We chose these because they represent some of the most important facets of the profession. Research occupies a central place for many academics. The most highly coveted jobs use selection and promotion processes that weigh research most heavily. In academia, fame and prestige (if only among a fairly niche crowd) come from research and its public presentation. Many who have achieved prominence through their research also affect the field when they write synthetic works such as textbooks. Teaching is also a central part of the profession, and our students are both our biggest audiences and the potential future of the field, and so this chapter closes with a brief study of gender in the most widely used textbooks in Jewish studies classrooms.

Faculty

Faculty are the beating heart of Jewish studies, and so it is crucial to understand the numbers of women, men, and nonbinary scholars who hold faculty appointments if we want to know about gender equity in the field. When we talk about who is in the field of Jewish studies, we are primarily talking about people who do research and teaching: faculty and graduate students. Faculty have more power and influence, and so we will concentrate our analysis there, but we will also draw on data about graduating PhD students since they are in the pipeline to become not only future faculty but also the future of the field.

Faculty positions are not all created equal. Across academic fields, tenured and tenure-track positions hold more prestige, offer more job security, and generally have larger salaries than non-tenure-track positions, which are more precarious, lower paying, and without health insurance.

In the 2020–21 academic year, 132 research 1 (R1) institutions in the United States had Jewish studies faculty.[6] At each of these universities, we counted everyone who was identified as core faculty by a Jewish studies program, center, or department web page, and we followed up with emails in all cases of ambiguity, such as

---

6. The Carnegie Classification of Institutions of Higher Education determines which institutions count as R1. It is updated every three years. Carnegie Classification of Institutions of Higher Education, accessed September 10, 2023, https:// carnegieclassifications.acenet.edu/.

whether a faculty member was still teaching there or whether a position was tenure track or not. We did not count emeritus or emerita faculty who occupy a space of full retirement or semiretirement and who are usually no longer teaching full time or expected to contribute to the university through service. Many universities do not list adjunct faculty, so we are certain we have undercounted these scholars—but adjunct positions do not come with the pay or prestige of tenure-track jobs. The numbers we collected do not capture every single member of Jewish studies departments and programs, but they do tell us about active faculty in the "top tier" of US colleges and universities, where much of the field's resources are concentrated and where the tone of the field is set.

Out of 1,312 total Jewish studies faculty at R1 institutions in the United States in 2020–21, 42.5 percent were women. Tenured and tenure-track positions totaled 1,054, of which 39.8 percent were held by women. In Jewish studies, like most other fields, women form a smaller proportion of tenure-track faculty and a larger proportion of non-tenure-track faculty.[7] These numbers are similar to statistics we see across all academic fields in the United States: one recent national survey shows that 46.7 percent of faculty are women, and 43.7 percent of tenure-track faculty are women.[8] But these numbers include STEM fields, many of which have large gender gaps.

7. Across fields including STEM, women are more likely than men to hold adjunct positions. Estimates of adjunct positions held by women range from 51 percent to 61 percent. If Jewish studies follows the patterns we see for humanities and social sciences, we would expect the field to have even higher percentages of women working as adjunct faculty. Kay Steiger, "The Pink Collar Workforce of Academia," Nation, July 11, 2013, https://www.thenation.com/article/archive/academias-pink-collar-workforce/.

8. According to the National Center for Education Statistics (NCES), in 2018–19, 388,530 of 832,119 professors were women. "IPEDS Data Explorer," National Center for Educational Statistics, accessed January 4, 2024, https://nces.ed.gov/ipeds/Search?query=faculty%20gender&query2=faculty%20gender&resultType=table&page=1&sortBy=relevance&collectionYears=2019-20&collectionYears=2018-19&collectionYears=2017-18&overlayDigestTableId=201365.

When compared to similar fields in the humanities and social
sciences, Jewish studies is lagging behind. Across the humanities,
in every year from the late 1990s to today, the majority of doctorates were awarded to women.[9] Jewish studies is part of that trend
(even though it is not entirely within the humanities, given its interdisciplinary focus and its inclusion of fields within the social
sciences). Newly awarded PhDs related to Jewish studies are difficult to count because people come from many different departments. The overwhelming majority of faculty members have a
PhD not granted by a Jewish studies department but by another
department. Departments that produce the vast majority of newly
minted PhDs in the field include history, religious studies,
languages and literature, English, comparative literature, and
Germanic studies. Anthropology and sociology make up a small
percentage of recent PhDs in Jewish studies.[10] The American
Academy of Arts and Sciences (AAAS) reports that, as of 2015,
women earned 54 percent of the doctoral degrees in the humanities: 43 percent of PhDs in history were awarded to women; in
religious studies and theology, 40 percent; in languages other than
English, 62 percent; and in English, 60 percent.[11] The AAAS ag-
gregates the small number of people who earn PhDs in Jewish
studies under the category of religious studies. (It is important to
note, as we describe later, that the field of "religious studies and

9. "Gender Distribution of Advanced Degrees in the Humanities," American
Academy of Arts and Sciences (AAAS), accessed December 3, 2023, https://www
.amacad.org/humanities-indicators/higher-education/gender-distribution
-advanced-degrees-humanities.

10. Women made up 64 percent of sociology PhD recipients and 65 percent of
cultural anthropology PhD recipients in 2019. "Survey of Earned Doctorates," National Center for Science and Engineering Statistics (NCSES), accessed December 3,
2023, https://ncses.nsf.gov/pubs/nsf21308/data-tables. See table 16 under "Field
and Demographic Characteristics of Doctorate Recipients."

11. See in particular data under "Degree Information" in "Higher Education,"
American Academy of Arts and Sciences (AAAS), accessed December 3, 2023,
https://www.amacad.org/humanities-indicators/higher-education.

theology" includes all the people who receive PhDs from Christian denominational seminaries, a group in which men far exceed women.) We also have more direct numbers from within the field of Jewish studies: between 2015 and 2022, of all the applications received by the Association for Jewish Studies (AJS) for dissertation completion fellowships, 58 percent came from women and 42 percent from men, judging by the names and pronouns available online.[12] ProQuest, the most widely used dissertation database, to which most universities require students to submit their dissertations, lists more than eight hundred doctoral dissertations from the past ten years in English about Jews, Judaism, or Jewishness. Women authored about 58 percent of them.[13] The precise number of graduates in Jewish studies, then, is difficult to pinpoint, but recent data suggest at least half of new graduates from PhD programs in the last two decades were women. The decade before that had only slightly lower percentages of women PhD recipients. Because women have earned PhDs in fields related to Jewish studies at about the same rate as men over the last thirty years, the fact that they hold only 39.8 percent of tenure-track appointments is cause for concern.

There is another gender gap that should concern us too. Only 25 percent of full professors are women. By now, scholars who received their doctorates in the late 1990s have been working in the field for more than twenty years, so if men and women were hired into tenure-track positions at R1 universities at the same rate

12. Amy Weiss (AJS Grants and Professional Development director), email message to Sarah Imhoff, June 28, 2002. All the applications were for the following academic year.

13. Gender nonbinary people, as best we could tell via pronouns available on the internet, authored under 1 percent. These data are the result of a search on ProQuest Dissertations and Theses Global, in which we viewed only English-language doctoral dissertations from the past ten years that used the words "Jew," "Jews," "Judaism," "Jewish," or "Jewishness" in the listed title. This may have missed some dissertations, but we have no reason to believe that the few we missed should contradict our findings on the overall gender balance.

at which they received their doctorates, we would see a number far greater than 25 percent. The 25 percent rate is especially concerning when examined from a comparative perspective. In 2018, about a third (34.3 percent) of full professors in the United States, across all fields, were women.[14] While the numbers are not precisely comparable because the 34.3 percent figure includes professors at all colleges and universities, not just R1 universities, the difference is notable.

One might speculate that the issue here is that many women faculty are getting "stuck" at the associate level. Across academia, women spend a slightly longer time as associates before promotion to full professor. There are many reasons for this, including larger service burdens, more time spent on teaching, and greater care responsibilities outside of the workplace.[15]

But this cannot be the main explanation for why there are so few women full professors in Jewish studies, because only 33 percent of associate professors in Jewish studies at R1 universities are women. If being stuck at the associate professor rank were the main cause, we should see many more at the associate rank. But we don't. This suggests that the proportion of women hired into tenure-track positions, say, seven to fifteen years ago, was much smaller than the proportion of men, even though women were earning PhDs at higher rates than their male counterparts.[16]

14. "Table 315.20: Full-Time Faculty in Degree-Granting Postsecondary Institutions, by Race/Ethnicity, Sex, and Academic Rank: Fall 2015, Fall 2016, and Fall 2017," IPEDS Data Explorer, National Center for Education Statistics, accessed December 3, 2023, https://nces.ed.gov/ipeds/Search?query=faculty%20gender&query2=faculty%20gender&resultType=table&page=1&sortBy=date_desc&collectionYears=2019-20&collectionYears=2018-19&collectionYears=2017-18&overlayDigestTableId=201365.

15. Amani El-Alayli, Ashley A. Hansen-Brown, and Michelle Ceynar, "Dancing Backwards in High Heels: Female Professors Experience More Work Demands and Special Favor Requests, Particularly from Academically Entitled Students," *Sex Roles* 79, no. 3 (2018): 136–50.

16. Though it is also possible that more women are leaving before making it to the associate level, the general data on leaving academia are mixed, though they

Beyond R1 universities, the numbers seem similar. In the 2018 AJS member survey, 51 percent of respondents identified as women, 44 percent identified as men, and 3 percent registered as gender-queer, nonbinary, or not listed.[17] Although these numbers might initially seem heartening, further research reveals they may not be. Research shows that women are more likely to fill out surveys than men are. One study specifically used university faculty to study this question.[18] Their research drew only from university faculty members of a large research university in the southeastern United States. (They did this to help control for other variables, such as internet access, education level, and socioeconomic status.) In that study, male faculty responded at a 24 percent rate, and female faculty responded at a 36 percent rate.[19] If men and women followed this pattern in filling out the AJS survey, it would reflect a membership that was in actuality 54 percent men, 42 percent women, and 3 percent genderqueer or nonbinary people—strikingly similar to the overall numbers we found for faculty at R1 universities.[20]

---

generally suggest that women and minority faculty report their reasons for leaving in distinctive ways. See Yonghong Jade Xu, "Faculty Turnover: Discipline-Specific Attention Is Warranted," *Research in Higher Education* 49, no. 1 (2008): 40–61.

17. And 2 percent declined to answer. *Association for Jewish Studies: 50th Annual Survey Report*, October 5, 2018, https://www.associationforjewishstudies.org/docs/default-source/surveys-of-the-profession/2018-ajs-survey-report-(1).pdf?sfvrsn=41e8a506_2.

18. William Grinell Smith, "Does Gender Influence Online Survey Participation? A Record-Linkage Analysis of University Faculty Online Survey Response Behavior," Education Resources Information Center (ERIC) Document Reproduction Service, ED501717 (2008), https://files.eric.ed.gov/fulltext/ED501717.pdf.

19. Smith.

20. We still need data on the rate at which gender nonconforming or nonbinary people fill out surveys—none of the studies we found included them as a group, so we kept that at 3 percent. The 2014 AJS survey had more respondents (1,353). In that survey, 52 percent identified as male and 48 percent as female. The 60 percent response rate of that survey was quite high, which makes it unlike most other voluntary online surveys and thus difficult to extrapolate from. Still, it seems fair to guess that male scholars make up just over half of AJS members.

Our focus is on the United States, and the most comprehensive data we have for comparison are from Israel, where the trends look similar to those in the United States. Women there are earning 54 percent of PhDs in the humanities.[21] However, they still make up only 17 percent of full professors and 29 percent of associate professors in all fields. And in spite of their high humanities PhD percentages, women make up only a small fraction of faculty in Jewish thought (where Jewish philosophy is studied) and Bible departments, and larger but still small percentages in Jewish history departments. The field of Talmud today is still dominated by men; as of this writing, Hebrew University has one woman, and Bar Ilan University has none. Yet there are distinguished women professors of Talmud; for example, Vered Noam, professor of Talmud at Tel Aviv University, recently received the prestigious Israel Prize in the field of Talmud, demonstrating that individual women scholars can excel in the field despite underrepresentation. One woman told us,

No women held tenure in the department where I studied. A junior woman, fabulous teacher, and brilliant scholar was told not to even bother coming up for tenure because there was no chance of it. She left for another university and years later became a world-famous scholar in her field. The message I got as a grad student: it's hopeless even if you are super-brilliant.

In all my years in graduate school, I never saw a woman get promoted or receive tenure. There was an unhappy atmosphere. The only woman teaching there had to leave after seven years.

Our overall data on faculty positions in the US reveal reasons to hope that we are moving closer to gender equity. Fifty-three percent of assistant professors in Jewish studies at R1 universities are women. This number is much closer to the proportion of PhD earners. These assistant professors still need the time, resources,

21. These data are from 2015–16 but used in a 2018 report. Michal Lerer and Ido Avgar, "Women in Academia," Knesset Report, June 18, 2018, https://m.knesset.gov .il/EN/activity/mmm/me040618.pdf.

and support to earn tenure and promotion if they are to climb the academic ladder. But these numbers suggest we should expect movement toward gender parity over time.

But our data also reveal reasons to be less hopeful. We already have several decades of women earning PhDs in fields related to Jewish studies at about the same rate as men, and that hasn't yet led to parity at higher levels. This suggests that women have been getting stuck on the ladder of advancement. It implies that if we keep doing what we have been doing, institutionally and as an academic culture, we cannot expect that these gender differences will fix themselves with time.

The increasing gender equity at the level of assistant professors reflects national trends across many fields, but other national trends still show that advancement is more difficult for women than for men. For example, study upon study shows that women faculty do "significantly more service" than men.[22] Service, such as serving on department committees, holding a position such as director of undergraduate studies, or serving on a search committee, is crucial to making universities run. Most service, however, is semivoluntary: sometimes you can decline, but there is often a cost for doing so. Sometimes projects or tasks even require volunteers, and volunteering turns out to be gendered: "Relative to men, women are more likely to volunteer, more likely to be asked to volunteer, and more likely to accept direct requests to volunteer."[23] A study of academic political scientists found that women were asked to provide more service than men, and they also agreed to serve more frequently than men. It also found that "the service women provide is more typically 'token' service, as women are less likely to be asked by their colleagues to serve as department chair,

22. Cassandra M. Guarino and Victor M. H. Borden, "Faculty Service Loads and Gender: Are Women Taking Care of the Academic Family?," *Research in Higher Education* 58, no. 6 (2017): 672–94.

23. Linda Babcock, Maria P. Recalde, Lise Vesterlund, and Laurie Weingart, "Gender Differences in Accepting and Receiving Requests for Tasks with Low Promotability," *American Economic Review* 107, no. 3 (2017): 714–47, quote on 744.

to chair committees, or to lead academic programs."[24] Token service might mean serving on smaller committees with few resources and little power, serving as director of undergraduate studies, or taking notes during faculty meetings. We have no reason to believe that the findings in these studies and other, similar ones across disciplines would be any different from what might be found in Jewish studies.

Even if we don't fully understand all the reasons why women do more service—and there are quite a few, such as women being socialized to be more likely to say yes when asked for help, or the need for diversity on committees resulting in underrepresented faculty members being called on more often—it is certain that greater service burdens result in less time to conduct research and publish. And, as we noted above, research and publishing are the pillars of tenure and promotion at research institutions. Even at liberal arts colleges and other teaching colleges, where teaching takes precedence, service is still generally counted as far less important (if it's counted at all). In an informal survey of our colleagues, we heard of exactly *zero* cases where a faculty member was denied tenure or promotion for insufficient service, and exactly *zero* cases where a faculty member was tenured or promoted primarily because of service.

Our informal investigations also reveal a related pattern that many in the field will recognize: on average, the period between tenure and promotion to full professor is longer for women than for men. Unlike tenure clocks, which have a set number of years until a tenure-track assistant professor must apply for tenure, promotion to full professor happens on an individualized calendar, if it happens at all. The time between earning tenure and promotion to full professor depends on each person's own career trajectory, which includes assessments of their work by department chairs or deans.

24. Sara M. Mitchell and Vicki L. Hesli, "Women Don't Ask? Women Don't Say No? Bargaining and Service in the Political Science Profession," *PS: Political Science and Politics* 46, no. 2 (2013): 355–69, quote on 355.

Given the studies that show people (both men and women) judge
a CV or résumé with a male-sounding name as more accomplished
than an identical one with a female-sounding name, we might wonder if women must work harder to seem "ready" for promotion to
their chairs or deans.[25] Moreover, each tenure and promotion case
requires letters from outside reviewers who are scholars in the field
at a higher rank than the candidate. This often means drawing on
male scholars of an older generation, some of whom are skeptical
of feminist scholarship. "National reputation"—hardly an objective
measure—is often one of the criteria for promotion, and it may be
driven in part by the ability to take many airplane trips to present at
universities and conferences. Faculty members who have small
children or are primary caretakers find that kind of travel far more
difficult than those who do not, and women are more likely than
men to have caretaking responsibilities.

Family roles and responsibilities represent another reason that
women across disciplines may be slower to promotion. One recent
study of academic parents is striking: across all disciplines,
"women who had children within five years of receiving their PhD
were much less likely than men with early babies to acquire tenured professorships."[26] Among tenured faculty, 70 percent of
tenured male professors were fathers, whereas only 44 percent
of tenured women were mothers.[27] It would be a mistake to chalk
these numbers up to choice. "The obstacle to parity is lack of institutional will," writes Kimberly Hamlin. "For example, policies

25. The classic study that discusses gender, hiring, and readiness for tenure is
Rhea E. Steinpreis, Katie A. Anders, and Dawn Ritzke, "The Impact of Gender on
the Review of the Curricula Vitae of Job Applicants and Tenure Candidates: A National Empirical Study," *Sex Roles* 41, nos. 7–8 (1999): 509–28.

26. Mary Ann Mason et al., *Do Babies Matter? Gender and Family in the Ivory
Tower* (New York: Routledge, 2013), 2. The conclusion is from a study by the Association for Institutional Research.

27. "Fast Facts: Women Working in Academia," American Association of University Women, accessed October 2, 2023, https://www.aauw.org/resources/article/fast
-facts-academia/.

intended to benefit mothers, such as [parental] leave, tend instead to benefit new fathers, who use the break from teaching to advance their research."[28]

Studies of STEM fields demonstrate that while women are well represented at the undergraduate level, there are fewer and fewer who rise up the academic ladder from graduate student to postdoc, and then to junior and ultimately senior faculty positions. Scholars such as Jennifer Thompson use the metaphor of the "leaking pipeline" to describe the same phenomenon in Jewish studies, illustrating that sexual harassment, lack of female mentorship, gender stereotyping, and even illegal sex discrimination cause women to leave or not be promoted.[29]

The leaking pipeline is distinctive in Jewish studies because of the relative paucity of nonacademic careers. A woman who earns a PhD in biochemistry can pursue a career within academia or with a pharmaceutical company. A woman with a PhD in history who researches Jews in France, by contrast, has far fewer obvious alternative career paths. This means that women with doctoral training in Jewish studies are more likely to exit the academic track because of push factors rather than pull factors, as Thompson demonstrates.[30]

In addition to these factors shared with many other academic disciplines, the field of Jewish studies faces some issues and

28. Kimberly Hamlin, "Why Are There So Few Women Full Professors?," *Chronicle of Higher Education*, March 30, 2020, https://www-chronicle-com.proxyiub.uits .iu.edu/article/why-we-need-more-women-full-professors; and Alexis Coe, "Being Married Helps Professors Get Ahead, but Only If They're Male," *Atlantic*, January 17, 2013, https://www.theatlantic.com/sexes/archive/2013/01/being-married-helps -professors-get-ahead-but-only-if-theyre-male/267289/.

29. Jennifer Thompson, "The Birdcage: Gender Inequity in Academic Jewish Studies," *Contemporary Jewry* 39, no. 3 (2019): 427–46; "leaking pipeline" appears throughout the article, beginning on p. 427. See also Joan C. Williams, "The Glass Ceiling and the Maternal Wall in Academia," *New Directions for Higher Education* 130 (2005): 91–105.

30. Thompson, "Birdcage," 427.

assumptions that many other fields do not. Unlike, say, physics or chemistry, where students and the general public recognize that experts in the field are scholars of physics or chemistry, people often see rabbis, cantors, and communal leaders as more authoritative than scholars. Although more women fill these roles than in the past, the majority are men, especially in Ortho-dox and ultra-Orthodox spaces. The people who serve in these public religious roles continue to shape what people—especially students, but also sometimes other scholars—see when they imagine authoritative figures. (We discuss this more in chapter 4, but it is worth mentioning here.)

This discussion of who people imagine as an authority in Jewish studies relates not only to gender, but also to religion and race. Most Jewish studies scholars are Jewish. Some are religious; some are not. But only a small percentage of people in Jewish studies identify with another religion, unless you count "agnosticism" or "atheism" as religions. Those who identify as atheists or agnostics often still do identify as Jewish. The 2018 AJS survey reported that 4 percent of respondents identified as Protestant, and fewer than ten people total identified as Buddhist, Catholic, Eastern Ortho-dox, or Hindu.[31] For scholars of Jews and Judaism, it is the norm to be Jewish. In our own experiences, students, colleagues, donors, and the general public assume that we are Jewish because we teach Jewish studies.

Also, most Jewish studies scholars are white. In that same AJS survey, 92 percent identified as white. (For comparison, 69.8 percent of faculty across US institutions identify as white.)[32] The survey included this explanatory note: "an exact breakdown of other races is not provided as the numbers are so small that they might unintentionally identify individuals and this is designed to

31. *Association for Jewish Studies: 50th Annual Survey Report*, 9.

32. "Digest of Education Statistics," National Center for Education Statistics, accessed December 29, 2023, https://nces.ed.gov/programs/digest/d18/tables/dt18_315.20.asp.

be an anonymous survey."[33] To reiterate: this international scholarly organization has so few nonwhite scholars that it fears that identifying someone as, for example, Asian will mean that others can figure out who that scholar is. Our colleagues who are not white often report that both their expertise and their identities are challenged. "Are you Jewish?" "You don't look Jewish." "Did you convert?" These are not appropriate scholarly questions, and yet we know our colleagues continue to face them.

These numbers demonstrate that, for Jewish studies, the norm is for the scholar to be white and Jewish. Subsequent chapters will deal more with the ways gender, race, and religion can intersect, but here it is important to note that experiences of exclusion or having their authority challenged can be compounded for women and nonbinary scholars who are not white and Jewish.

Leadership, Prestige, and Fellowships

The leaking pipeline may also contribute to the paucity of women who hold senior endowed chairs in Jewish studies. Our research shows that only 32 percent of endowed chairs in Jewish studies are held by women. Endowed chairs are usually given to professors with a significant academic profile or who show particular promise, and they almost always come with additional benefits such as research accounts, student fellowships, or other funding. Because this funding comes from large donations and subsequent earnings on that investment rather than regular university operating budgets, people with endowed chairs have more resources than those who do not. (Both of us, Susannah and Sarah, have these positions, and we are grateful, even as we point out the gender disparities.)

Prestigious fellowships and appointments also show a gender gap. The American Academy for Jewish Research (AAJR) promotes itself this way: "The Academy represents the oldest

---

33. *Association for Jewish Studies: 50th Annual Survey Report*, 9.

organization of Judaic scholars in North America. Fellows are nominated and elected by their peers and thus constitute the most distinguished and most senior scholars teaching Judaic studies at American universities."[34] As of 2020, women constituted only 24 percent of AAJR membership.[35] We know from many studies that women are less well integrated into men's professional networks, as men are more likely to have men in their networks.[36] The AAJR's election process is primarily a network-based one: you can be nominated only by a current member, so a current member must know you or your work. Here we see an example of how a process can perpetuate the status quo, even if no one harbors sexist plans.

A comparison of two additional prestigious research fellowships gives us insight into the issue—and also into a possible solution. The Katz Center at the University of Pennsylvania and the Frankel Center Institute for Advanced Judaic Studies at the University of Michigan each run an annual funded fellowship for a group of scholars. These fellowships have an outsized effect on the field because fellows are paid to spend either one semester or a full academic year in residence—that is, concentrating on research with few teaching and service responsibilities. Over the years, the Katz Center has awarded more than seven hundred such fellowships, and the Frankel Center almost two hundred.

Since its inception in 2007, 50 percent of the Frankel Center's fellowships have gone to men, 49 percent to women, and 1 percent to gender nonbinary people. Since the Katz Center began offering

34. "About," American Academy for Jewish Research, accessed December 7, 2023, http://aajr.org/about/.

35. "Current Fellows," American Academy for Jewish Research, accessed December 7, 2023, http://aajr.org/fellows/fellows-2/.

36. Daniel J. Brass, "Men's and Women's Networks: A Study of Interaction Patterns and Influence in an Organization," *Academy of Management Journal* 28, no. 2 (1985): 327–43. Similarly, for social networks, see Miller McPherson, Lynn Smith-Lovin, and James M. Cook, "Birds of a Feather: Homophily in Social Networks," *Annual Review of Sociology* 27, no. 1 (2001): 415–44.

its programming in 1993, 63 percent of its fellowships have gone to men and 37 percent to women. (For comparison, from 2007 on, the Katz Center reports that it has had 60 percent men and 40 percent women.) Throughout the years, the topics for each have ranged across time periods and methods. The only two years in which women outnumbered men at the Katz Center before 2019 had the themes "Modern Jewry and the Arts" and "Jews beyond Reason: Exploring Emotion, the Unconscious, and Other Dimensions of Jews' Inner Lives," both subfields and themes in which women are well represented. In 2007–8 and 2008–9, the Katz Center's sixty fellows included only seventeen women. In the most recent two cohorts (2019–20 and 2020–21), twenty-nine fellows of fifty-four total have been women. In 2007–8 and 2008–9, Frankel had fourteen women out of twenty-seven fellows, and for the most recent two cohorts, women have been twelve out of twenty-eight. Although the Frankel Center's numbers have stayed relatively even, the Katz Center's numbers have moved from favoring male scholars toward balance. So what accounted for the earlier differences, and what had changed?

These seemingly stark differences—both between the Frankel Center and the Katz Center, and in recent years at the Katz Center—made us wonder: What were the processes of awarding these fellowships to faculty? And how were topics chosen? Were men applying at greater rates? The last is the most straightforward: over the last twelve years, men have made up 56 percent of applicants to the Frankel Center program, and the numbers for the Katz Center are similar in recent years. Thus, men are applying at slightly higher rates than women, but they apply in proportion to their representation at R1 universities.

One of the reasons for the difference in their numbers in the past may have to do with the people in power. One former director of the Frankel Center is Deborah Dash Moore, who entered the field when women scholars were a smaller minority. The Katz Center has not yet had a woman director. A woman center director may make women more likely to apply or to take the fellowship if offered, as has been shown in corporate settings.[37] However, the fact of having a woman director, even one who pays attention to gender, cannot by itself ensure the full inclusion of women.

Current directors of both centers told Sarah that they generally found that years with more diversity (with respect to the identity of scholars as well as their methods) were more intellectually vibrant. They also did more than pay lip service to diversity: both of them described steps that they or their predecessors had taken to build gender diversity into the selection system. In composing the two decision-making committees, the Frankel Center directors now strive for "as diverse a group of advisory members as possible," Jeffrey Veidlinger explained to Sarah, with respect to field, types of institutions, and gender, as well as including international scholars. Committees with diverse representation are more likely to yield fellowship cohorts that are more diverse.

Diversity is also an explicit goal in the process of selecting fellows out of the applicant pool at the Frankel Center. In that process, overall diversity of the cohort of fellows is one of the main objectives. The center strives for a mix of gender, institution size, methodology, and geography (especially international scholars). One challenge is that some fellows will turn down the fellowship, and then the center will move down the waitlist. If the goal is a diverse cohort, that requires paying attention to which scholars tend to be able to say yes to a residential fellowship once it is awarded.

It is easier for able-bodied scholars, scholars without school-age children, scholars who have partners with flexible jobs, scholars who are single, and scholars who do not have primary child-care or elder-care responsibilities to say yes to a residential fellowship. Given the gendered nature of care responsibilities, women scholars are somewhat less likely to have the flexibility to take up a

---

37. "Network Trends Report: Gender, Equity, and Gen Z," Handshake, accessed December 7, 2023, https://joinhandshake.com/wp-content/themes/handshake /dist/assets/downloads/network-trends/Gender-Equity-And-Gen-Z__Hand shake-Network-Trends.pdf?view=true.

position at a residential fellowship. The 2020–21 year, marked by Covid-19, forced new accommodations, especially with respect to whether or not a fellow should be physically present. The Frankel Center had already installed video-conferencing equipment to facilitate remote participation. Video conferencing matters for gender equity precisely because it allows the participation of people with caregiving responsibilities, and people with caregiving responsibilities are more likely to be women.

Like the Frankel Center, the Katz Center has multiple governing bodies—a board of advisers, a faculty advisory council (composed mostly of University of Pennsylvania faculty), and an international advisory council. Each year, the director solicits themes via their own networks, as well as hosting an open process for proposing via the website. Each theme proposal usually involves two to three scholars working together, and all proposals (there are typically three or four) are brought to the faculty advisory council for evaluation. A different committee—which includes four people (mostly faculty from institutions other than Penn), plus the director and the assistant director—then evaluates the proposals. The directors seek gender equity as well as diversity of disciplinary perspectives on that committee. Final decisions about the fellowship are made in a collective conversation rather than strictly by ranking. That committee receives instructions about creating a diverse cohort with respect to rank, gender, discipline, and national location. Yet, director Steven Weitzman reports, it depends on the subfield whether it is possible to achieve as diverse a cohort as they would like. We would like to add that achieving diversity takes work, and in some cases it takes more work than in other cases.

Over the last several years, the Katz Center has made several changes to increase gender diversity specifically. One move was to bring more women into the leadership structure. Also crucial was empowering these boards and committees to make decisions (in this case, especially about the fellowship themes), rather than have committees as decorative features in a system where a director wields all the decision-making power. The center has also moved toward considering themes that stretch beyond the discipline of history, as well as paying special attention to themes that intersect with gender studies.

This discussion of the process of selection for prestigious fellowships indicates something important: creating a program that serves diverse scholars depends on whether diversity appears explicitly in the criteria a committee uses when choosing a theme, whether selection committees are required to consider it when they offer fellowships, and whether the committees themselves must be diverse in terms of gender. Our focus here has been gender equity, but we see very similar processes with respect to other kinds of diversity, such as race and ability. If welcoming scholars of color is important, scholars of color should be included on decision-making committees, and racial diversity needs to be an explicit criterion when choosing themes and offering fellowships. To include disabled scholars, the same principle applies, and the directors and committees need to make additional considerations about accessibility. If directors, committees, and other decision makers do not prioritize these kinds of inclusion, they are unlikely to happen by themselves.

The Gender of Citations

In the academic world, citations matter. "Citation is the currency of academia," writes Kecia Ali.[38] It is an "intellectual economy," explains Annabel Kim.[39] Citation is the way authors credit ideas. It is one way we name who we are in conversation with. Citations also signal that an author has "done the homework" of reading canonical sources in the field. When you read a paper, you want to check where the information came from—and you may often want to

---

38. Kecia Ali, "The Politics of Citation," *Gender Avenger*, May 31, 2019, https://www.genderavenger.com/blog/politics-of-citation.

39. Annabel L. Kim, "The Politics of Citation," *Diacritics* 48, no. 3 (2020): 4–9.

read those books or articles. And when you're a faculty member, the number of times your work is cited can be used to assess the importance of your work to the field. Many institutions use citation data as part of the criteria for promotion and tenure.[40]

Our research shows that women authors made up only 27 percent of authors cited in articles published in recent years in five major Jewish studies journals, despite the fact that women constitute 42 percent of tenure-track faculty in the field. Our findings also show that the gender of an article's author was the greatest factor in predicting the rate of women cited: women were more likely to cite women, though even then the rate was well below 42 percent.

To learn about citations in Jewish studies, we performed a bibliometric analysis. Bibliometrics, the quantitative study of citations, has been more widely used in STEM disciplines than in humanistic ones, largely because citations in the sciences are much more uniform and easier to count by algorithm. In fact, bibliometrics is so closely associated with the sciences that the bond between the two is assumed in common definitions. For example: "Bibliometric analysis is defined as a statistical evaluation of published scientific articles, books, or the chapters of a book, and it is an effectual way to measure the influence of publication in the scientific community."[41] Bibliometrics, then, can help us see trends in Jewish studies and allow us to compare the gendered issues in Jewish studies with other fields.

Our data on citations come from journal articles. While humanities scholars within Jewish studies often publish books— and indeed, those are at the center of tenure and promotion

40. For an excellent set of reflections on citational practices, race, and gender within the anthropology of religion, see the introduction to the forthcoming special issue of *Studies of Religion*: Britt Halvorson and Ingie Hovland, "The Problem of Citation in the Study of Religion: Who Do We Cite and Why?"

41. Pulwasha M. Iftikhar et al., "A Bibliometric Analysis of the Top 30 Most-Cited Articles in Gestational Diabetes Mellitus Literature (1946–2019)," *Cureus* 11, no. 2 (2019): e4131.

cases—journals offer better points of comparison. Journal citations can also reflect demographic changes in the field more quickly than books do. Graduate students and early-career faculty can and do publish journal articles, arguably at even greater rates than more senior faculty, some of whom choose to concentrate on writing books once they have tenure or become full professors.

Bibliometric studies in STEM fields and philosophy have identified a phenomenon known as the "Matthew effect," wherein having a significant reputation and track record of awards make one much more likely to receive future accolades and rewards.[42] Unsurprisingly, the Matthew effect has a significant gendered aspect: the research of men tends to be deemed more important than that of women, especially in fields where men significantly outnumber women. Scientists have hypothesized that the gendered problem is driven in part by the size of the gender gap in faculty, so fields where men vastly outnumber women would see an even more dramatic gap in citations.[43]

Given this hypothesis, we would not expect to see such a significant citation gap in a field such as Jewish studies because it already has a critical mass of women scholars. Yet men are still cited more often than women in Jewish studies journals. Studies in the sciences have demonstrated a "Matilda effect,"[44] wherein peer reviewers on average deem women authors less competent, even when their research has had similar impact factors.[45] Scholars in other non-STEM fields, especially social sciences, also show

42. A classic publication is Robert K. Merton, "The Matthew Effect in Science," *Science* 159, no. 1380 (January 5, 1968): 56–63.

43. Michelle L. Dion, Jane L. Sumner, and Sara M. Mitchell, "Gendered Citation Patterns across Political Science and Social Science Methodology Fields," *Political Analysis* 26, no. 3 (2018): 312–27.

44. Anne E. Lincoln, Stephanie Pincus, Janet Bandows Koster, and Phoebe S. Leboy, "The Matilda Effect in Science: Awards and Prizes in the US, 1990s and 2000s," *Social Studies of Science* 42, no. 2 (April 2012): 307–20.

45. C. Wennerås and A. Wold, "Nepotism and Sexism in Peer-Review," *Nature* 387 (1987): 341–43.

strong trends of citing both white women and people of color at rates well below their presence in the field.[46] Women in the field of environmental history, for example, have documented a growing number of cases in which publications relied on women's scholarship but did not cite it.[47]

To explore trends in citation, our study looked at every article published from the year 2018 to 2020[48] in six journals: *AJS Review, Jewish Quarterly Review (JQR), Modern Judaism, Jewish Social Studies, Prooftexts,* and the *Journal of the American Academy of Religion (JAAR)* (the last was from a related field for comparison).[49] We included only citations deemed to be secondary sources. If an article was about a person, we did not include citations of that person's work (so an article about Jacques Derrida did not include in its count any of the citations of Derrida). We did not count anything before 1950, which mainly meant excluding older, often philological, scholarship published exclusively by men.[50] If we had

46. Paula Chakravartty, Rachel Kuo, Victoria Grubbs, and Charlton McIlwain, "#CommunicationSoWhite." *Journal of Communication* 68, no. 2 (2018): 254–66; Carrie Mott and Daniel Cockayne, "Citation Matters: Mobilizing the Politics of Citation toward a Practice of 'Conscientious Engagement,'" *Gender, Place and Culture* 24, no. 7 (2017): 954–73; Joshua Reno and Britt Halvorson. "The Gendering of Anthropological Theory since 2000: Ontology, Semiotics, and Feminism." *Current Anthropology* 64, no. 5 (2023): 475–97; Christen A. Smith and Dominique Garrett-Scott, "'We Are Not Named': Black Women and the Politics of Citation in Anthropology," *Feminist Anthropology* 2, no. 1 (2021): 18–37.

47. 12 Women Scholars, "A Disturbing Pattern," *Chronicle of Higher Education,* August 27, 2021, https://www.insidehighered.com/advice/2021/08/27/entrenched -inequity-not-appropriately-citing-scholarship-women-and-people-color.

48. These were the most recent years that all journals had published when we ran our final analyses on data in 2021.

49. We did not count book reviews, editorial notes, or non-peer-reviewed reflections, such as on the work of a recently deceased scholar.

50. The year 1950 was an arbitrary cutoff, but we wanted to be sure to appropriately count earlier canonical scholarship that is still cited as such. For example, the historian Jacob Katz and the Talmud scholar Hanoch Albeck each published scholarship well before 1970 that scholars continue to cite. Still, the overall number of cited works predating the 1980s in our sample is comparatively very small.

included any of these categories, our data would have reflected an even wider gender gap.

Using our criteria meant we had a total of 8,326 included citations in Jewish studies journals alone. To create data that paralleled bibliometric studies in other fields, we began by using Genderize (a software interface) to predict the gender of the cited author. Genderize gives a percentage likelihood based on the first name. For any percentages under 95 percent, we checked individually using web searches to find the pronouns used for that scholar. We coded each article according to the gender of its author (or, in some cases, authors), the rough time period it addressed (ancient, medieval, or modern), and a broad characterization of its subfield (history, philosophy, literature, textual studies, or contemporary/theoretical studies). Here we did not include multiple citations of the same author. If we had, the gender gaps would be even wider; we also found that male authors were more likely to have multiple citations within a single article. We should stress that these data rely on the *names* of scholars, not their own gender identity. That is why there is no representation on our graphs for nonbinary or genderqueer scholars. We need better ways of tracking citation of nonbinary and genderqueer scholars, but names are not the way to do this. (The same could be said about tracking the racial or ethnic profile of cited scholars. Much work remains to be done.) The data presented below represent men and women, which we know is not the full picture.

Women publish slightly less often than men. But only slightly. In the Jewish studies journals we looked at for the years 2018–20, women authored 39 percent of the single-authored articles we evaluated, and men authored 61 percent. The religious studies journal we used for comparison had a breakdown of 48 percent female and 52 percent male. For Jewish studies, these numbers are only slightly lower than the numbers we see in tenure and tenure-track positions.

Moreover, publishing is not simply an exercise in meritocracy. Most peer reviews are anonymous, sometimes in hopes of decreasing bias, but other inequalities persist. For example, Robert Boice and Ferdinand Jones draw on Diana Crane's concept of the "invisible college" to explain how one's scholarly networks make a difference: "The road to getting published includes membership in an invisible college—a group of individuals who can exert enormous influence on the popularity of topics in journals."[51] When most journal editors are men (seven of eleven editors were for most of the years our data cover), and men disproportionately have other men in their networks, this tips the scales. We'll discuss more about networking below.

Kecia Ali also notes that sometimes women's work appears under men's names, or is otherwise assumed to be written by men. She writes, "Attributing women's scholarly achievements to men is a time-honored practice that spans fields and disciplines."[52]

Women are not cited in proportion to their presence as researchers in the field. Only 25 percent of authors' citations in Jewish studies journals were of works of scholarship by women, while the remaining 75 percent of citations were of scholarship by men (see figure 1). Since we know that women currently constitute 42 percent of faculty in Jewish studies in tenure-track jobs at R1 universities, this discrepancy cannot be attributed to a stark demographic imbalance in the field. We also noted that in our data, women published at only a slightly lower rate than men (39 percent

---

51. Robert Boice and Ferdinand Jones, "Why Academicians Don't Write," *Journal of Higher Education* 55, no. 5 (September–October 1984): 571; and R. K. Blashfield, "Feighner et al., Invisible Colleges, and the Matthew Effect," *Schizophrenia Bulletin* 8, no. 1 (1982): 1–12.

52. Kecia Ali, *The Woman Question in Islamic Studies* (Princeton, NJ: Princeton University Press, forthcoming). Ali offers the examples in Kishonna Gray, "#CiteHerWork: Marginalizing Women in Academic and Journalistic Writing," http://www.kishonnagray.com/manifestmy-reality/citeherwork-marginalizing -women-in-academic-and-journalistic-writing.

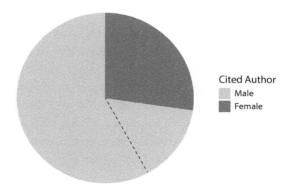

FIGURE 1. Gender of cited authors (dotted line at 42 percent)

of articles by women). So what could explain this difference in citations? Perhaps a closer examination of a particular subset of the data would yield answers. One journal might be bringing the numbers down. Or perhaps one subfield was a particular offender, while the others were more equitable. But no finer-tuned examination of the data—focused on one journal, or one subfield or time period—had a proportion of women authors cited that came close to 42 percent. We saw some significant variation across those groups, but none exceeded 32 percent.

As one female scholar said to us: "When my work is not footnoted, even in places where it would be the perfect citation, I wonder if the scholar just doesn't know it or if my work is somehow forgettable. Is there a gender thing at work, or am I being paranoid?" We can't know an individual author's reasons behind their citation choices, and we suspect any oversights are rarely malicious in intent, but, as this colleague expressed, missing citations matter to scholars and their careers.

Women across academic fields have noted citation gaps, so in this way, Jewish studies is not unique. The Cite Black Women collective, for example, notes the relationship between citation and who and how we read; its tenets "read Black women's work" and "acknowledge Black women's intellectual production" call for both reading and citing Black women's work.[53] When there are few Black women scholars in the canons of our scholarly literature, it means that authors may not feel required to cite them as part of signaling that they have read the requisite or canonical material. As Elizabeth Pérez notes, graduate students and junior scholars are encouraged to "cite upwards," that is, to invoke the intellectual giants of the canon—a canon whose authors are still largely white and male.[54] When citations are about cementing status, it advantages an author to cite the towering figures of the scholarly past, and in Jewish studies, as in most other fields, those figures are rarely women.

Male authors of articles cite female scholars at lower rates than female authors cite female scholars. This was one of the most striking differences we found. Neither male nor female journal article authors cited women as much as they cited men, but the difference was much more pronounced for male authors (see figure 2). We found that men were significantly more likely to cite men: overall, when an author was male, he was 2.1 times as likely to cite a male author. Moreover, neither male nor female authors cited women at a rate close to 42 percent (the estimated percent of women in the field) or even 39 percent (the percent of women authors of journal articles we studied). This difference is striking, but it did not come as a surprise to us because we have seen similar data from other fields.[55] In Jewish studies journals, 19 percent of male authors' citations were to scholarship by women, whereas 34 percent of female authors' citations were to scholarship by women. For male-authored articles,

53. Cite Black Women Collective, "Our Praxis," accessed January 5, 2024, https://www.citeblackwomencollective.org/our-praxis.html.

54. Elizabeth Pérez, "Sorry Cites: The (Necro)politics of Citation in the Anthropology of Religion," *Studies in Religion*, forthcoming.

55. Sara M. Mitchell, Samantha Lange, and Holly Brus, "Gendered Citation Patterns in International Relations Journals," *International Studies Perspectives* 14, no. 4 (November 2013): 485–92.

fewer than one in five citations was to a woman's scholarship. In religious studies, men cited women at roughly the same rate (19 percent), while women cited women in 41 percent of their citations.

A small part of this gap may be because of self-citation. Studies in other fields have shown that men are more likely to cite themselves: "In the last two decades of data, men self-cited 70 percent more than women," one study concluded.[56] The explanations offered run the gamut from men thinking more highly of themselves and being socialized to self-promote to men merely being overrepresented as accomplished researchers. Men did cite themselves more often than women cited themselves in our data, but not at a rate that could account for these differences.

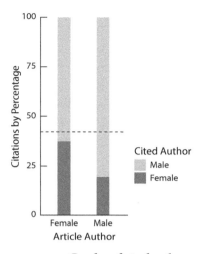

FIGURE 2. Gender of cited authors by gender of article author (dotted line at 42 percent)

We suspect that one of the most important reasons for this citational gender gap concerns the makeup of scholarly networks. Scholars can cite only work they know about. They can engage substantively only with work they have read. Even the most widely read of scholars cannot know about all the current work in their field. They are more likely to have read a work by someone they know, either personally or by reputation—that is, someone within their own scholarly networks. Sometimes, for example, the

56. Molly M. King, Carl T. Bergstrom, Shelley J. Correll, Jennifer Jacquet, and Jevin D. West, "Men Set Their Own Cites High: Gender and Self-Citation across Fields and over Time," *Socius* 3 (2017), https://journals.sagepub.com/doi/10.1177/2378023117738903.

acknowledgments section in a book written by a man lets us know that his intellectual companions have been all or mostly men.

We know from sociological studies that men are more likely to network with men.[57] Similarly, working professionals are more likely to network with people of their own race.[58] We have fewer data for queer and trans professional networking, but there are good reasons to assume parallels there too. Professional networks, like personal ones, tend to mirror the traits of the person.

Studies that compare men and women also suggest that men network more "effectively"—that is, they are more likely to reap professional benefits from their networks, in part because they are more likely to ask for things that benefit them.[59] If men are better networked, it also means that they tend to be better known among other male scholars.

Our interviews affirmed the perceived strength and benefits of these networks. One senior, tenured woman scholar recalled,

> *A senior male colleague once told me that he felt like he should write on behalf of the promotion of a male colleague "because his father wrote for my promotion." I have also read recommendation letters that mentioned connections of this very sort, such as that a candidate "went to yeshiva with my son." Such statements strike me as exemplary of the male-dominant networks that shape the field, from which most if not all women are habitually excluded.*

Although this explicit statement of personal connection is unusual, the overall picture is this: white male scholars are likely to have scholarly networks that include a disproportionate number of white men. And there is a relationship between knowing more male scholars and reading or citing more male scholars. We believe

57. Brass, "Men's and Women's Networks."

58. Matthew O. Jackson, *Social and Economic Networks* (Princeton, NJ: Princeton University Press, 2010).

59. Elena Greguletz, Marjo-Riitta Diehl, and Karin Kreutzer, "Why Women Build Less Effective Networks Than Men: The Role of Structural Exclusion and Personal Hesitation," *Human Relations* 72, no. 7 (July 2019): 1234–61.

that this networking issue—men knowing and reading a larger than proportional number of men—drives some of the difference between men's and women's citation rates of women scholars. This is also critically important because of its relationship to professional advancement. One study about professional status noted men's greater integration into other men's networks and concluded that "promotions were significantly related to centrality in departmental, men's, and dominant-coalition interaction networks."[60]

We suspect that networking is one major driver of the difference in citations, but it is unlikely to be the whole explanation, especially because even women article authors do not cite women at a rate equal to their presence in the field. These may be results of an additional set of reasons for citation continue to privilege citing male scholarship, such as the pressure to "cite up" and refer to more famous authors, to cite canonical or foundational authors in the field and thus prove oneself as a legitimate scholar, and to put one's work into conversation with big names, all of which skew male.

Women are cited at different rates in different subfields. We coded the articles by rough subfields: textual studies (such as biblical studies and rabbinics), philosophy/Jewish thought, history, literary studies, and anthropology/sociology/cultural studies. Then we labeled each article according to what we judged to be its primary subfield. We did this by reading at least the first two pages of the article and carefully looking at the bibliography to see which scholarly audience or conversation the author was seeking.

We found a clear, statistically significant difference (see figure 3). Articles published in philosophy/Jewish thought cited women at a rate of 17 percent. (Recall that we counted only citations of secondary literature: the canon of Jewish thinkers is overwhelmingly male, so the vast majority of these articles were also about male thinkers, but we didn't count the citations of those

---

60. Brass, "Men's and Women's Networks," 327.

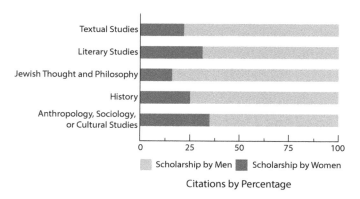

FIGURE 3. Citations by subfield

male thinkers because they were primary sources.) These percentages indicated substantial differences from other subfields.

In both literary studies and anthropology/sociology/cultural studies, citations of women were about one-third of total citations. History and textual studies articles had slightly lower rates with, respectively, about 25 percent and 22 percent of cited works authored by women. The relative ordering of these percentages may be explained in part by the gender of faculty working in these fields: women make up more than half of PhD earners in literary studies and sociology, but slightly less than half in history. Moreover, these percentages were fairly consistent across the published articles in Jewish studies and religious studies, suggesting that many of the causes may be shared. But even if the relative order is unsurprising, the numbers themselves should be. Why do women authors make up only a quarter or a third of secondary source citations when they make up about half the faculty in these subfields?

Some reasons are shared across fields. For example, certain types of academic work have broader applicability because they are sweeping or theoretical. "Classic" works in Jewish history, textual studies, philosophy, and literary studies are mostly authored by men. Doctoral qualifying exam reading lists bear this out. Some of this is a function of age (there were proportionally more male academics in the past), and some of it may be a function of men's greater likelihood of authoring broad, sweeping texts.

These differences are certainly driven in part by the fact that some fields have more male scholars (who we know are more likely to cite men), but they cannot be explained *solely* by the gender of faculty in these fields. Jewish thought has more men than women, but by any measure (faculty positions held, articles published, conference papers submitted), it has a significant and growing number of women. By none of our informal counts did women number below about a third. It is worth noting that the *average* percentage of women cited in Jewish thought articles was 16 percent. In 2018 articles, it was only 11 percent. Many articles cited even less.

These rates are on the lower end even when compared to other philosophical fields. Philosophy of science, for example, sees about 18 percent of articles and books cited authored by women, while women constitute 20 percent of the field.[61] The American Philosophical Association has reported that women make up about 21 percent of professors, but they make up smaller numbers at elite institutions and at the full professor rank. Philosophers have written at length on the reasons for these low numbers, and the causes they name include conceptual and methodological assumptions, as well as historical trends. Causes are not reducible to numbers or percentiles but instead are deeply entwined with the content of the discipline.

We believe that many of the reasons for the difference in citation rates across subfields are intellectually particular to the history, methods, and assumptions of these subfields. We explore

---

61. Evelyn Brister and Daniel J. Hicks, "Contributions of Women to Philosophy of Science: A Bibliometric Analysis," in *The Routledge Handbook of Feminist Philosophy of Science*, ed. Sharon Crasnow and Kristen Intemann (New York: Routledge, 2020), 65.

some of these intellectual and historical differences among sub-fields in chapters 4, 5, and 6.

Women are cited at different rates in scholarship on different historical eras. We also sorted our data to compare the citational rates across scholarly articles on different time periods: modernity, the medieval period, and antiquity (see figure 4). We found that more women were cited in articles about the modern era (26 percent of cited authors were women) than those about antiquity (23 percent of cited authors were women). Bringing up the rear with 17 percent were citations of women in articles concerning the medieval period. This last statistic may be surprising, given that medieval studies has become an exciting field for the study of women, gender, and feminist theory—but it would seem this scholarship is not as widely cited as one would imagine. Here again we believe these differences are driven by the gendered makeup of faculty as well as by the history of scholarship in these fields.

Citation rates are different across journals. We also investigated whether specific Jewish studies journals have different citation rates. This question is connected to our previous questions since many journals focus on a particular subfield or time period. As figure 5 shows, *Jewish Social Studies* and *Prooftexts* each had citation rates of women scholars at near 30 percent. The religious studies journal we analyzed had a similar citation rate. The *AJS Review* had citation rates of women of 25 percent. In *Jewish Quarterly Review* (*JQR*) women constituted 22 percent of cited scholars, and only 19 percent of cited scholars in *Modern Judaism* were women. Some of this relates back to the issues we saw in subfields, particularly because *Modern Judaism* leans heavily toward modern Jewish thought. And yet it also restricts itself to the modern period, which we have seen has the highest rate of women cited of the three broad time periods we examined. Our data suggest correlation between the gender ratio of the editorial board and the gender of scholars cited (see table 1).

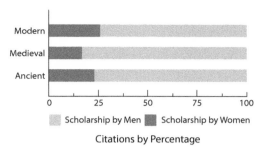

FIGURE 4. Citations by time period

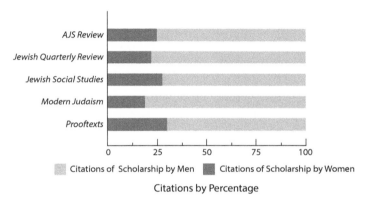

FIGURE 5. Citations by journal

We suspect that the correlation between citation rates and the composition of the board is not a simple causative one. Instead, we suspect the citation rates of women correlate with a number of factors related to the culture of a particular journal, including the genders of the editors and board members, but also particular policies about diversity, the culture of submissions (such as whether and how editors solicit submissions, and whether and how they publish special issues), how much the editorial board is involved in decision making, the role of the managing editor,[62]

62. Interestingly, for most of the time under study, every managing editor was a woman. (*Modern Judaism* calls this position "editorial assistant.") Some managing

TABLE 1. Correlation between the Gender Ratio of Editorial Boards and the Gender of Scholars Cited

	Editors by gender, 2020	Editorial board by gender, 2020	Women as percentage of editorial board, 2020	Rate of citation of women-authored scholarship, 2018–20
AJS Review	1 man, 1 woman	6 men, 5 women	45%	25%
Jewish Quarterly Review	1 man, 1 woman	15 men, 5 women	25%	22%
Jewish Social Studies	2 men, 1 woman	14 men, 11 women	44%	28%
Modern Judaism	1 man	8 men, 2 women	20%	19%
Prooftexts	1 man, 1 woman	11 men, 10 women	48%	30%

and the gender makeup of the subfield. We note that journal editors and editorial boards change over time; even since we collected our citation data, we have seen significant changes in editors' genders and in the gender makeup of boards of several of these journals.[63]

Journals also demonstrate the rule of "like attracts like." This works in benign ways, such as articles on a particular topic clustering in one journal. It can also work in ways that undermine inclusion: if a journal publishes articles by men who largely cite other men, then these men are more likely to read the journal, to see their own work reflected there, and to send in submissions. This

---

editors hold PhDs, and some are advanced graduate students. It is a position that does a lot of the paperwork and correspondence but has relatively little say over editorial decisions, such as acceptance, rejection, and the intellectual trajectory of the journal.

63. While we were writing this book, *Jewish Quarterly Review* made significant changes in its editorial board, including reaching 50 percent women. Full disclosure: Sarah agreed to be part of the editorial board after being asked to join and reading of its interest in increasing gender equity.

reveals, yet again, the importance of networks and also of representation. If a journal is not including voices like yours, it is harder to imagine your own work published there.

Overall, Jewish studies journal articles cited women at a slightly lower rate than did religious studies articles. (In statistical terms, we found that if an article appeared in a religious studies journal, the likelihood that an author cited a woman increased by 18 percent.) Given the different citation rates we see in journals, it seems likely that the gap between Jewish studies and religious studies articles may be driven more by the articles in *JQR* and *Modern Judaism* rather than being uniform across publications. We also noticed that *JAAR* and *AJS Review*, each of which is the journal of the learned society for its respective field (religious studies and Jewish studies), had very similar citation rates. This too suggests that the difference we see in Jewish studies journals may not be field-wide but isolated to particular subfields or journals.

Which of these factors matter most? When we analyzed the data overall (using a regression analysis), we found that the gender of the author of the scholarly article was the greatest factor in predicting the rate of citation of women. Of secondary importance was the subfield, closely followed by the composition of the journal's editorial board. Time period had comparatively little importance.

We also found evidence for optimism: between 2018 and 2020, the rates of citation of women increased overall, though many individual areas and journals saw it decrease. We recognize that three years is a small time difference, so our optimism is guarded. However, those years also marked a time of increasing awareness of gender issues both in the wider culture (the #MeToo movement, for example) and within academic cultures.

In the Classroom

Jewish studies scholars shape the field not only by publishing work, but also by their pedagogy in classrooms. At most universities, professors have near autonomy in designing their syllabi, including choosing readings. A number of criteria go into those choices: an instructor usually has an idea of which topics, time periods, geographical areas, and intellectual concepts they want to cover. They must also choose readings that are appropriate for undergraduates and, often, for students with no background in Jewish studies.

Which authors appear most often on syllabi? And what place do women and gender have in the most popular books assigned in Jewish studies classrooms? We gathered more than thirty introductory syllabi publicly available on the internet, such as on university websites and at academia.edu, as well as through interpersonal requests. We looked specifically at introductory courses, like those often called "Introduction to Judaism," "Judaism," "Jewish History," "Introduction to Jewish Studies," "Introduction to Jewish Civilizations," and similar titles. We also used social media to solicit answers to the question: "What textbooks do you use in introductory courses?" We received nineteen additional responses from faculty who used textbooks in their courses (some do not). We counted only syllabi from the last ten years.

Faculty members who share syllabi publicly via the internet are mostly a self-selecting group. Others shared which textbooks they used in response to social media queries on Facebook or X (formerly Twitter), so they are part of our own scholarly networks. Overall, we received responses from those who teach at research universities and small liberal arts colleges, at public and private institutions, and in several departments (mainly those focusing on Jewish studies, religious studies, and history). The syllabi available online represented more male professors, and social media responses represented more women professors; overall about half of the total number were created by women professors.

Among these forty-nine syllabi, we kept seeing the same textbooks assigned repeatedly, so we are confident that these texts represent the ways that hundreds of students are encountering Jewish studies. It is true that many instructors (both of us included) sometimes teach readings with which we disagree, so we cannot take the very fact of a text appearing on a syllabus as an endorsement of it. Still, readings strongly shape what students take away from a classroom.

Looking at the syllabi as a group, almost all the syllabi we collected had at least one reading by a woman author, but almost all also had a majority of readings by male authors. Our count excluded primary sources, such as biblical or rabbinic texts, even though it is fair to assume male authorship of those texts too. As one professor told us, on many syllabi, "women are like decorations."

We also examined the books most often used in introductory Jewish studies classrooms: the textbooks that play a central role in creating the narrative of the class. Many of these do not look like the hardcover introductory textbooks you might expect to see in an undergraduate biology class or in an introduction to microeconomics course, but nevertheless students treat them as authoritative. Students often assume these textbooks' narratives are true, and that the facts they impart are the most important ones, so they are important for forming many undergraduates' impressions of Jews and Jewish history. (We did not count primary sources or readers, though they would provide an additional way to examine what students are learning.) Reading lists thus both reflect faculty choices and shape students' received narratives.

Only one of our six most popular texts was authored by a woman—Leora Batnitzky's *How Judaism Became a Religion*—and it was the one least often assigned. The other five were Michael Satlow's *Creating Judaism*, Raymond Scheindlin's *A Short History of the Jewish People*, Barry Holtz's collection (of all male scholars) *Back to the Sources*, Aaron Hahn Tapper's *Judaisms*, and *The Jews* by John Efron, Matthias Lehman, and Steven Weitzman. We chose the top six because they appeared on many syllabi, and the seventh most popular appeared only on two.

Once we identified the most popular texts, we asked three questions: (1) What generalizations does this book draw about women, gender, and/or Jews? (2) How extensive is the coverage of gender in this book? And (3) what conclusions would a student draw from this book? We took note of mentions of women, discussions of women, mentions of gender, and discussions of gender. We coded something as a mention when someone was merely named in a single sentence, such as a sentence naming Miriam's Song of the Sea in the Bible or a timeline that includes Golda Meir becoming Israeli prime minister.[64] We coded something as a discussion if it was longer than one sentence about a woman, even if it had nothing to do with her gender, such as a mention of Mary Antin describing pogroms. We coded something a discussion of gender if it recognized the constructed, social nature of gender in any way, such as how *tekhines* (prayers) were associated with women's rituals.[65] We also coded instances of women mentioned or discussed in a sidebar rather than within the main text. None of these textbooks included discussions of gender beyond a gender binary (such as, say, the *tumtum* or *androginos* of rabbinic texts). Kathryn Cooper, an undergraduate at Indiana University, also created extensive notations for each of these textbooks, noting mentions and discussions as well as writing about what conclusions a student could draw from reading these. We integrate her analyses here; she played a central role in the way we understand these texts.

Our research helps us examine (1) the way women can seem incidental to history or thought by appearing only as a name or other brief mention rather than as a subject in an extended discussion, (2) how appearance in a sidebar can include women while still keeping them outside the central narrative, and (3) how the shared assumptions about textbooks indicate that gender is an ancillary issue or a topic of special interest.

---

64. Raymond Scheindlin, *A Short History of the Jewish People: From Legendary Times to Modern Statehood* (New York: Macmillan, 1998), 236; and Barry Holtz, *Back to the Sources: Reading the Classic Jewish Texts* (New York: Summit Books, 1984), 41.

65. Michael Satlow, *Creating Judaism: History, Tradition, Practice* (New York: Columbia University Press, 2006), 275.

Every textbook included mentions of women or gender that went no further than a name or a single fact. Any textbook that seeks to introduce a wide historical or intellectual tradition will need to do this. But in many cases, women appear only in these single-sentence mentions. *A Short History of the Jewish People* can serve as an example: in the course of the entire book, women appear twenty-five times in 288 pages. This is a tiny fraction of the book, but the breakdown of these appearances is even more telling: it has twenty-two mentions and only three discussions. (We were also very capacious in counting mentions. One sentence about King Ferdinand and Queen Isabella counted as a mention, for example, as did a sentence about Jews and Muslims seeing each other as "sisters in monotheism.")[66] Seven of the mentions are about women as wives or consorts, and women are never the main characters, even for a small section. Gender is never mentioned and never appears as an analytic tool.

Other textbooks include more attention to women and gender, but in many sections, they appear primarily in sidebars, such as inserted text boxes, images, or timelines. While this is better than complete absence, it allows the main story to continue without them. *The Jews* provides an example of this. It is in its third edition, and women have appeared slightly more in each successive version. Women are mentioned several times in each section, which puts this book ahead of others in terms of showing the involvement of women in a wide cross section of Jewish life. However, it includes the most lengthy discussions of women in its inserts, not in the main text, giving students the impression that men's stories are central to Jewish life while women's stories are relevant only as supplementary reading. These supplements can be fascinating reading; it's not that they are dull or fail to illuminate larger themes in Jewish life. Rather, it seems that the authors have started with a historical narrative that centers on men. Naturally, in writing a textbook, authors must rely on others' scholarship: we cannot

66. Scheindlin, *Short History of the Jewish People*, 73.

write a history of Jews entirely from our own investigations of primary sources. One of the problems with our inherited scholarly narratives, however, is that most center on men. Fully integrating women would mean turning the narrative upside down with respect to themes, continuities, change, or key events. This is no mean feat, especially when we must write about areas outside our own area of research expertise.

Convention also drives textbooks in another way: when gender analysis is not integral to the genre. Here, *How Judaism Became a Religion* is most telling. Batnitzky writes that "issues of gender and feminism are beyond this book's scope."[67] She introduces modern Jewish thought and modern Judaism through male, European thinkers with little attention to women and almost no use of gender as an analytic tool. Thus, it might come as a surprise to know that Batnitzky herself has been an astute observer of gender in the canonical texts of modern Jewish thought. She has noted gendered issues in her own analytical work.[68] Why would an expert who thinks about gender when writing a different scholarly book decide it was "beyond the scope" of a more general book? We assume that Batnitzky carefully considered the expected audience and reception of the book. Perhaps this led her to conclude—as it seems other authors also did—that gender is "niche" or special interest, that the field itself has positioned it as peripheral, or that it is of lesser importance for Jewish studies students. These genre conventions and assumptions, then, affect even scholars whose research interests include gender.

Some textbooks did offer ways for students to think about gender—a trend that suggests that scholars have tools available to them to improve textbooks. One mode we saw infrequently but

67. Leora Batnitzky, *How Judaism Became a Religion: An Introduction to Modern Jewish Thought* (Princeton, NJ: Princeton University Press, 2013), 4–5.
68. For just one example of Batnitzky's work on gender, see "Dependency and Vulnerability: Jewish and Feminist Existentialist Constructions of the Human," in *Women and Gender in Jewish Philosophy*, ed. Hava Tirosh-Samuelson (Bloomington: Indiana University Press, 2004), 127–52.

effectively was an acknowledgment of how gender and power shape what is knowable. *The Jews*, for example, acknowledges the archival gap in documenting women's stories from history. Over more than five hundred pages, it includes 119 mentions of women or gender, twenty-one discussions of women, and eight discussions of gender. It includes much about women in chapters that cover recent history such as the Holocaust and the present day. Students could then connect the dots to understand the fact that there are more sources to draw from about women from these eras. Hahn Tapper's *Judaisms* explicitly discusses how Jewish women have been excluded, as well as how particular discourses have "reinforced the notion that men are the norm and women are the exception."[69]

Gender and sexuality were best integrated into Hahn Tapper's *Judaisms*, which was the most common textbook assigned in our solicited syllabi but appeared on only one of the syllabi we found online. Perhaps some of the difference lies in our own scholarly networks (which include feminist scholars at a higher rate than the field as a whole, we suspect), though the recent publication date of *Judaisms* (2016) also means that it was unavailable for some of the earliest syllabi we studied. It focuses more on the present day than on history and more on lived religion than on text or history, yet it thematically covers a wide range of topics appropriate to an introductory course. Both women and gender appear central to the story, occurring in both the main text and sidebars, and on almost every page.

Michael Satlow's *Creating Judaism* demonstrated another trend: discussing women beyond their relationships to men, an analysis that was bolstered by drawing on women scholars who have studied women. The book's discussions of women go beyond terms of wife, daughter, or whore and delve into women's participation in religious Judaism and Jewish scholarship. The book frequently

69. Aaron J. Hahn Tapper, *Judaisms: A Twenty-First Century Introduction to Jews and Jewish Identity* (Berkeley: University of California Press, 2016), 90.

cites female scholars of Jewish studies, such as Susan Starr Sered's *Women as Ritual Experts*. It has no sidebars, and it has twenty-seven mentions of women or gender, nineteen discussions of women, and twelve discussions of gender in 340 pages. Many of these discussions are lengthy, and some are interconnected. A student reading this book would conclude that women's participation in religious Jewish life is historically important (even if there are still some obstacles to full participation) and, as acknowledged only in this book and *Judaisms*, that lesbians also participate in religious life. When scholars encounter structures that figure women primarily in relationship to men, it can make it more difficult to see women who are not heterosexual, and these two books present compelling alternatives.

The maleness of religious study leaks into books used in undergraduate and adult education classrooms as well. One popular introduction to the study of Jewish texts—a collection edited by Barry Holtz, *Back to the Sources: Reading the Classic Jewish Texts*, first published in 1984 and still assigned to students today—includes eight articles by ten men that present the genres of Jewish texts and demonstrate how they should be read and interpreted. This is not for lack of accessible work on these texts: for example, some recent publications demonstrate how to study Talmud and why it remains relevant; one edited volume foregrounds women Talmud scholars who grapple with what it means to be a woman for whom these texts were not written.[70] The connection between the maleness of religious study and the perceived expertise of male Jewish scholars is perhaps clearest for scholars who continue to work with these canonical texts and their later cousins. Such texts form a central set of sources for scholars who study premodern materials. The imagined body of the expert reader of Jewish texts has remained stubbornly that of an adult Jewish man. The segregation of knowledge about women, gender, and sexuality

70. Paul Socken, ed., *Why Study Talmud in the Twenty-First Century? The Relevance of the Ancient Jewish Text to Our World* (Lanham, MD: Lexington Books, 2009).

reinforces the misidentification of Jewishness as male and scholarship as masculine.

Overall, these popular classroom texts demonstrate a wide range of engagement (and nonengagement) with women and gender. The syllabi we studied showed a trend of moving toward books that discuss gender more and more centrally, and we are hopeful that trend will continue. We also hope that faculty can teach students to be good critical readers of these texts and note for themselves when and where women appear as part of the story or gender appears as a category of analysis.

There is also much new scholarship on gender that is ripe for inclusion in new textbooks. Gender analyses of rabbinic texts, for example, uncover fascinating aspects of Jewish self-definition, particularly in relation to Christianity.[71] And examination of the gendered violence of rape during the pogroms of Eastern Europe reveal how this violence created lasting physical and emotional horror for women and consequences for their families and communities, shaping Jewish political thought in the modern era.[72] Contemporary scholarship in Jewish women's history also features analyses of the homoeroticism in the purported "manliness" of Zionist thought; surveys of women who served as Jewish religious leaders long before the twentieth century; and portraits of women writers of Hebrew and Yiddish literary traditions and those who wrote in the multitude of other vernaculars, including those who participated in the Nahda, the modern Arab intellectual renaissance of the Middle East.[73] (We recognize that this a problematic term for its Eurocentrism—"Middle" of what? "East" of what?—yet it is still the most widely recognized label, so we use

71. These include scholars such as Israel Yuval, Gailt Hasan-Rokem, and Rafe Neis.

72. Irina Astashkevich, *Gendered Violence: Jewish Women in the Pogroms of 1917 to 1921* (Boston: Academic Studies, 2018).

73. These include contributions by Ofri Ilany, Ilana Szobel, Lital Levy, and Tarek El-Ariss, in *The Arab Renaissance: A Bilingual Anthology of the Nahda*, ed. Tarek El-Ariss (New York: Modern Language Association of America, 2018).

it in this book.) Introductory textbooks that accord women equal attention can spotlight the scholarly discoveries that make this an exciting era for the field of Jewish studies.

Jewish studies textbooks should not present the normative Jew as male, sideline women in the narrative, or ignore feminist scholarship. Discussion of women should appear in all historical time periods, locations, and textual sources, even when their words have not been preserved directly. And gender can be a useful analytical tool to understand when and where silences take place, as well as the many spaces in which women and genderqueer people are not silent.

As our numbers show, women are underrepresented in Jewish studies faculty posts and editorial positions. They are even more dramatically underrepresented in citations. Presentations and analyses of women and gender appear only unevenly in the most popular textbooks of Jewish studies. How did women come to occupy the sidelines of Jewish studies, and what factors hinder women from greater prominence in the field?

Part II

2

Discrimination and Harassment

A male scholar at a Jewish studies conference put his hand on my knee and said he would give me a postdoc if I had sex with him. He was an attractive man and presented his offer as transactional: sex for a postdoc. What do you do with such an offer? How do you respond without creating an enemy in the field who will do damage to your career behind your back? To whom do you complain, knowing that no one will ever do anything to protect you or any other woman from male predators who also happen to be tenured, respected professors?

This "offer" of career advancement in exchange for sex took place a few years ago and exemplifies unethical behavior in the academy, which takes a multitude of forms. Note here that the graduate student who was propositioned walked away, but she feared that her refusal might lead to career damage: the man who propositioned her might one day be on a hiring committee or determine if she receives a grant or tenure or an invitation to lecture at an important conference. To whom can she complain? And without witnesses, will she be believed? If she were to file a complaint, what would be the outcome? Would a tenured scholar be excommunicated from the field solely based on her charge that he would no doubt deny? What if others saw *her* as the problem?

When we discussed our research on harassment in Jewish studies, some colleagues responded with comments that suggested changing the culture would spell the end of friendly relationships or unnecessarily police people's personal lives. We heard: "Does this mean we can no longer flirt?" and "I like your scarf! I guess I'm not supposed to say that anymore." Others even blamed the people who faced harassment: "You can't stop people from having erotic fantasies." We heard several variations on the idea that it was particularly women's responsibility to deter harassment, such as, "When I was her age, I knew how to handle such men."

Why is sexual harassment prevalent in the field of Jewish studies, as it is in so many other academic fields? The previous chapter presented quantitative data demonstrating the marginalization of women in faculty positions, fellowships, and citations. We did not gather quantitative data on harassment, but we do have the results of interviews with over eighty women and nonbinary scholars, ranging from postdocs to tenured full professors, and all but three gave us vivid accounts of witnessing or experiencing discrimination, exclusion, harassment, or assault. Even when incidents occurred decades ago, many remembered the precise details and could still feel the powerful emotions they had felt at that moment, particularly shame, shock, and rage. Some told us that the experience had lasting consequences for them emotionally, and that they remained suspicious that their career advancement had been affected in ways they would never know.

We heard similar stories over and over, leading us to realize that these were not occasional aberrations. We heard from our interlocutors about the consequences—for instance, people who experienced harassment or witnessed harassment directed against a colleague described feeling demoralized, as if not only their work but also their very ability to function as a scholar had been thrown into question. We have also spoken to victims of sexual assault, criminal acts that they sometimes did not report to the police out of feelings of shock, embarrassment, hopelessness, and concern that they would not be believed, that their careers would be damaged irreparably if they pursued criminal charges, or that they would lose valuable time and emotional resources if they had to return again and again to explain the incident.

We report experiences anonymously, changing only details that might identify the people involved. Some of the people we interviewed were relieved to tell their stories. Many were angry that they could not report what happened out of fear of retaliation or because there were no administrative officials who would act on their behalf. Some feared gossip, but many wished they could warn others about those who had harassed them.

Harassment, discrimination, and exclusion are related, but not identical. Discrimination is fundamentally about unjust exclusion or marginalization, which contradict ethical norms of scholarship; scholarship demands consideration of all evidence and engagement with all legitimate scholarly interpretations. Sexual harassment is unwanted verbal or physical interactions of a sexual nature. It can also function as a particularly egregious form of discrimination, undermining the feeling of legitimacy for a scholar, and turning that person into a representative for an entire group: harassment of one woman undermines the feeling of belonging for all women; harassment of one trans scholar undermines all trans scholars. We also track what some have called "gender harassment," or nonsexual acts repeatedly committed against a person because of their gender. There are also cases that may lurk in the borderlands between harassment and discrimination, such as repeated comments that a woman should bake snacks for faculty meetings, or cutting remarks about gender scholarship not being "real scholarship." These may not have sexual content, but they foster disrespect and undermine membership in the academic community. We are less interested in a taxonomy of what exactly constitutes harassment and more interested in showing the ways that harassment, discrimination, and even sexual assault overlap and work together in the current culture of Jewish studies.

This chapter's primary goal is to give voice to women's experiences of discrimination, exclusion, harassment, and assault within the field of Jewish studies. Although we focus primarily on experiences of women because women formed the largest portion of our interviewees, we know that many historically marginalized people also face harassment, and we see some of this overlap in our inter-locutors' accounts. We argue that when women and nonbinary people are not treated as equal colleagues, it contributes to a cul-ture that tolerates marginalization, denigration, and even harass-ment. While supporting academic freedom and freedom of speech, we argue for a culture of dignity and professionalism within the academy that would make harassment unthinkable.

Although we did not collect quantitative data about sexual ha-rassment in the field of Jewish studies, we have evidence from other academic fields. According to a report issued in 2018 by the National Academies of Science, Engineering and Medicine (NASEM), coauthored by Frazier Benya (senior program officer at NASEM), Sheila E. Widnall (Massachusetts Institute of Technology), and Paula A. Johnson (president of Wellesley Col-lege), 58 percent of female faculty and staff in academia reported experiencing sexual harassment, the second-highest industry rate after the military at 69 percent.[1] In science, medicine, and engineering—fields long dominated by men—female faculty who experienced harassment said that male colleagues' inappropriate behavior was often ignored or minimized, particularly if they were part of the "old guard," whose conduct had been excused for years. According to a 2018 study issued by the University of Texas, "3,831 students (20.0 percent) reported experiencing sexual harass-ment perpetrated by a faculty or staff member; 3,343 (17.4 percent) reported experiencing sexist hostility, 1,411 (7.7 percent) reported crude behavior, 595 (3.1 percent) reported unwanted sexual atten-tion, and 240 (1.3 percent) reported sexual coercion."[2]

1. Frazier F. Benya, Sheila E. Widnall, and Paula A. Johnson, eds., *Sexual Harass-ment of Women: Climate, Culture, and Consequences in Academic Sciences, Engineering, and Medicine*, National Academies of Science, Engineering, and Medicine (Wash-ington, DC: National Academies Press, 2018), 1, https://www.ncbi.nlm.nih.gov/books/NBK507206/.

2. Kevin M. Swartout, "Appendix D. Consultant Report on the University of Texas System Campus Climate Survey," prepared for the Committee on the Im-pacts of Sexual Harassment in Academia of the National Academies of Sciences,

Benya, Widnall, and Johnson conclude: "Too often, schools have created policies and training that focus on symbolic compliance with current law and avoiding liability, and not on preventing sexual harassment."[3] The report calls for a "systemwide change to the culture and climate in higher education."[4] The journal *Scientific American* titled its analysis of the three-hundred-plus page NASEM report "When It Comes to Sexual Harassment, Academia Is Fundamentally Broken."[5] Another study, this one of field research sites away from the university campus, also found extensive sexual harassment of women, primarily by men who outrank them professionally, and also harassment of men by their peers.[6]

These studies reflect campus-wide cultures. A 2016 University of Oregon survey of 525 graduate students in all fields found that 38 percent of female students and 23 percent of male students said they had been sexually harassed by faculty or staff; almost 58 percent of women and 39 percent of men said they had been harassed by fellow students.[7]

Most of the women with whom we spoke agreed that the legal system is inadequate to create change; academic culture has to change. "It's not just about toughening the laws," Anita Hill once said in an interview. "You also have to change the mind-set of

Engineering, and Medicine, of the National Institutes of Health, National Center for Biotechnology Information, US National Library of Medicine, accessed June 12, 2024, https://www.ncbi.nlm.nih.gov/books/NBK519462/.

3. Benya, Widnall, and Johnson, *Sexual Harassment of Women*, 2.

4. Benya, Widnall, and Johnson, 22.

5. The 500 Women Scientists Leadership, "When It Comes to Sexual Harassment, Academia Is Fundamentally Broken," *Scientific American*, August 9, 2018, https://blogs.scientificamerican.com/voices/when-it-comes-to-sexual-harassment-academia-is-fundamentally-broken/.

6. Kathryn B. H. Clancy, Robin G. Nelson, Julienne N. Rutherford, and Katie Hinde, "Survey of Academic Field Experiences (SAFE): Trainees Report Harassment and Assault," *PLoS ONE* 9, no. 7 (2014): e102172.

7. Marina N. Rosenthal, Alec M. Smidt, and Jennifer J. Freyd, "Still Second Class: Sexual Harassment of Graduate Students," *Psychology of Women Quarterly* 40, no. 3 (2016): 364–77.

people who may believe that they're above the law."[8] Ending harassment also requires changing the gender politics of the academy. Federal law has required for decades that educational opportunities as well as employment be open to all, regardless of sex, race, and religion, but law alone has not solved the problem.

We want to be clear: harassment is unethical because it damages human lives as well as careers. Talented scholars suddenly find themselves unable to pursue their research interests if they want to avoid repeated exposure. Some confessed perpetrators may continue to participate in conferences and workshops, much to the horror of their victims. More broadly, the field of Jewish studies is damaged by harassment and assault that harm scholars physically and emotionally and decrease trust. We speak in the present tense to convey the impact of harassment and assault: for many victims, it is never forgotten and is always looming in their life.

On the personal level, harassment and assault can constitute a terrible and permanent blow. Women spoke to us of feelings of shame, guilt, loss of self-esteem, a sense of betrayal, insecurity, fear, outrage, horror, disgust, rejection, anger, depression, helplessness—feelings that last for years. Some were young graduate students hoping for encouragement and guidance from professors they trusted and who turned out to be manipulating them. Some were tenured faculty who found themselves shut out of the cohort of their colleagues or who had to stay away from certain academic gatherings to avoid men who had harassed or assaulted them in the past. We have learned about senior male faculty who defame women's scholarly reputations to deflect attention from having harassed those women. In some cases, women told us they simply accepted the harassment as part of the price they had to pay for entering a male field; a few said they blamed themselves (or were

8. Jodi Kantor and Arya Sundaram, "How Cuomo Took Advantage of #MeToo," *New York Times*, August 7, 2021, https://www.nytimes.com/2021/08/07/nyregion /andrew-cuomo-metoo.html.

told to blame themselves) for going alone to meet a male professor. Such self-abnegating responses by victims horrify us. Let us be clear: no victim is at fault for an immoral and sometimes illegal act.

Among the examples of harassment we heard are comments made in private and in public regarding marital and family status, disabilities, race, sexuality, and religious practices, and we heard complaints of an overall "bro" culture of men enjoying male-only company. Our interlocutors told us many stories of people who were supportive in some ways but participated in a culture of sexism in other ways. The overall picture is not one of just a few bad individuals but of a culture steeped in inequality and tolerance for sexist structures and behaviors. Here are some of the women's experiences we collected.

Sexuality

Sexual harassment and discrimination are both rooted in cultural imbalances of power that are subtle as well as overt. Discrimination can be subtle, even hidden from view, and harassment can be enacted verbally or physically or can involve the exclusion of students or colleagues from professional opportunities. All are exercises of power. Harassment can take the form of a quid pro quo that might seem innocuous: professors asking students, male or female, to undertake chores—babysit, type papers, do basic research, translate publications—with the implication that students who agree will win favors, such as a good grade, a letter of recommendation, or help obtaining jobs, grants, or other academic goodies. In some cases, this functions as "grooming," when men cultivate a seemingly innocuous, trusting relationship with women and then assault them or demand sexual relations as payment. By working together with women, these men present themselves to the field as supporters of women scholars, which discourages the women they assault to come forward—who would believe such a man would harass women? For example, Elaine Pagels's recent memoir reports that a distinguished professor at Harvard in a field adjacent to Jewish studies was admired for accepting numerous female students into his graduate program, but he then sexually harassed and assaulted many of them, sometimes while they were babysitting his children at his home. His behavior was known and whispered about for decades but never censured. Who would believe a graduate student's accusation against such a distinguished scholar and supporter of women students? Teaching and advising women doctoral students helped him stave off accusations of sexual assault.[9]

I tolerated that my graduate adviser would embrace and lightly kiss me when I came to his office to discuss my work. I put up with it because he was encouraging and enthusiastic about my work, gave me lots of his time to talk, and taught me so much, unlike the other male professors who were aloof and utterly unhelpful. It felt like [his kissing was] the price I had to pay, and it was stressful because I had the feeling that I had to somehow keep him under control and prevent him from going too far.

He could be charming to women he liked, but he was always on the edge, saying to a woman graduate student, "What are we going to do about the chemistry between us?" And then [he would] manipulate which woman would win the postdoc. There are different ways to harass—tantalize one woman with a job and keep out a different woman—the first effort justifying the second.

I arrived as an assistant professor fresh out of graduate school, and my department chair gave me a tour of the university campus. As we were walking, he started telling me about his experiences in his home country. He told me about one of his female students who had told him her husband was beating her, and he told her—so he recounted to me—because she was in the university, she had given up all rights to protection as a woman. I have no idea why he told me this, and I felt physically threatened by the story.

9. Elaine Pagels, *Why Religion? A Personal Story* (New York: Ecco, 2018).

Women, men, and nonbinary people can both experience and commit sexual harassment, and the harassment may range from pervasive, inappropriate comments about gender to posting pornographic images at the workplace. Harassment can be implicit, subtle, or suggestive, drawing on age-old stereotypes. Even when unintentionally hostile, comments and behavior may constitute harassment. After all, the denigration of women, including as scholars, has long been cultivated simply by employing the social norms and stereotypes that surround us.

The situation can be worse for trans students and faculty. Some told us they kept central aspects of their personal lives secret from advisers and colleagues out of fear of harassment; one trans person waited to complete physical transition until they earned their doctorate. Another felt they had to conceal their trans identity while in graduate school. Harassment conveys the message: you don't belong, and I/we have power over you.

He was always complimenting what we were wearing, and someone finally told him to stop. His response: I learned that I should never give anyone a compliment.

About five years ago, a group of Jewish history graduate students and faculty were on a field trip (which felt like one long harassment), taking photographs of each other when one of my professors called out, "She should take her shirt off." I confronted him, and he apologized, but it made me feel the only reason women are here in grad school is to take off your shirt. Standing up to him allowed me to keep going, though he thought it was a joke.

I first attended the AJS Annual Meeting when I was a graduate student, and as a woman then in my twenties, I honestly did not feel physically safe there, so I did not return to attend the meeting again for many decades. "Oh, now there's much less sexual harassment at AJS than there used to be!" a number of people told me, apparently not realizing how creepy that sounds and how strange it is to have to say something like that about an ostensibly professional event.

Senior male scholars have talked to me knowing I am a lesbian about the weird heterosexual sex they're having because their assumption was that we're bonding as two perverts. I was so nonconfrontational, I just listened. I found it fascinating because it was so inappropriate.

These accounts reflect that harassment affects populations unequally. Sexual harassment and violence occur at a higher rate against LGBTQ+ people and against people who are marginalized.[10] Graduate students, adjunct and untenured faculty, postdocs, researchers, and staff are in positions of marginality, job insecurity, and, frequently, financial insecurity. Race too plays a significant role in the academic culture of sexual harassment and assault, though it is often overlooked, thus rendering invisible people of color who face harassment.[11]

The impact of harassment can undermine scholarly careers. People who had been harassed told us they lost self-confidence after being propositioned by their graduate advisers or colleagues: "Did he admire my scholarship or just want to get me into his bed?" Several told us about graduate advisers who asked intrusive sexual questions or talked about their own sexual lives, often under the guise of "offering advice," damaging the professional relationship the students had expected from a mentor. One woman told us that a fellow graduate student pursued her sexually and ultimately became an enemy when she rebuffed him. Another woman told us that a male graduate student in her program had a crush on her, and when she made it clear that she was not interested in him,

10. "LGBT People Nearly Four Times More Likely Than Non-LGBT People to be Victims of Violent Crime," Williams Institute of UCLA Law School, October 2, 2023, https://williamsinstitute.law.ucla.edu/press/ncvs-lgbt-violence-press-release/; and Robert W. S. Coulter and Susan R. Rankin, "College Sexual Assault and Campus Climate for Sexual- and Gender-Minority Undergraduate Students," *Journal of Interpersonal Violence* 35, nos. 5–6 (2020): 1351–66.

11. Nancy Chi Cantalupo, "And Even More of Us Are Brave: Intersectionality and Sexual Harassment of Women Students of Color," *Harvard Journal of Law and Gender* 42, no. 1 (Winter 2019): 1–81.

he became angry and spread gossip about her. Several women told us about feeling uncomfortable about being the only woman in a graduate seminar dealing with the sexual images in kabbalistic texts. We heard about predatory behavior by male graduate students who became aggressive and demeaning toward women graduate students after such seminars, especially if women had raised feminist arguments. Harassment from fellow graduate students put a damper on the possibility of the open intellectual exchange that doctoral programs are supposed to foster.

When the problem persists over time, it fosters an environment where exclusion and harassment can become normalized. At one Jewish institution, several male faculty members had harassed and assaulted female students with impunity for decades—and at least two of the five male presidents who presided over the institution during those decades had themselves engaged in harassment or assault.[12] If the presidents had been engaging in harassment, how could the female students and faculty expect adjudication and protection from the institution? The claim of presidents to have been unaware of the misdeeds seemed disingenuous, given the small size of the college, the extent of the harassment, and how long it had persisted. It is also possible, however, that the atmosphere of allowing harassment simply seemed normal to them, so they did not feel anything was out of the ordinary even when they saw it take place.

Marital Status and Children

Family obligations disproportionately affect women's careers. Two major academic organizations, the Modern Language Association (MLA) and the American Historical Association (AHA), have carried out studies of the status of women in the profession. The

12. Grace E. Speights, Sharon P. Masling, Martha B. Stolley, Jocelyn R. Cuttino, and Ira G. Rosenstein, *Report of Investigation into Misconduct at Hebrew Union College–Jewish Institute of Religion*, November 3, 2021, https://huc.edu/wp-content /uploads/HUC-REPORT-OF-INVESTIGATION-11.04.21.pdf.

MLA study of 2009 found that "men disproportionately held positions of higher rank than women and moved through the ranks more rapidly than women."[13] Caring for spouses and children was one factor limiting women's time for research and publication. Family obligations may also prevent a woman from accepting a fellowship far from home or undertaking a long-term research project in another country. A 2010 AHA survey of historians found that almost twice as many female senior faculty members were divorced or separated at the time of the survey as their male counterparts (11.8 percent of the responding women historians, as compared to 5.6 percent of the men), and 13.5 percent of the women respondents had never married, compared to 4.9 percent of men. Among those who reported a committed relationship, women were significantly more likely to have a spouse or partner with a doctoral degree: 54.7 percent of the female professors in a relationship reported that their spouse or significant other held a PhD, compared to 30.9 percent of their male counterparts.[14] Analyzing statistics for the academy at large, Troy Vettese writes, "That men rarely make sacrifices to help their scholarly wives is possibly why so few tenured female professors ever marry or stay married. More than half are divorced or have never wed, and few have children. Yet 70 percent of their male peers are married and have children. Childless single women are actually more likely to get tenure than childless single men."[15]

13. The Modern Language Association of America, *Standing Still: The Associate Professor Survey Report of the Committee on the Status of Women in the Profession*, April 27, 2009, https://apps.mla.org/pdf/cswp_final042909.pdf.

14. Robert B. Townsend, "Gender and Success in Academia: More from the Historians' Career Path Survey," *Perspectives on History* 51, no. 1 (January 1, 2013): 15–18.

15. Troy Vettese, "Sexism in the Academy: Women's Narrowing Path to Tenure," *n+1* 34 (Spring 2019), https://www.nplusonemag.com/issue-34/essays/sexism-in-the-academy/. Vettese cites the *Atlantic*, July 29, 2013, https://www.theatlantic.com/sexes/archive/2013/07/for-female-scientists-theres-no-good-time-to-have-children/278165.

At my job interview, a famous professor asked me, "Do you contem-plate marriage to a man?" It was illegal, of course, but no one said anything.

At department meetings, male faculty members sometimes talk openly about the marital statuses and possible reproductive plans of female prospective graduate students and job applicants alike (and never [of] their male counterparts!), speculating about how that relates to whether they would take an offer or should be ex-tended one; they are even more explicit in private.

Several women told us that their social interactions with male colleagues suddenly improved once they became coupled. One woman told us she wanted to spend time talking to a senior male colleague but sensed that he felt uncomfortable meet-ing her for a meal at a restaurant. Another woman told us she was the only woman and the only unpartnered person in her graduate school cohort and was excluded from the social gath-erings (and therefore informal intellectual exchanges) of her fellow graduate students. Men may hesitate to invite a single woman colleague for a meal, afraid their intentions might be misinterpreted; without invitations from their colleagues, women may feel they are not respected. In either case, the ab-sence of collegial exchange is unfortunate and even detrimental for both.

I started my first tenure track job at twenty-seven. When I became engaged at thirty-four the social change was almost instantaneous. We—as a couple—were suddenly invited to dinner parties, soirees, events, restaurants, Shabbat tables with academics particularly, and others connected to the academic world, invitations that I had rarely received as a single woman.

At a faculty retreat we were asked to say something about what's going on in our life. We went around the room, and all the men talked about their wives and children, but the only two women fac-ulty who were present were single.

Child- and family-based discrimination can cut both ways: some women with children also experienced exclusion by or resentment from their colleagues.

> *I was the first woman faculty member of my department to have a baby. Behind my back, I was told, there was resentment that I got a maternity leave. Once I had the baby, I found myself excluded from social gatherings—dinners and parties.*

> *What was particularly awful, however, was that over the next five years I watched many women in Jewish studies take time off from their PhDs first to get married and later to have children. The "joke" was that after one child you could try to go back; after two children it was clear you were never going to finish. Frequently these women were married to male Jewish studies scholars who would themselves go on to have academic careers.*

Sometimes genuine concern can be phrased in an inappropriate way, and sometimes the particular concern itself is inappropriate:

> *After returning to graduate school following a serious illness, one of my professors asked me, "Will you still be able to have children?" So inappropriate. And it was a signal for me from the person who symbolized authentic Jewish studies, making it clear that I didn't belong there, that he didn't take me seriously as a scholar.*

> *I think there have been a lot of positive changes to the Jewish studies academic environment in the past ten years. I think there's been more awareness raised on topics such as sexual harassment [and] gender bias, and at the very least colleagues can articulate that they understand that these problems exist even as they do appalling things to demonstrate they don't really understand. One of the things I worked to achieve was forcing the AJS to recognize that child care wasn't a specific women's issue that women had to fund-raise for but a responsibility of the organization. I would love to see changes, but I think these are societal changes. I would love to see more balance*

in home and child-rearing responsibilities. Even my college dean is expected to go home and make dinner despite having a retired husband.

Cultural norms also shape women scholars' experiences, and the Israeli academic environment differs from the North American one. Israelis expect much less privacy around reproduction. They are more likely to ask questions about whether a woman has children or plans for children, even in professional settings. However, because the culture also has a strong streak of pronatalism, there are structures and social support for women's childbearing and child rearing. The result is that women scholars are subject to questions that would be unprofessional in North American environments, but at the same time there are more spaces and flexibility for children, which can allow scholars who are parents of young children more ease of access than they might find elsewhere.

One woman scholar recently encountered an Israeli colleague's desire to chat publicly about reproduction alongside sexual harassment:

> *I was at a conference, and I was seven months pregnant. An Israeli guy on my panel turned to me in the moments before I was going to speak. He said, "It looks like you're expecting!" and then, "Does your husband find you very attractive?" I responded: "Don't ever say that to a colleague!" And that was the end of that. It's kind of shocking when it occurs.*

Openness around reproduction may have opened the door to its occurrence, but sexual harassment is in no way a necessary outcome of Israeli cultural norms about childbearing. The incident similarly does not imply that sexual harassment is so rampant in Jewish studies or Israel studies as to be par for the course: the woman scholar expressed her shock that this had happened. The experience does suggest to us, however, that harassment can be shaped by a distinctive set of cultural norms.

Racism

We interviewed women of color in the field of Jewish studies and found that they had experiences similar to those of just about all the other women we talked to. Intellectual condescension and exclusion from intellectual discussions and from administrative leadership on campus predominated. The crucial difference was their sense of uncertainty: Were they being treated in this way because they were women or because they were Asian or Black? Or was it something about her own personality, one woman mused, that evoked negative reactions from her colleagues? Scholars of color told us their academic credentials were often questioned, as were their reasons for entering the field of Jewish studies, making them feel like oddities rather than respected colleagues. Most concluded that their experiences were shaped by their intersectional identities, meaning that being female inflected the racism and vice versa.

Every single scholar of color reported microaggressions, and many reported experiencing discrimination. For example, several reported being mistaken for another scholar of their race, which is especially significant when there are so few nonwhite scholars in the field. They also reported repeatedly fielding questions about why they were at a Jewish studies conference and whether they were Jewish. Sometimes scholars asked for their personal stories rather than their scholarship: Where are you from? How did a person like you become Jewish? Two white male scholars were speaking English with a scholar of color at a Jewish studies conference. "Is she Jewish?" one male scholar asked the other in Hebrew while she was still standing there. These are not questions that white Jewish scholars must answer very often.

At other times, the women didn't have to wonder if race was a factor because someone commented on their race out loud. One woman told us that some of her Jewish colleagues were astonished that a Black woman was a Jew. Others connected their personal experiences in Jewish studies to broader cultures of sexism:

My personal experience is pretty particular because of the virtually total lack of women of color in Jewish studies of my particular generation as well as the extremely widespread and socially acceptable anti-Asianness in Jewish studies circles.

I actually find it quite heartbreaking that my experiences teaching in Jewish studies programs and departments have been marked by a degree of explicit and everyday sexism (not even to mention anti-Black, anti-Arab, and anti-Asian racism) that I have never encountered in any other professional setting. To be sure, I have found Jewish studies programs and departments to be far more family-friendly than other settings, but the persistent and pervasive sexism still remains striking.

As we noted in chapter 1, the field of Jewish studies is overwhelmingly populated by white scholars, and so even in situations where no one directly expresses racism, scholars of color may be very aware of their minority status. We have heard from Asian scholars in Jewish studies that their very credentials as scholars are sometimes questioned, and their own voices of authority are challenged or simply disregarded. After a presentation at AJS, an older, white, male scholar asked an Asian scholar in several ways, "Are you Jewish? Did you grow up Jewish?" until another scholar came and asked him, very politely, "Can you tell me how an answer to that question would affect the evaluation of her scholarship?" In addition, the racist eroticization of Asian women is particularly disturbing in an academic setting where sexual harassment is already a problem, and Asian women told us they feel they are expected to "handle" aggressive men. Moreover, Samira Mehta has argued, when Jewish scholars of European descent disavow their own whiteness because of their discomfort with white racist histories or the idea that experiencing antisemitism negates whiteness, it can alienate Jewish scholars of color who do not experience white-skin privilege.[16]

---

16. Samira Mehta, "Amid the Other Others: Jews and the Navigation of Race in the United States," keynote address, Society of Jewish Ethics, January 9, 2022.

One Asian American scholar told us that they feel similarly marginal in both Jewish studies and other academic spaces. They also remarked, however, that being marginal or an outsider allows certain insights:

> *I can understand why white non-Jewish women might walk into a Jewish studies space and feel alienated. . . . In Jewish spaces, I'm a foreigner, and that doesn't really bother me. I will always be on the outside, but that means I might be able to perceive things that I wouldn't if I were solidly in the center.*

Expectations about gender and race mix to influence perceptions of scholarship. Stereotypes link Asians to STEM fields and women to humanities. An Asian Jewish woman scholar told us that men are expected to present quantitative data while women are expected to present qualitative analysis; the former are considered hard science, the latter soft science. Her work involves both, but she finds that when she presents her findings at a conference, men on the panel either are given more time or simply take more time for their presentations, an observation reiterated by many of the women we interviewed.

Several Black scholars reported to us that other scholars questioned their motivations for entering the field, their knowledge of Hebrew, and their facility with Jewish texts. Moreover, they were not always accepted as authorities in their field in Jewish studies. One told us that her dean, trying to create a Jewish studies program, consulted many faculty, including non-Jews and scholars who were themselves Jewish but unaffiliated with the field, but not her. Some universities, writes Lewis Gordon, "boast about 'having' Black scholars as though one can have Black people through the 'possession' of one or two." He adds, "the most dominant feature of racist ideology is the extent to which it is premised upon a spirit of evasion"—the evasion of Black inclusion. That evasion, Gordon argues, is the failure to recognize "how race functions in a racist society," the identification of Black people and not white people as raced, and a "'multicultural' discourse, a full-fledged self-bewitchment which confuses antiracial rhetoric with the achievement of antiracial reality."[17] Using the language of possession is a reminder that many US colleges and universities originated with the wealth produced by enslavement.[18] Black Jewish women in the field spoke to us about their double consciousness—being aware of what they think but simultaneously attentive to how others are perceiving them:

> I see a pattern: when I have felt excluded or marginalized or talked over, I haven't always noticed it at first. When I have, I interpret it as encountering people who see me not the way I see myself. This is the American racial lens.

Experiences vary, but what is constant is the uncertainty of how one is perceived as a Black person in Jewish studies:

> Sometimes it's as if I am speaking to the air—or to an interest that is curiosity, that puts me in a box—or I'm just like everyone in the room. Is it me, my personality, or is it because I'm a woman, because I'm Israeli, because I'm Black? Is it all three interacting? And I wonder, am I assertive or am I aggressive or am I Israeli?

To be Black in the field of Jewish studies is often to be marginalized or simply ignored.

The intersection of racism and sexism is not unique to Jewish studies. Women of color teaching at British universities have described feeling at times invisible and at other times hypervisible.[19] The constant shift from being excluded to being wanted (often as displays of alleged university "diversity") is compounded by the

17. Lewis Gordon, untitled essay, in Tricia Rose et al., "Race and Racism: A Symposium," special issue, *Social Text* 42 (Spring 1995): 40.

18. Craig Wilder, *Ebony and Ivy: Race, Slavery and the Troubled History of America's Universities* (New York: Bloomsbury, 2013).

19. Elizabeth Ettorre, *Autoethnography as Feminist Method* (London: Routledge, 2016); and Shardé M. Davis et al., "Writing Ourselves into Existence: Black Women Researchers' Collaborative Autoethnographic Reflections on Addressing Exclusion in Academia," *Departures in Critical Qualitative Research* 10, no. 1 (2021): 4–27.

combination of racism and misogyny. Quite a few women, both in a British study and in our interviews, described the burden of trying to balance expressing their academic authority with not being perceived by male colleagues or students as offensively aggressive.[20] For women of color in Jewish studies, the dilemma is particularly acute as they cope with racism as well as sexism in a field in which they are a distinct minority at present.

Jewish Religious Practice

Though it is an academic field, Jewish studies sometimes becomes a religious event. Gatherings sometimes include religious practices, such as prayers at conference banquets, or conference attendees organizing prayer services. Such religious practices are often geared to suit the stringent requirements of the Orthodox men in attendance, which means that others can be excluded or marginalized. One woman told us she attended a workshop with two other women and twelve men, and all three women were asked to leave the room so that the men could hold a service at which one of the men could say kaddish for his father. While respecting his wishes to honor his father, she wrote, it transformed the dynamics of the workshop, making the women feel marginalized.

Jewish scholars from across the religious spectrum can experience conflict between their observance and professional obligations. Both women and men, Orthodox and not, told us they had been pressured by their departments or colleagues to attend social gatherings on the Sabbath and holidays and worried that their refusal would harm their chances for tenure and promotion.

At a department dinner attended by a guest speaker, one of my colleagues announced that she had voted to hire me because I had ordered a cheeseburger for lunch during my job interview; it showed

20. "Power in the Academy: Staff Sexual Misconduct in UK Higher Education," National Union of Students, accessed June 20, 2024, https://1752group.com/wp-content/uploads/2021/09/4f9f6-nus_staff-student_misconduct_report.pdf.

her that I wasn't "too Jewish." I was shocked by what I considered blatant antisemitism and by her obvious lack of concern about showing it.

I learned it's best not to try to explain to my colleagues that I keep kosher; better to simply say I am vegetarian. Kosher seemed to imply something exclusive and a demand for special consideration, while vegetarian or vegan evoked positive feelings, even admiration.

How should we reconcile allowing for religious practices *and* upholding gender inclusion in academic spaces? Maintaining Orthodox religious practices is difficult in the American academic world. Conferences and convocations (as well as classes) sometimes take place during Jewish holidays, and absence from such events may be viewed as shirking one's faculty duties. These are institutional practices that imply that being religious and being an open-minded, critical scholar as impossible.

Some religious Jewish women told us that their Orthodox upbringing had taught them to be modest, quiet, and respectful, especially of male authorities, and they felt uncomfortable in classes in which other students undertook lively debates, even criticizing the professor. A few nonreligious students told us they were annoyed when religious women dropped out of graduate programs to marry and raise children because it encouraged male professors to view women students as recreational students, not as serious scholars. An Israeli scholar, looking back at her graduate school days, told us,

I found my fellow graduate students who were Orthodox men intimidating, and I was upset that Orthodox women didn't remain long in the program. Graduate study was just an extra thing they were doing temporarily. Then they would disappear.

These impressions were not universal, however. A few of our interlocutors expressed concern that Orthodox male professors dismissed women, especially women who were not religious, as having inadequate preparation in classical Hebrew texts. Seen from outside the field, Orthodox men are sometimes viewed as more "authentic" Jews than nonreligious men or women. Yet while an earlier generation of senior male scholars declared that only those who completed rigorous yeshiva training in Talmud could ever be a serious scholar in Jewish studies, the next generation saw several women become professors of rabbinics at distinguished universities.

An anthropologist in a Jewish studies program offered some striking observations about what she calls the "tribalism" that distinguishes the field from other disciplines. At her large university, located in a town with a sizable Jewish community, her students and colleagues who are Orthodox Jewish men leave campus each afternoon to join a minyan (prayer quorum). While women are not excluded from praying, they are not counted in the Orthodox minyan and are not invited to join the men in their trek to the local Hillel or synagogue. That all-male daily minyan ritual, she told us, establishes their male bonding, a sort of locker room for Jewish male academics, creating an intense masculine bond:

> *The daily minyan is a community, men being there for each other, establishing that climate, believing they are the backbone of the community and that whatever happens, they are there for each other. They don't want women in there. No matter what women do, that is an inviolable bedrock of Jewish bonding and communal solidarity that is impermeable, designed to be impermeable to women and to non-Jews.*

Ultimately, these male faculty may have to abide by Title IX regulations, but attending the Orthodox minyan reinforces their male power and authority. Some Jewish women support the Orthodox minyan and its separation of men from women, while to other women their separation feels degrading. Similar feelings exist among non-Jews in the field who are excluded from the prayers. Reconciling Orthodox religious commitment with the full participation of non-Orthodox and non-Jewish women and men is a problem the field has to address.

One woman wrote about a weeklong conference that included attending an Orthodox synagogue service: "We weren't required to go to the synagogue, but our meals were served there." She sat in the women's section, behind a low bar that had been erected and placed behind the men's section, while her male colleagues from the conference were called to the Torah. The separation of the synagogue, she realized, created an "invisible *mehitza*" (curtain) within the conference itself: "it broke the sense of scholarly camaraderie I had been fighting for all week." Several women spoke to us of similar situations, such as being asked to leave the room while the men at the conference constituted themselves as an Orthodox minyan to pray. Jodi Eichler-Levine's published account of her own experience at the Orthodox synagogue to which conference participants were taken is powerful:

> I broke personally. That moment of exclusion shredded my Jewish sense of self. . . . I broke professionally. I had wanted to impress these male colleagues on equal footing. . . . When they ascended the *bema* while I couldn't, it was clear that I was not, in fact, their equal. I had never felt more vulnerable. But most of all: I broke because I felt ashamed. "How will I face them in the seminar room tomorrow?" I thought. "How can any of them respect me after this? How can any of them see me as their colleague in the same way they see the men beside them?" . . . That *meḥizah* is why Jewish Studies has a gender problem. How can Jewish Studies ever be a truly equitable field when male-only homosocial spaces have played, and continue to play, such an enormous part in our guild's networks? . . . If only I had simply been born a Jewish man, I thought. No one should still feel that way in our field.[21]

Gila Silverman, an anthropologist, reflected on her experience of saying kaddish, the mourner's prayer, at an AJS conference

---

21. Jodi Eichler-Levine, "The Invisible Meḥizah," *AJS Perspectives* (Spring 2021): 74–76, quote on 75.

during the year after her mother's death. She first went to the advertised egalitarian minyan where people of all genders would pray together. When only three people showed up, all looking for a place to say kaddish, the attendees of the "traditional" minyan invited them to join. The "traditional" minyan had different gender practices:

> Several men wearing *kippot* were standing in the hallway, trying to gather people to make the "traditional" *minyan*, and they kindly invited us to join them in the room next door. I explained to them that I was saying *Kaddish*, and asked if that would be a problem for anyone. I knew that some Orthodox men would not want me to say the *Kaddish* out loud, and I knew that if I joined their *minyan*, I would do so in a way that respected their *minhag* [custom]. They welcomed me and said that was more than fine.
>
> But when we entered the room, I realized that a floor-to-ceiling black curtain had been set up as a *mehitzah* [divider], enclosing the "women's section" from three sides (with the back wall of the room as the 4th side). I wanted to respect the more observant expectations of this *minyan*, but I also knew that I could not say *Kaddish* while standing behind an opaque curtain that separated me completely from the community that would say "Amen." Feeling slightly queasy, I quietly asked those who had welcomed me if I had to sit behind the curtain, and asked if they would feel comfortable if I sat in the back of the "men's section." With their agreement, I quietly pulled a chair out from behind the curtain and sat in the back corner of the room. The other woman who was also saying *Kaddish* did the same. Although we received several confused glances, no one said anything to us, and when we stood to say *Kaddish*, I thought I felt a collective nod of understanding and support in the Amens that answered us.

I left the room shaking slightly, realizing later that not only had the male mourner not needed to clarify that he could be there, but that he was also asked to lead the service, while I—if I had not spoken up—would have *davenned* [prayed] invisibly behind a thick black barrier. Outside of that room, these men and I were peers and colleagues, sharing our scholarship and debating ideas at a professional meeting. But inside that room, I was clearly not equal.[22]

The gendered practices of Orthodox Judaism are not just a matter of study for some in Jewish studies, as Silverman's reflection shows. This is not a story of sexist men degrading women, but a story of how religious practice, gender, and power intertwine to make some belong and others feel like interlopers. Plenty of women feel comfortable sitting behind a barrier at religious services; plenty do not. Again, the problem is an unresolved conflict between religious practice and gender equality.

Intellectual Condescension

Ideally, collegiality, mutuality, and reciprocity are central in professional interactions and teaching students. Most scholars need intellectual exchange and support for intellectual stimulation—learning about new methods, trying out ideas and arguments. Although as scholars we spend much of our time in isolation, interaction with colleagues—attending conferences, sharing ideas and debating issues, and writing and editing joint projects—sustains and stimulates us. Yet we enter academic environments that have not fully integrated women and nonbinary scholars. Many of us in the field of Jewish studies experienced working with only male professors when we were students, and some of us teach in departments with almost entirely male faculty, especially at the senior level. We have male colleagues who may never have studied

22. Gila Silverman, "It Takes a Community to Say Kaddish, Especially as a Woman," *Hadassah-Brandeis Institute Blog*, August 3, 2017, https://blogs.brandeis.edu /freshideasfromhbi/it-takes-a-community-to-say-kaddish-especially-as-a-woman.

with a woman or experienced women as senior colleagues with academic authority over them. Many may have gone through graduate programs in Jewish studies without having considered women's experiences in Jewish history or a feminist critique of classical Jewish texts, and they view such projects as lying at the margins of the field.

Discrimination against women in an academic context often takes the form of intellectual condescension. Although some women's stories may not rise to the level of harassment, they all indicate a discriminatory culture. When bystanders observe bias or discrimination and do nothing, it perpetuates the sense that such bias is normal and acceptable. Consider the following examples:

> In one case, a female applicant's physical attributes came up as a concern in a search committee meeting. In one departmental meeting, a senior male faculty member even spoke on behalf of his junior female colleague, who was sitting right next to him, as if she was unable to talk (and actually saying the opposite of what she thought of the matter under discussion!). Upon news about male colleagues accused of sexual harassment, I have had male colleagues barge into my office, upset because "Why would those women want to ruin a man's whole life like that . . . ?" Celebrated, conversely, are those wives who do editorial work for their husbands' books. My female colleagues and I actually nicknamed one of our department hallways "Misogyny Avenue"—and we had gotten so accustomed to it that we were actually surprised when a new faculty member found that surprising.

Women often told us they felt their authority was belittled. Such experiences may well happen to any scholar, but women and nonbinary scholars are often left with a sense of uncertainty, compounding the feeling of being out of place in a man's world:

> When I joined my university with tenure, I outranked two men in the department. Nonetheless, they spoke to me in a patronizing way for years.

I don't know any woman who hasn't been patronized at the university; it's intrinsic to the culture.

At my first annual pretenure review, the provost looked at my list of publications and said, with a tone of sarcasm, "Well, aren't you a little overachiever!" He noted my youthful appearance and said, "You will have problems with the students respecting you because you look like you could be one of them."

A doctoral candidate at another university asked me to serve on his committee. Yet whenever we met, he talked down to me. It was as if the only way he knew how to be a professional man was to patronize women, even those who supervised his work.

Two senior men organized a two-day conference on a topic I had written a major book about. I was invited to give one of the short talks. For the opening keynote, they chose a senior male professor whose work had tangentially engaged the topic, but not directly. I knew they chose him because he was a man, and I also knew I would have been asked if I were a man. In fact, I was the only woman invited to speak at the conference. This field [modern German-Jewish thought] is hopeless for women.

Sometimes colleagues denigrate or ignore women's intellectual accomplishments:

At a department faculty party, a colleague said to me about the recently published book he coauthored with his wife, also an academic, "I busted my ass writing that for her."

I told a male colleague about a study I was writing on a rabbinic concept, and he replied, "What, you think you can write about a rabbinic concept like a man who has spent twenty years in a yeshiva studying these passages?"

My work [in Jewish history] was never taken seriously, and my promotion was delayed for fifteen years. Colleagues claimed I probably copied or translated someone else's scholarship, and that my blue eyes were all that filled my research file.

Discrimination in hiring is forbidden in most university contexts, yet it continues in sometimes subtle ways, including in confidential decisions regarding hiring, tenure, and promotion.[23] At a job interview, a tenured full professor with numerous publications and widespread respect in her field asked a question of a job candidate, and immediately one of her male colleagues said, "Let me ask that question better." Would a man who speaks that way to his female colleague be free of gender bias in hiring and tenure decisions? In selecting a candidate for a tenure-track appointment, a man said about a female candidate, "She's too short." About another female job candidate, "She's going to have a second child." One woman reported to us:

> Ten years ago, I was the only woman on a search committee for my department. We had two excellent finalists, a man and a woman. I said we should hire the woman. The head of the department turned to me and said, "Why are you whining?" No one said a word, no one supported me, and he never apologized. They hired the man. Today that might not happen—younger men don't talk that way—but those words left me furious for weeks. I didn't say anything because I didn't have tenure.

The atmosphere that is created may become so toxic that women simply give up trying to change it:

> I see the wreckage of brilliant women who just couldn't do it. Their lives have been ruined. They dropped out or finished the PhD and had kids and couldn't get back in.

For Jewish women, feeling accepted sometimes came more readily from non-Jewish professors than from Jewish professors. Some

23. The University of Maryland has published a summary of social science research on bias in academic hiring: K. O'Meara and D. Culpepper, *How Bias Emerges in Academic Hiring: A Research Brief for Faculty Search Committees*, Inclusive Hiring Pilot Materials, ADVANCE program (College Park: University of Maryland, 2018), https://advance.umd.edu/sites/default/files/2021-04/5.%20Bias%20in%20Hiring%20Handout.pdf.

complained that Jewish professors, especially in courses devoted to text study of classical Hebrew writings, created what they called a "clubby" atmosphere with the male students, whereas other professors welcomed Jewish students regardless of gender.

I was silent as a graduate student in the courses taught by Jewish men, but not by Christian men. In my classes with Christian professors, I felt more empowered. All this time I've taken it personally. Flip the feeling of invisibility, and put it on the sin of omission: it's about them, not about us.

The professor I had for medieval texts was fabulously brilliant, but sarcastic and nasty to anyone who had trouble reading the Hebrew text—men and women—even if they had great interpretations of the texts. He created an intimidating atmosphere that was not conducive to learning, just about him showing off. The intimidation was worse for me as the single woman in the class of twelve men.

In my first semester of graduate school, we were asked on the first day by the male professor to prepare the Hebrew texts for his seminar in "hevruta," that is, in pairs. After class, I asked the other students—all male—who was available. One of them, very tall, walked over and stood an inch from me and said, "We're all taken." From day one, I was not wanted. I was left to prepare alone, which I explained privately to the professor. He was totally unsympathetic and said to me that the male students didn't like the way I dressed. So much for academic study.

In one department, a distinguished senior male historian had to be excluded from the dissertation committees of the women doctoral students in his department because he was widely known to be impossibly discouraging and rude to women students—yet he was permitted to continue teaching undergraduates, including women. A woman at another institution told us:

A senior, male distinguished professor in my graduate department, not my adviser, asked me one day, "Tell me about your dissertation.

*Are you writing about women?" That was not my topic, and I real-
ized how my scholarship could be stereotyped because I am a
woman.*

One of the difficulties women have found in entering the profession is not being regarded as academic authorities, even when they
hold tenure and have published extensively. Some women we interviewed blame Jewish religious tradition for assuming that men
are the sole authorities—from the rabbis, back to Moses, back to
God, all of whom are conceptualized as male. Women, too, can be
imbued with assumptions and rhetoric that diminish the academic
authority of women. One woman told us,

> *A Jewish feminist professor at my university, not in Jewish studies,
> was concerned about homophobic statements she was hearing from
> members of the local Jewish community and asked a few of us, all
> Jewish women, to meet with her and discuss a response. Her sugges-
> tion was to hold a meeting at which the local male rabbi would
> speak about what she called "Judaism's views on homosexuality"
> while she would talk about "what it feels like to be lesbian." He
> would be the "authority," she would offer "feelings." I couldn't be-
> lieve this was coming from a so-called feminist. And all this in front
> of me, a scholar of Jewish women's history and an activist for years
> on Jewish feminist issues.*

For women scholars of color, it is sometimes not clear if their
femaleness or their race plays the greater role in the way they are
dismissed, assumed not to be the professor but a staff member or
student, or spoken to (and about) by colleagues as if they were
children.[24] Some Black women told us they thought they would be
taken far more seriously if they were men; as men they would

24. There is a large literature on women of color in academia; see, for example,
Gloria D. Thomas and Carol Hollenshead, "Resisting from the Margins: The Coping
Strategies of Black Women and Other Women of Color Faculty Members at a Re-
search University," *Journal of Negro Education* 70, no. 3 (Summer 2001): 66–75; and
Nina Asher, "Race, Gender and Sexuality," in *The Routledge Companion to Race and*

be invited to represent African American thought, but as women they were viewed as voices of Black women. For example, a senior scholar in Jewish studies told us about some of her experiences: In her presence, a male archivist, referring to her, remarked, "I'm here with this little girl." When she was a junior faculty member, a senior faculty member thrust his hand into the pocket of her skirt and said, "What do you keep in those pockets?" On another occasion, seeing her meeting with several male students, he commented, "There's mama hen with her chicks." While she was working in a collaborative project with four men, one of them referred to her as "child," "sweetheart," and "baby."

> Why am I not viewed as an authority, even on a topic that I have researched more thoroughly than anyone else?

> So often at social events [at my university] my expertise is ignored. People will raise a question about the Bible—which is my field of scholarship, as they all know—but instead of asking me, they ask the male rabbi. And he puffs himself up and pompously gives an answer—again, without acknowledging my presence and my expertise, as if a male rabbi automatically outranks a female scholar and deserves greater acknowledgment of his authority.

> I'm often on panels in public or on Zoom with a man who is thanked by the moderator with his title—Dr. or Professor or Rabbi or Reverend—while I am thanked with my first name.

Another woman told us that from the moment she arrived at her university, appointed to a tenured, endowed professorship, she was treated with hostility both by the two older male faculty members in Jewish studies and by male Jews on the faculty in other fields:

> To this day, I am not quite sure what turned the men in Jewish studies against me even before they met me, but the hostility has been

Ethnicity, ed. Stephen M. Caliendo and Charlton D. McIlwain (New York: Routledge, 2020), 68–77.

palpable for years. They don't even greet me when we pass each other on campus, let alone engage with me in discussion about our scholarship or about new developments in our field. Not once has a male colleague sent a student to meet with me or take a course with me; there is simply no collaboration of faculty in Jewish studies at my college. Why? Is it because I'm a woman? Because I write on gender? I'll never know—they won't tell me because they would incriminate themselves.

Another told us a similar story:

I was hired as a full professor at a large university where three men were also full professors in Jewish studies. I quickly discovered that those three men held "faculty meetings" and excluded me. They made all the decisions about who would teach which courses in which semester and at what time slot, who would be the guest speakers that year, which students would receive financial assistance, and so forth. I could have complained to the university administration, but those men would have immediately known I was the complainant, and they would have been even more nasty to me.

Exclusion

It can be tempting to think that antidiscrimination laws will prevent exclusion, but federal and state laws and campus regulations do not cover all the damaging behaviors that create the culture of discrimination that pervades segments of our field, nor have those laws eliminated exclusion in the areas they do cover. No professor is legally obligated to include women or nonbinary colleagues in a workshop he organizes, though it ought to spark outrage if he invites only men. Excluding women from a conference or a book project may not violate antidiscrimination laws, but it lies at the heart of a discriminatory culture when women scholars are consistently excluded from academic gatherings.

When I was in graduate school, I knew that the male professor of Jewish studies used to go out for lunch and coffee with the male students. I was never included. He invited the male students and their wives (all but one was married) to his home for dinners and to stay overnight for Shabbat and holidays. I was never invited. I was angry because informal discussions of ideas are part of graduate education, a way to learn how to formulate arguments, hear about new books, and grow intellectually.

More than once I have invited a senior, male distinguished scholar to lecture at my college and find that my male colleagues "bond" with the visitor and arrange to spend private time, from which I am explicitly excluded—even though I am the visitor's host.

Just because people are physically present does not necessarily mean there is no atmosphere of exclusion. Non-Jewish scholars can feel particularly vulnerable at conferences peopled entirely by Jews; one told us that she was uncomfortable with the "in-group" language she heard at a workshop where she was the only non-Jew and the only woman:

The Jewish male scholars were calling each other by Hebrew nicknames, showing off by dropping rabbinic and biblical passages in Hebrew, using Yiddish expressions and creating the atmosphere of Jewish summer camp more than an academic workshop.

While some scholars enjoy Hebrew names, Yiddish jokes, or references to rabbinic idioms, such in-group comments may marginalize non-Jews within the field of Jewish studies. Scholarship is not improved by this kind of chummy language, and it sends a signal to other scholars who are not in the know: you do not really belong here. The patterns that denigrate or exclude women, people of color, nonbinary people, and non-Jews reinforce one another, often drawing on stereotypes and appealing to biases.

Women and nonbinary scholars share with others in academia that, for career advancement, they must travel to where jobs are located, but once there, they may find themselves in a small town. This can produce multiple problems: if they are single, it may not be an easy place to find a suitable partner. The town may not have places for worship that are welcoming or accommodating. Religious and ethnic foods or ritual supplies may not be available. Small towns are less likely to have multiple social groups that welcome LGBTQ+ adults.

> I struggled for years to be accepted in a Jewish community which doubted my expertise, all the time telling me that I was such a young woman—what could I know? I had similar experiences with an older, male dean who treated me at age thirty like I was a child.

Jewish scholars may not be welcomed by everyone in the local Jewish community, and the community may not view them as academic authorities:

> When I first arrived to teach at a small, remote liberal arts college, I was the only "visible" Jew on the faculty. I was coming into a world without Jews, which is actually a normative Christian situation. Some Jewish women in town asked me to help organize a women's seder, which I did. That made the local Orthodox rabbi furious, and he compared the women's Haggadah that I put together to Holocaust denial.

> I had a male colleague, now retired, who never published, never attended academic meetings, taught outdated and outmoded courses, and yet always spoke with a tone of condescension and pomposity and managed to convince the local Jewish community that he was a genius; the rabbi would say to me, "Now he is a real scholar." Yes, women can also be condescending, but I can't imagine a woman carrying off that pomposity without being mocked, hated, and called a bitch.

> I've taught for decades at a university in a small town with just one synagogue. Not once have I been invited to give a talk about my work—in fact, I've never once been invited to the home of anyone in the local Jewish community. I have no idea why they are so unwelcoming.

Bro Culture

Sexism may come in the form of a brief moment or an inappropriate comment or gesture; or it may be more serious, such as when the comments of women students and faculty are repeatedly dismissed; or it may be in the form of persistent remarks with sexual innuendo or gender or racial deprecations made in passing, as if obvious or perhaps humorous. Such experiences accumulate, and the atmosphere can become demeaning, exclusionary, and intimidating. The cumulative effect of microaggressions can be strong, undermining the self-confidence needed for scholarly work.

One anthropologist used her ethnographic expertise to describe her faculty meetings to us: her male colleagues speak in a kind of shorthand, shifting from serious, abstract discussion to humor in a nanosecond, and talking among themselves as if they were all pals with each other, creating a language for what she calls their "bro culture." They police the boundaries, she said, with a "wink and a nod," saying, "We have to find a woman to speak," or asking, "Does so-and-so [a man] have a MeToo problem, or can we bring him to speak?" Cognizant of Title IX regulations, they adapt to them while retaining male privilege. Some Jewish studies scholars, she said, are used to functioning as independent entities on campus, sometimes defending their independence from disciplines and administrators they perceive to be politically problematic. Some women scholars who are not feminists participate in the "bro culture" and acknowledge the men's mastery because they want a seat at what she calls "the table of tyranny." Some of those women, she added, "have the feeling that these male scholars are their sons who are special and do not have to play by [what they consider] stupid Gentile rules." She observed that although the diversity coordinator conducts workshops for the faculty, and the faculty seek out women as speakers on campus, decisions are still being made in a language of male shorthand from which she is excluded.

Even when good men recognize male colleagues to be horrible human beings, they can pass off their friendship saying—well but he's been friendly to me, or I've never seen that behavior though I can imagine it from him—traditional bystander language that facilitates ongoing poor behavior. There is also now a generation of "woke" men—men who ostentatiously present their leftist credentials—who systematically and regularly harass women, holding their scholarship hostage through the control of journals and conferences (as well as serving on hiring committees or as writers of letters of recommendation or letters of promotion). Using their power, they establish patriarchal systems that continue to punish women.

I found myself a woman mentor in another department. The absence of seeing any successful women in grad school and witnessing what the women faculty who were there had to go through was awful. Only when I started teaching at a liberal arts college did I find women mentors who were well-rounded, complete human beings and talked about the same challenges I had faced.

Gossip

Within academic cultures, gossip has two sides. Nasty gossip can destroy a person's career, but gossip can also help save someone from assault or harassment. The power of gossip is enormous; as the anthropologist Robin Dunbar writes, "language evolved to allow us to gossip."[25] In discussing the work of psychologist Nicholas Emler, Dunbar continues, "One of the most important things that gossip allows you to do is to keep track of (and also influence) other people's reputations as well as your own. Gossip, in [Emler's] view, is all about the management of reputation."[26] Since

25. Robin Dunbar, *Grooming, Gossip, and the Evolution of Language* (Cambridge, MA: Harvard University Press, 1996), 87.

26. Dunbar, 123.

career advancement in the research world is based heavily on reputation, gossip plays a major role in academic careers.[27]

Gossip can undermine job performance. Promotion, research grants, and other awards come not only from the learned evaluations of faculty but also from networking. As we discussed in chapter 1, studies find that men sometimes prefer to network with men more than with women or nonbinary people, leading to male-male collaborations on research and publications, something that is widespread in Jewish studies.[28] Exclusion is sometimes created and maintained through gossip. The familiar kinds of gossip about women's bodies and sexuality carry over into the academy and can become a tool to wield maliciously against women who have spoken against discrimination.

The other side of gossip is its potential to protect the vulnerable. When someone has harassed colleagues or students, gossip may be the only way to warn others. Scholars call this "prosocial gossip," reflecting the idea that sharing information about a person's reputation can protect others from exploitation or hurt.[29] Gossip is often one of the only tools that those who are harassed have. For example, several women we interviewed told us that they had been warned by friends or colleagues to avoid someone who later admitted to sexual assault, and they all expressed appreciation that they were forewarned. Without gossip, there might have been more victims.

An American postdoc who had completed his studies in New York recently spent a year in residence at Oxford, where I was a graduate

27. Stefanie Ernst, "From Blame Gossip to Praise Gossip? Gender, Leadership and Organizational Change," *European Journal of Women's Studies* 10, no. 3 (2003): 277–99.

28. Sarah-Jane Leslie, Andrei Cimpian, Meredith Meyer, and Edward Freeland, "Expectations of Brilliance Underlie Gender Distributions across Academic Disciplines," *Science* 347, no. 6219 (2015): 262.

29. Matthew Feinberg, Robb Willer, Jennifer Stellar, and Dacher Keltner, "The Virtues of Gossip: Reputational Information Sharing as Prosocial Behavior," *Journal of Personality and Social Psychology* 102, no. 5 (2012): 1015.

student, and he explained "the ropes" of Jewish studies to me. He explained that no one talked to me (a single woman, still a graduate student) at the AJS conference because I was female, and the male graduate students understood that women doing PhDs in Jewish studies were looking for husbands, and so weren't serious scholars. Thus, unless they wanted to sleep with them, it was a waste of time to talk to the women at the conference. Instead, their networking (and time) was better spent speaking to other male students or professors. He himself had been married (and divorced), [been] engaged, [and] dated a significant number of women in Jewish studies. He served as my guide at the AJS a few years later. He introduced me to many scholars—both junior and senior—but it was because he was seen with me that people took an interest in who I was. It was the currency of gossip that gave me an access pass. I was noticed because I was a female who could be gossiped about, not because I was a scholar.

The content of gossip is often gendered. For example, we have heard gossip suggesting that a woman received a fellowship because she slept with someone, but a similar claim might not be applied so easily to a man receiving a fellowship because men hold many positions of power as well as because of sexist norms that reward men for sex but punish others. The most common gossip that seeks to undermine women's credibility accuses them of being "sluts" who use sexuality to advance their careers. There is no term equivalent to "slut" for a man; as a headline in the *Guardian* proclaimed, "What Makes a Slut? The Only Rule, It Seems, Is Being Female."[30] Leora Tanenbaum—the author of SLUT! *Growing Up Female with a Bad Reputation*, a memoir of her high school experiences at Ramaz, the Orthodox day school in New York—illustrates the uses of gossip that aims to destroy the reputations of women who may be social outsiders or outspoken women's

30. Jessica Valenti, "What Makes a Slut? The Only Rule, It Seems, Is Being Female," *Guardian*, June 23, 2014, https://www.theguardian.com/commentisfree/2014/jun/23/slut-female-word-women-being-female.

rights advocates, and the near impossibility of countering that gossip.[31] With the rise of social media, the use of the term has grown considerably.[32] The term "slut" is not directed against heterosexual men (except with a kind of ironic affection), and its meaning for Black women is complicated by the history of enslavement during which Black women were treated as property and used for sexual exploitation and propagation of more slaves, often through rape by white men.

Gossip itself is neither positive nor negative; it can function for the good of a culture, as it does in protective prosocial gossip, or it can damage. The key is to create a culture that encourages prosocial gossip while not tolerating antisocial gossip that reinforces sexism, racism, transphobia, or other biases.

Israeli Universities

In Israel, gender is also joined by religion and race in issues of discrimination. Students tend to be older than American students, in part because Jewish Israeli citizens are required to serve in the military (three years for men, two for women) before they enter universities. Palestinian citizens of Israel are not required to serve; for Druze Israelis, military service is optional. Religious commitments keep some Jews, especially men, away from universities. However, increasing numbers of Haredi men are attending secular universities and requesting male-only classes taught by male professors. Wanting to encourage university education, many departments are complying, making gender equality subservient to religious regulations that enshrine gender separation.

Where does that leave women professors? One example is the field of Talmud. Although the field of Talmud has historically been

31. Leora Tanenbaum, SLUT! *Growing Up Female with a Bad Reputation* (New York: Seven Stories, 1999).

32. Leora Tanenbaum, *I Am Not a Slut: Slut-Shaming in the Age of the Internet* (New York: Harper Perennial, 2015).

overwhelmingly populated by male professors, in the last two decades more women have climbed the academic ranks and now train graduate students. However, a religious man studying Talmud may refuse to have a woman as his doctoral adviser for religious reasons, or to take a class at a university in which women students are also present, and the university administration will accommodate him out of respect for his religious commitments. The ramifications for women scholars, however, are dangerous: Will a department hire women faculty, knowing that many religious male students will not study with them? With fewer students, the department may suffer financial cuts from the university—yet another reason not to hire a woman.

Religion is a sphere in which women's secondary status conflicts with gender equality, but university administrators, mostly secular, are the gatekeepers who approve requests for male-only classes. Such requests for male-only authorities are not granted by hospitals, courts of law, or other public spaces, and there is no reason a public university should turn its back on the equality of women faculty and students in the face of religious requests.

At the same time, women at Israeli universities have launched groundbreaking initiatives against sexual harassment and assault. A 1998 Israeli law criminalizes sexual harassment, thanks primarily to the efforts of legal scholar Orit Kamir, and it applies to the army, workplaces, and universities.[33] (There is no US law that similarly criminalizes discrimination; rather, students and faculty can bring a civil lawsuit against a university for failing to adhere to Title IX, and the US Department of Education can also sue a university for failing to adhere to its regulations.) In the early 2000s, a group of women at Tel Aviv University established the university's first hotline to report sexual violence. The hotline provides women with information about how to report the violence to an

33. Orit Kamir, "Dignity, Respect, and Equality in Israel's Sexual Harassment Law," in *Directions in Sexual Harassment Law*, ed. Catherine A. MacKinnon and Reva B. Siegel (New Haven, CT: Yale University Press, 2004), 561–81.

office at the university—though that office exists primarily to protect the university.

We learned from women we interviewed that the group also trained volunteers to answer the phone and began intensive educational programs on campus with groups of students and presentations to classes. When a woman called the hotline, volunteers offered to meet her immediately to give her both emotional support and advice about pursuing legal action. Many students in those first years did not even realize that what happened to them was illegal. Most of the phone calls to the hotline concerned male faculty harassing female students, both undergraduate and graduate students in all fields, and most of the harassment reported concerned physical assault. And yet, if legal adjudication is the only focus, we lose sight of victims' other needs. Most victims require emotional support and academic advice before they can even begin to think about legal actions. Most of all, they need to recover from the trauma of the experience.[34]

Each country has its own unique configuration of gendered assumptions and inequalities, and within each country there are different subcultures, affected by a host of factors, from economics to ethnicity to religiosity. In explaining the academic culture in Israel, one woman told us:

> As Israeli women, we are educated to certain roles as partner, mother—then we go to the army, one of the most sexist environments in Israel, where most women are given jobs as secretaries and harassment is rampant, and our self-esteem is damaged, then to college, maybe graduate school. Just when you are starting to create yourself as an intellectual, an adviser refers to you as a sexual object, and immediately you are transformed into a sexual object, not an intellectual. A woman professor at Tel Aviv University, Tova Rosen,

34. An extraordinary village for women's recovery from sexual assault—called Ohela: Land Where Women Heal—was created in Israel by a midwife, Marva Zohar, herself a survivor of rape. Information is available on their website, accessed May 1, 2024, https://www.ohelaenglish.org/.

was such an important influence for us, a unique model—along with Hannah Naveh and Orly Lubin—who were on campus because of their intellectual capacity. That's why sexual harassment is so harmful—just at the moment when you are born as an intellectual at a university, it starts, before you have the tools to reject the gaze.

Since adjudication of assault and harassment is conducted privately, it is also possible for harassers to simply transfer to another university, which some have done. Others remain in place, so that women who have been assaulted may continue to encounter the assaulter in classes, in a dorm, at the library, in the cafeteria, or elsewhere on campus. Moreover, widely circulating reports of harassment lawsuits leave some women fearful of filing a complaint because the adjudication may take a long time and the process may become public knowledge, as we discuss in chapter 3. One Israeli woman we interviewed who is now teaching in the United States called attention to female staff at universities who are also subject to harassment and whose jobs can be precarious. How discouraging must it be to the janitors, she said, who sometimes see what is transpiring but dare not intervene lest their own jobs be jeopardized. Staff, she said, notice a great deal because they are usually ignored. Yet they, too, can be targets of harassment and assault.

Israel is a small country, and the academic community knows what happens to colleagues. One Israeli academic mused to us, "What happens when a harasser marries his student? Female graduate students who have had relationships with their professors sometimes leave the field and abandon their ambitions. How do we address this?" Another Israeli professor said she was haunted by the case of a married male professor who had an affair with his female graduate student. He left his wife, who had also been his student, and married the new graduate student, who was then forced to leave the graduate program on the grounds of nepotism. The power imbalance in relationships between professors and students may easily derail students' careers.

Are all romantic relationships between professors and students, tenured and untenured faculty, necessarily harassment? We think there are ways that a relationship within a university-related power dynamic could be acceptable, but we also see this as an area in which everyone should move very cautiously. A simple rubric of consent is not sufficient. Moreover, what begins as consensual can become stickier: If a student enters a relationship with an instructor consensually, what happens when they are considering exiting that relationship, and their grades, letters of reference, or reputation in the department remain at stake? Important considerations also include whether there is a direct relationship (such as between a teacher and a graduate student, or between a department chair and an untenured faculty member) and whether there is at-work contact (such as with a postdoc and a full professor in the same department). Some universities forbid all romantic relationships between faculty and undergraduate students, fearing that the power held by faculty might be used to manipulate students or disrupt their educational experience. Other institutions prohibit sexual or romantic relationships between professors and their students or advisees. One scholar has argued that, in these situations, the person with greater power may be drawn to a student out of narcissistic desire, and students who fall in love with a professor may confuse envy with desire; they may actually be in love with the scholarly enterprise.[35] In any case, the weight of the ethical responsibility falls on the person with greater power not to misuse that power. Even then, good intentions are not always sufficient to guarantee there is no harm.

This chapter has discussed scholars' experiences of discrimination and harassment in the field of Jewish studies, but we found that very few of our interlocutors responded by turning to their college's or university's procedures as a remedy. This leads us to the troubling question of why people do not report discrimination and harassment more frequently. The next chapter explores why.

---

35. That is the argument put forward by Amia Srinivasan, *The Right to Sex: Feminism in the Twenty-First Century* (New York: Farrar, Straus and Giroux, 2021).

3

Reporting Sexual Harassment
and Assault

TWO CASE STUDIES

WHY DON'T MORE PEOPLE REPORT HARASSMENT? Sometimes people think the reporting will change nothing, and they are often right. One scholar told us she reported a violation of EEOC (Equal Employment Opportunity Commission) regulations to the proper office in her university because a faculty member had asked private questions related to gender and reproduction as part of a job interview.[1] The administrator asked her, "Do you think she [the candidate] will sue?" When the scholar said no, the administrator said, "That's good," and then did nothing at all, not even talk to the faculty member who had violated the regulations. Some victims fear retaliation. (One 2020 report on the workplace found that 72 percent of women who experienced workplace sexual harassment faced retaliation.)[2] Others just want to stop thinking about

---

1. The Equal Employment Opportunity Commission is a federal agency that enforces laws forbidding discrimination in the workplace.

2. "Seventy-Two Percent of Workers Who Experienced Sex Harassment Faced Retaliation, Says New Report by NWLC Based on TIME'S UP Legal Defense Fund Data," National Women's Law Center, October 15, 2020, https://nwlc.org/press-releases/seventy-two-percent-of-workers-who-experienced-sex-harassment-faced-retaliation-says-new-report-by-nwlc-based-on-times-up-legal-defense-fund-data/.

what happened to them, which becomes impossible if there is a process with interviews, forms, and repeated invocations and re-tellings of the event.

In this chapter we examine two egregious cases—one involving scholars in Jewish studies, the other in an adjacent field—to dem-onstrate that even when people *do* choose to report, the culture and the systems that are supposed to protect people and discipline offenders let them down. The difficulties we recount in these two cases reinforce a widespread concern that reporting is not worth it. We chose cases that have been discussed extensively in other publications; our goal is not to bring new cases to light but to show the inadequacy (and sometimes failure) of the systems that are supposed to prevent harassment or assault and to discipline offenders.

Sexual harassment and assault represent not just one person acting badly. A culture of ignorance or acceptance allows and sometimes fosters sexist behavior. It may even protect the careers of perpetrators at the expense of those they have harmed. Some of our interlocutors who have filed complaints in the past have been disappointed because when they reported discrimination, nothing changed. Thus, as our analysis highlights, one of the reasons reporting harassment or assault does not fix the problem is because the problem is not simply one of rules or punishment, but of what is acceptable in an academic culture.

We are not proposing more or better reporting as the solution. We do not think that increased reporting will stop harassment or assault, and we know there can be real costs to the careers and well-being of people who report. Until we have widespread soci-etal consensus that harassment and assault are unacceptable, such acts will not cease, and disciplinary procedures will not function effectively. Right now, it is clear that the systems in place cannot fully protect victims, whether they report or not. The two cases we discuss illustrate the hurt caused to individuals, and they also show some of the deficiencies in the systems, policies, and proce-dures designed to address harassment or assault. These cases are high-profile examples, and so they are not typical of every instance of discrimination in the field, but in our judgment, they lay bare the shortcomings and failures of these systems.

The first case we discuss concerns Steven M. Cohen, a well-known, well-published senior scholar of Jewish sociology whose work received financial support and acclaim from Jewish organizations for decades. During those same decades, according to internal investigations undertaken by his employer, Hebrew Union College (HUC), and by investigative journalist Hannah Dreyfus, Cohen harassed and assaulted numerous women, even as he mentored other women. At the time, Cohen was a research professor of Jewish social policy at HUC and director of the Berman Jewish Policy Archive, an electronic database at Stanford University.

Cohen was finally exposed after an untenured woman scholar, Keren McGinity, in the same field, Jewish sociology, published an article in a Jewish newspaper in June 2018 describing in detail an assault she had endured in December 2017 without naming the assailant. She wrote that she had been pleased when a senior male scholar in her field came over to her at the annual AJS meeting and invited her to meet for dinner and discuss her research. After returning to the conference hotel, he joined her in the elevator, exited when she did, and followed her down an empty corridor—and assaulted her.[3] She broke free, horrified, and raced to her room. Initially, she kept quiet, fearful for her career and aware that without witnesses her word might not be accepted.[4]

Yet she was far from alone. One of Cohen's female colleagues told Dreyfus that Cohen would place his hand "on her knee,

3. Keren McGinity, "American Jewry's #MeToo Problem: A First-Person Encounter," *New York Jewish Week*, June 21, 2018, https://jewishweek.timesofisrael.com/american-jewrys-metoo-problem-a-first-person-encounter/.

4. McGinity has since published an extensive analysis of harassment and assault in Jewish, Muslim, and Christian religious communities: Keren McGinity, *#UsToo: How Jewish, Muslim, and Christian Women Changed Our Communities* (London: Routledge, 2023).

shoulder or back" and ask her intimate questions about her love life; another woman said that Cohen stared at her name tag at a conference and then put "his hand on her left breast."[5] The stories went back many years. In 1992, Cohen reportedly sexually assaulted an organizational consultant.[6] Another woman colleague reported that she arrived at his apartment for a scheduled meeting to work on an article they were coauthoring, and he answered the door wearing only his underwear and requested "sexual activity"; one woman professor, a lesbian, reported that during their research collaboration, Cohen made "blatantly homophobic comments about my sexual orientation," including asking "how lesbians get pregnant."[7]

While some women had informed appropriate authorities over the course of the decades, nothing was done until the allegations appeared in the press. Cohen did not deny the charges against him and issued this statement shortly after Dreyfus's article appeared: "I recognize that there is a pattern here. . . . It's one that speaks to my inappropriate behavior for which I take full responsibility. I am deeply apologetic to the women whom I have hurt by my words or my actions." What Cohen calls "inappropriate behavior" was often physical sexual assault, and "hurt" does not encompass the trauma experienced by his victims. In his statement, Cohen said he would undertake a process of "education, recognition, remorse and repair" in consultation with clergy, therapists, and professional experts and would "seek to apologize directly to, and ask forgiveness from, those I have unintentionally hurt" when the "time is right."[8] To this day, those of Cohen's victims who spoke

5. Hannah Dreyfus, "Harassment Allegations Mount against Leading Jewish Sociologist," *Jewish Telegraphic Agency*, July 19, 2018, https://www.jta.org/2018/07/19/ny/harassment-allegations-mount-against-leading-jewish-sociologist.

6. Dreyfus.

7. Dreyfus.

8. Steven M. Cohen quoted in Dreyfus. See also "Several Women Accuse Leading Jewish Sociologist of Sexual Misconduct," *Jewish Telegraphic Agency*, July 19, 2018, https://www.jta.org/2018/07/19/united-states/several-women-accuse-leading

to us have not heard from him. The statement he issued exemplifies what Leigh Gilmore calls the "nonapology," which "hijacks sympathy for the victim and transfers it to the abuser, who, through no fault or responsibility of his own, was, if you think about it, equally a victim of a misunderstanding"—according to the statement.[9] To retain power, the apology is devised to be vague and to sound heartfelt: nonspecific—to "anyone who might have been offended," adding a promise to consult therapists, clergy, and other vaguely referenced professionals—as if this were not a crime but a misunderstanding that "offended" a woman, perhaps because of a psychological flaw, at worst a sin for which one receives absolution. The "nonapology," Gilmore writes, is "an attempt to gain absolution by spinning sex, including sexual violence, into discourse. Specifically, by recycling the myth that rape is sex gone wrong."[10] While Cohen was not accused of rape and did not use the language of offense, much of Gilmore's analysis is apt. Some members of the wider community applaud such apologies and immediately turn to discuss how the offender might be rehabilitated because the importance of his work outweighs his "misconduct."

But if the problems were problems of the norms of the academic community, then some of the responses were necessarily communal responses. Thanks to the courage of McGinity and the tenacity of Dreyfus, Cohen's case became a decisive moment in Jewish studies. Prompted by their articles, HUC, where Cohen held a faculty position, launched a Title IX investigation. Before the investigation was concluded, Cohen resigned, ending the investigation. In the wake of the Cohen case, additional reports

---

-jewish-sociologist-sexual-misconduct; and "Leading Jewish Sociologist Out at 2 Organizations following Sexual Misconduct Allegations," *Jewish Telegraphic Agency*, July 25, 2028, https://www.jta.org/2018/07/25/united-states/leading-jewish-sociologist-2-organizations-following-sexual-misconduct-allegations.

9. Leigh Gilmore, *The #MeToo Effect: What Happens When We Believe Women* (New York: Columbia University Press, 2023), 65.

10. Gilmore, 66.

came to light of sexual harassment, predatory behavior, and sexual assault by HUC faculty, including a former president of the institution, over the last several decades, leading HUC to establish a Teshuvah (repentance) working group.[11] In May 2023, the working group issued a series of recommendations, including an offer of revised graduation diplomas purged of the names of accused faculty abusers.[12] In 2018, the UJA-Federation of New York as well as several other organizations announced that they would not engage in further work with Cohen.[13]

Yet within two years, and despite Cohen's acknowledgment of his sexual assaults, some scholars began an effort to return him to academic and communal respectability. Several of his colleagues organized a series of private workshops and invited other scholars to join them. In addition to the ethical problems raised by holding behind-the-scenes private workshops with someone banned from public academic settings in the field, scholars who were invited to participate found themselves in a compromised situation of either

11. Arno Rosenfeld, "Reform Seminary Investigation: 'Good Old Boys' Culture Has Left Scars," *Forward*, November 9, 2021, https://forward.com/news/477909 /reform-seminary-huc-investigation-hebrew-union-college-sexual-misconduct/. The HUC's Teshuvah (repentance) working group's website, accessed June 12, 2024, is at https://pr.huc.edu/email/2022/06/teshuvah/.

12. Hebrew Union College has announced that it accepts the recommendations, including issuing new certificates, diplomas, and ordination documents to replace those signed by abusers or offenders or containing gendered language that recipients would like changed; see HUC website, accessed June 20, 2024, https://huc.edu/for -alumni/reissuing-of-diplomas-and-ordination-documents-as-part-of-huc-jirs -teshuvah-process/.

13. Eric S. Goldstein, "Learning from #MeToo," UJA [United Jewish Appeal]- Federation of New York, July 27, 2018, https://www.ujafedny.org/news/learning -from-metoo; "Statement from the AJS Women's Caucus," Association for Jewish Studies, March 23, 2021, https://www.associationforjewishstudies.org/about-ajs /gender-justice/statement-from-the-ajs-women-s-caucus; and "Statement from the Executive Committee on Recent Meetings Involving Steven M. Cohen," Association for Jewish Studies, March 24, 2021, https://www.associationforjewishstudies.org /about-ajs/press-room/news-events/news-detail/2021/03/24/statement-from -the-executive-committee-on-recent-meetings-involving-steven-m.-cohen.

choosing to meet with a known assaulter or declining the invitation and risking possible retaliation from powerful senior colleagues. Some accepted and joined the gatherings, while some who were invited and declined to attend told us they felt coerced by the invitation. Again, Hannah Dreyfus investigated and published reports of the private meetings in the press.[14] Within hours after the press reports appeared, over five hundred Jewish clergy signed a statement condemning the workshops; the signatures soon reached close to one thousand. It explained, "we condemn the attempts to try to rehabilitate unrepentant abusers."[15] The Women's Caucus of the AJS also condemned the workshops, writing, "The Women's Caucus views these efforts as unacceptable and deeply troubling, because they jeopardize the position of junior and contingent scholars as well as re-victimizing women targeted by Cohen."[16] When the public learned that the president of the AJS had participated in a workshop with Cohen, he voluntarily resigned his presidency. Ruth Wisse, a renowned scholar of Yiddish literature and professor emerita at Harvard University, wrote in defense of Cohen, saying the outrage over the private meetings "has turned into a campaign to reframe the perpetuation of Jewishness as a dystopian project of enforced reproduction."[17] Two anthologies of American Jewish thought were published and included articles by Cohen, which sparked further outrage. One

14. Hannah Dreyfus, "Steven M. Cohen, Shunned by Academy after Harassment Allegations, Makes a Stealthy Comeback—and Provokes Uproar," *Forward*, March 23, 2021, https://forward.com/news/466437/steven-cohen-shunned-after-harassment-accusations-trying-to-make-a-stealth/.

15. The statement, accessed June 12, 2024, condemning the private workshops involving Steven M. Cohen and signatures can be seen at https://docs.google.com/document/d/1hTVWgCqrIce8gFagLLiQanzd_-n27mvlg7RS4bQRqGw/edit?fbclid=IwAR2oMS2b6UlmC2TfWRW8wBg4PDCu6HgMLynfuqGsmUgduYDNsf_4eCp5Rmk.

16. "Statement from the AJS Women's Caucus."

17. Ruth Wisse, "The Hounding of Noam Pianko," *Mosaic*, May 13, 2021, https://mosaicmagazine.com/observation/politics-current-affairs/2021/05/the-hounding-of-noam-pianko/.

volume, entitled *The New Jewish Canon*, included works by Cohen and two others who had been accused of harassment, Leon Wieseltier and Ari Shavit, although the editors acknowledged that all three had been accused of "patterns of sexual impropriety." The editors wrote that they recognized "that the power and charisma that allowed them to succeed professionally and to promote their ideas is the very same power and charisma that they are accused of abusing in their predatory actions."[18]

Others denounced the efforts to rehabilitate Cohen as minimizing sexual assault and ignoring its impact on women. As Melissa Weininger, scholar of Hebrew literature, commented, a "closed and secretive network to rehabilitate Cohen is really an attempt to reinscribe the power dynamics that are central to harassment behavior in the first place."[19] Another colleague told us, "I am not surprised by the defenses of Steve Cohen. Some people just don't know what it means to work in an environment where you are excluded, denigrated, and patronized." Although Cohen has been banned from AJS meetings, he has continued to appear at some Zoom workshops, horrifying some of his victims when they suddenly see his face on their computer screens.

Cohen was able to assault women over the course of decades thanks to numerous forms of protection, many of which reflect a larger social and economic culture in Jewish studies: He employed women as part of his research projects, cultivating a reputation as a man supportive of women; indeed, women were among his colleagues and collaborators. While a Title IX office existed at the institution where he taught, the administration was apparently unaware of his harassment. Women held few positions of power in relation to Cohen, a pervasive culture denigrating to women was expressed by Cohen's defenders, and no effective mechanisms for reporting and adjudicating assault existed at many of the

18. Yehuda Kurtzer and Claire E. Sufrin, eds., *The New Jewish Canon: Ideas and Debates, 1980–2015* (Boston: Academic Studies, 2020), xxii.

19. Weininger quoted in Dreyfus, "Steven M. Cohen."

institutions that employed him. The fact that HUC technically had a procedure for reporting, but the procedure was opaque and ineffective, illustrates that the fundamental issue is the culture of our institutions and not just the actions of a single person.

Reports of Cohen's sexual harassment and assault also led to debates over his publications regarding American Jewish families and links between what critics saw as sexist assumptions in his scholarship and his sexual harassment. Articles in the April 2020 issue of the journal *American Jewish History* elucidated those links.[20] For example, Cohen's demographic surveys of US Jews concluded that assimilation, intermarriage, and smaller families were creating a declining population of Jews. Promoting "Jewish continuity," Cohen concluded that Jewish women should have more babies to counter the shrinking number of Jews that he forecast. Continuity, Cohen argued, required increasing Jewish fertility. Rokhl Kafrissen wrote, "Put simply, how surprised can we be that a man whose entire worldview hinged on women having more babies turned out to have no respect for women when it came to personal sexual boundaries?"[21]

Several scholars criticized the "large and expensive social research apparatus, driven by male leadership and sustained by aggressive boundary policing," that controlled academic research through its grants in conjunction with the communal demand for in-marriage and increased fertility.[22] Michal Kravel-Tovi sees the enormous power and authority within the Jewish community that Cohen garnered through his demographic studies as key to his

20. *American Jewish History* 104, no. 2/3 (April/July 2020).

21. Rokhl Kafrissen, "How a #MeToo Scandal Proved What We Already Know: 'Jewish Continuity' Is Sexist," *Forward*, July 18, 2020, https://forward.com/opinion/406271/how-a-metoo-scandal-proved-what-we-already-know-jewish-continuity-is-sexist/.

22. Lila Berman, Kate Rosenblatt, and Ronit Stahl, "How Jewish Academia Created a #MeToo Disaster," *Forward*, July 19, 2018, https://forward.com/opinion/406240/how-jewish-academia-created-a-metoo-disaster/.

transgressions as well as his biopolitical approach that quantifies human life.[23]

What was so compelling about Cohen's scholarship that brought him so much attention and major grants, especially from Jewish community federations, over the years? Gilah Kletenik and Rafael Rachel Neis pointed out that the continuity agenda is "tethered to an idealized patriarchal heteronuclear family that stigmatizes and erases increasingly more common forms of kinship and networks of care."[24] Those who fail to reproduce biologically, argues Barbara Dobkin, are marginalized or even shunned, as if they are not fully committed to Jewish life.[25] Yet some defenders of Cohen argue that promoting fertility is not necessarily sexist. Some women, Mijal Bitton points out, want to have many children but lack the societal accommodations to care for children and earn a living.[26]

The policy conclusions drawn by Cohen from his demographic studies led to major financial investments over the course of several decades by Jewish organizations with programs to prevent intermarriage, promote greater numbers of children, and cultivate the Jewish commitments of young Jews. Numerous scholars, including McGinity, have pointed to the absence of attention in this so-called Jewish continuity project to changing social dynamics,

23. Michal Kravel-Tovi, "Accounting of the Soul: Enumeration, Affect, and Soul Searching among American Jewry," *American Anthropologist* 120, no. 4 (December 2018): 711–24.

24. Gilah Kletenik and Rafael Rachel Neis, "What's the Matter with Jewish Studies? Sexism, Harassment, and Neoliberalism for Starters," *Religion Dispatches*, April 19, 2021, https://religiondispatches.org/whats-the-matter-with-jewish-studies-sexism-harassment-and-neoliberalism-for-starters/.

25. Barbara Dobkin, "Why the 'Jewish Continuity' Conversation Must Change in the Era of #MeToo," *eJewish Philanthropy*, October 5, 2018, https://ejewishphilanthropy.com/why-the-jewish-continuity-conversation-must-change-in-the-era-of-metoo/.

26. Mijal Bitton, "Is Jewish Continuity Sexist? On Jewish Values and Female Bodies," *Sources: A Journal of Jewish Ideas*, March 19, 2021, https://www.sourcesjournal.org/articles/is-jewish-continuity-sexist.

including the commitment to Judaism of single parents, same-sex parents, gay and lesbian Jews, nonpartnered Jews, converts, and intermarried couples, many of whom felt marginalized within the Jewish community.[27]

Strikingly, Cohen's promotion of fertility in the 1980s began precisely when women with children began pursuing careers, yet he did not publicly encourage Jewish leaders to support women as they entered their professions by creating programs to end gender discrimination and sexual harassment, establishing day-care centers, providing financial assistance for reproductive technologies, or advocating paid parental leave, as women were demanding. The fertility Cohen promoted did not demand Jewish communal support for noncisgender men and women, or for single parents, nor did Cohen challenge male dominance in Jewish communal affairs and demand an end to gender discrimination. Cohen's push for more babies has particularly problematic consequences for women academics, whose childbearing years coincide with graduate school and efforts to achieve tenure—and yet he did not support and promote the changes to institutional and societal structures advocated by feminists. Moreover, Cohen's use of binary, heteronormative categories ignored research in his own field, sociology, since the 1980s, which demonstrated that binary, static categories fail to convey gender fluidity and nonconforming gender identities constructed and performed in societies around the globe. Nor was his work attentive to the intersectionality of identities regarding gender, sexuality, ethnicity, religion, race, and other categories that have become central to the work of academic sociologists.[28]

27. Keren McGinity, *Marrying Out: Jewish Men, Intermarriage, and Fatherhood* (Bloomington: Indiana University Press, 2014); and Keren McGinity, *Still Jewish: A History of Women and Intermarriage in America* (New York: New York University Press, 2009).

28. Candace West and Don Zimmerman, "Doing Gender," *Gender and Society* 1, no. 2 (1987): 125–51; R. W. Connell, "Making Gendered People: Bodies, Identities, Sexualities," in *Revisioning Gender*, ed. Myra Marx Ferree, Judith Lorber, and Beth B.

Imagine if Cohen's research recommendations had included that paid parental leave be mandated by federal law; that overcoming sexism be placed prominently on the agenda of the Anti-Defamation League; that the federal government or Jewish Federations fund day-care centers; that Jewish day schools and summer camps be made affordable and be mandated to teach antiharassment and antiracism curriculums; that the American Jewish Committee direct its resources toward supporting the Equal Rights Amendment; that all Jewish organizations develop strict rules about harassment and sexual assault; that equal numbers of women and men serve on the boards of all Jewish organizations; that equal pay be instituted for employees of Jewish organizations at all levels; that more women be appointed as executive directors of Jewish organizations; that all Jewish schools, synagogues, and camps be made accessible to anyone with disabilities; and that conferences take place to talk about what needs to be done, on the ground-floor level, to eliminate sexism in every Jewish community.

Reporting Sexual Harassment

We found in our interviews that many women had stories of harassment that they had never told anyone beyond a partner, spouse, or therapist. We were struck that almost none had ever reported what had happened to them, and we asked why. In some cases, they told us, there was no one to tell—no ethics committee, no administrator, no one who monitors and works to challenge, prevent, or punish harassment. Others did file reports, and nothing happened. Although supervisors sometimes believed their accounts and sometimes had received prior complaints about the same man, they declined to intervene, perhaps because the man was "too important" or "too powerful"—in other words,

---

Hess (Thousand Oaks, CA: Sage, 1999), 449–71; and, more recently, J. E. Sumerau, "A Tale of Three Spectrums: Deviating from Normative Treatments of Sex and Gender," *Deviant Behavior* 41, no. 7 (2020): 893–904.

the women were too unimportant. In other cases, as one senior scholar told us, "it wasn't that the people to whom it was happening didn't try to tell. They did. But when they did, they got a big 'Huh?'" The most common reason—which sometimes accompanied others—was that they didn't think any action would be taken. Some women did not report harassment because they feared confidentiality was impossible, or they feared retaliation; although Title IX forbids retaliation, it nevertheless can still occur.[29] Others told us the costs were too high: graduate students in small, specialized fields could not switch advisers and continue their research.

Statistics about rape also point to the futility of reporting.[30] The Rape and Incest National Network indicates that only 23 percent of rapes are reported, compared to over 60 percent of robberies and assault and battery crimes. In hard numbers, Michelle Bowdler summarizes, "230 out of 1,000 rapes are reported. Of those 230, 46 cases lead to arrest, 9 to prosecution, and 5 to felony conviction. Only 4% of all *reported* rape cases ever see the inside of a courtroom, translating into 1 percent of every 1,000 rapes committed. About 2 percent of rapes reported and one half of one percent of every 1,000 rapes lead to conviction and/or incarceration."[31] Such data discourage women from reporting rape and sexual assault, despite the seriousness of those crimes. Jewish studies scholar Laura Levitt describes her experience of ineffectual police and an unprocessed rape kit, and then the arrest, prosecution, and conviction that never happened. Like other

29. Amicus Brief USA Statement of Justice Civil Action No. 1:22-cv-10202-JGD, accessed January 8, 1024, https://drive.google.com/file/d/1NEvm-tXKdr1-mBhy53tj_RcNiGa-CBWP/view.

30. Melissa S. Morabito, Linda M. Williams, and April Pattavina, "Decision Making in Sexual Assault Cases: Replication Research on Sexual Violence Case Attrition in the U.S.," National Institute of Justice, US Department of Justice, Washington, DC, February 2019, https://www.ojp.gov/library/publications/decision-making-sexual-assault-cases-replication-research-sexual-violence-case.

31. Michelle Bowdler, *Is Rape a Crime? A Memoir, an Investigation, and a Manifesto* (New York: Flatiron Books, 2020), 5.

survivors of sexual predation and assault, she writes of the trauma that remains.[32] When something as violent as rape is ignored by police and courts of law in the United States, it should not be surprising to learn that people are reluctant to report sexual harassment.

What can we do? Disciplining or educating perpetrators is crucial, and those who have abused require attentive management to prevent further destructive behavior.[33] If the harassment or assault takes place on campus, victims can turn to Title IX offices because that 1972 US law holds universities that receive federal funding responsible for equal access, prohibiting discrimination based on sex. Harassment and assault are forms of discrimination, requiring universities to respond promptly, provide supportive measures, and offer a process to resolve complaints and prevent the recurrence of violations. Title IX administrators are expected to investigate, adjudicate, and remediate claims brought to them.

What reparation is possible for victims of harassment and the trauma that may ensue? Judith Herman, writing about survivors of trauma, calls for victims to be heard, and we agree.[34] Justice, she writes, is "a major part of the process of healing from psychological trauma."[35] Leigh Gilmore puts it bluntly: What do survivors want? The answer: for those in power to "remove abusers from positions of authority and hold them accountable, and to replace the structures that enable abuse."[36] Witnessing, Gilmore writes, is our ethical responsibility.[37] In speaking to victims of assault,

32. Laura Levitt, *The Objects That Remain* (University Park: Pennsylvania State University Press, 2020).

33. Guila Benchimol, "It Takes a Village: Communal Guidance from an Orthodox Criminologist," *18Forty*, May 18, 2022, https://18forty.org/articles/it-takes-a-village-communal-guidance-from-an-orthodox-criminologist/.

34. Judith Herman, *Truth and Repair: How Trauma Survivors Envision Justice* (New York: Basic Books, 2023), 45.

35. Herman, 53.

36. Gilmore, *#MeToo Effect*, 99.

37. Gilmore, 163.

however, we concluded that various forms of restorative justice, in which victims face the perpetrators or meet with a "moral community" that offers witness to their trauma, may be important options for some, while others find such processes retraumatizing. Herman suggests saying to the perpetrator, "Ask yourself a hard question: What can I possibly do to enable people to trust me again?"[38] Yet we also question whether restorative justice for harassment prevents recidivism and acts as a deterrent. If harassment is facilitated by perpetrators' holding positions of power and authority, prevention ultimately requires a reconfiguration of hierarchical models and a change in the field's norms.

As a start, we want the world to listen when victims tell the stories about what was done to them—not as a confession but as part of the narrative activism created by the #MeToo movement. Tarana Burke, the founder of #MeToo, defines the importance of shifting from shame over trauma to empowerment by way of narrating the experience.[39] In their memoirs, Chanel Miller and Lacy Crawford write of wanting to overcome the silencing and shaming they experienced from the institutions that were supposed to protect them after they were assaulted.[40] Miller, whose name was concealed during the trial of the Stanford student who raped her, wrote to reclaim her identity, especially after hearing the trial judge express sympathy for the rapist. As a fifteen-year-old, Crawford was raped by two men, high school seniors and fellow students at her elite boarding school, St. Paul's. She writes that the students who assaulted her spread vicious gossip about her, that the school administrators did nothing to punish the rapists or support her, and that the institution worked for thirty years to prevent authorities from investigating the crime. She analyzes the gendered power that protects men and

38. Herman, *Truth and Repair*, 129.

39. Tarana Burke, *Unbound: My Story of Liberation and the Birth of the Me Too Movement* (New York: Flatiron Books, 2021), 157.

40. Chanel Miller, *Know My Name: A Memoir* (New York: Penguin Books, 2019); and Lacy Crawford, *Notes on a Silencing: A Memoir* (New York: Little, Brown, 2020).

shames women, and she sees shame as a weapon that extends the assault and punishes women for having been assaulted. One woman scholar told us that only by reading such memoirs did she come to realize that the teasing and public humiliation she experienced from a teacher at her yeshiva elementary school was sexual harassment.

After the rape came the harassment. Lacy Crawford suggests that women's silence is the goal of harassment. She concludes her memoir: "It's so simple, what happened at St. Paul's. It happens all the time. First, they refused to believe me. Then they shamed me. Then they silenced me. On balance, if this is a girl's trajectory from dignity to disappearance, I say it is better to be a slut than to be silent. I believe, in fact, that the slur slut carries within it, Trojan-horse style, silence as its true intent. That the opposite of slut is not virtue but voice.[41]

The Consequences of Reporting Harassment

What happens when women report harassment? Crawford writes that to be harassed is to be silenced. Those who dare report harassment may experience further marginalization and even more harassment, as happened to Simona Sharoni, professor of women's and gender studies at Merrimack College in Massachusetts. Sharoni published an important account of the efforts to silence and shame her after she complained about an inappropriate comment by the political scientist Richard Ned Lebow, professor emeritus at Dartmouth College, during the annual meeting of the International Studies Association (ISA) in April 2018.[42]

Neither Lebow nor Sharoni is a scholar fully within the field of Jewish studies, but each has published on topics adjacent to the field, including some with relevance to Israel studies, and each has

41. Crawford, *Notes on a Silencing*, 382.

42. Simona Sharoni, "Speaking Up in the Age of #MeToo and Persistent Patriarchy, or What Can We Learn from an Elevator Incident about Anti-feminist Backlash," *Feminist Review* 120 (2018): 143–51.

had engagement with the Israeli academic world. Sharoni's analysis of what transpired, Lebow's public self-defense, and the ensuing media attacks of Sharoni provide an excellent example of why some women hesitate to report harassment. Writing in the journal *Feminist Review*, Sharoni describes what happened:

> One of the only two women in the elevator populated mostly by middle-age white men, all attending the conference, I stood next to the buttons and therefore offered to press them for the passengers who could not reach. As people asked for their floor numbers, one person called out "ladies lingerie." Several men in the elevator laughed. I exchanged glances with the young woman standing next to me, whom I had not met prior to the incident, and made a mental note to myself to remember the name tag of the man who made the comment: Dr. Richard Ned Lebow. As he exited the elevator, the woman standing next to me, also a conference attendee, turned to me and another young man who remained in the elevator, remarking that we should have said something, and we all parted ways.[43]

Following the ISA's established protocol, Sharoni reported Lebow's comment as a violation of the ISA's code of conduct, claiming that "a comment with sexual innuendo was both unprofessional and inappropriate in a public setting, especially at an academic conference." Sharoni's complaint was turned over to the Professional Rights and Responsibilities Committee of the ISA for adjudication, a confidential process. The committee agreed with Sharoni that Lebow had violated its code of conduct, which calls for "dignity and respect" and prohibits "unwanted conduct affecting the dignity of people or individuals,"[44] and it asked Lebow to

---

43. Sharoni, 143.

44. An updated ISA Code of Conduct from 2020 is at https://www.isanet.org /Portals/0/Documents/ISA/ISACodeofConduct0420.pdf. It states, "Unwanted conduct affecting the dignity of men and women. It may be related to age, gender, gender identity, sexual orientation, race, disability, religion, nationality, or any personal characteristic of the individual, and may be persistent or isolated. The key is

write a note of apology to her. Instead, Lebow wrote to Sharoni and said her complaint was "frivolous" and that attention should be paid to "real offenses, not those that are imagined or marginal."[45] He refused to apologize and appealed the decision, but it was upheld by the ISA.[46]

Violating the confidentiality of the process, Lebow went to the media, asserting that Sharoni misunderstood his "joke" and presenting himself as a victim of "political correctness."[47] The case was widely reported in newspapers in the United States and England, on television, and on social media, with sympathy directed to Lebow. The day after Sharoni was attacked on Fox News, she received over one hundred email messages—including one telling her to "get cancer and die"[48]—primarily from self-identified men, ranging "from crude misogyny, racism, antisemitism and xenophobia to ableist, homophobic and transphobic comments."[49] Merrimack College supported her, but she was shocked not to receive any public support from the ISA, which remained silent.

Even liberal media outlets such as the *Washington Post* and the *Atlantic* published articles supporting Lebow and bemoaning Sharoni's attack on a distinguished scholar with nary a word about Sharoni's own scholarship. Journalist Ruth Marcus called Lebow's

---

that the actions or comments are experienced as demeaning and unacceptable by the recipient."

45. Ruth Marcus, "She Called His Elevator Joke Offensive. He Called Her Complaint 'Frivolous.' Who's Right?," *Washington Post*, May 3, 2018, https://www .washingtonpost.com/opinions/she-called-his-elevator-joke-offensive-he-called -her-complaint-frivolous-whos-right/2018/05/03/43ba4084-4ee1-11e8-af46 -b1d6dc0d9bfe_story.html.

46. Lebow described his appeal to the ISA and its response to him in *Quillette*, November 23, 2018, https://quillette.com/2018/11/23/warning-telling-a-lame-joke -in-an-elevator-can-endanger-your-career/.

47. Caleb Parke, "Male Professor Faces Sanction for Elevator Joke, Calls It 'Chilling Example of Political Correctness,'" Fox News, May 9, 2018, https://www.foxnews .com/us/male-professor-faces-sanction-for-elevator-joke-calls-it-chilling-example -of-political-correctness; Sharoni, "Speaking Up in the Age of #MeToo," 144.

48. Sharoni, 146.

49. Sharoni, 148.

remark "a lame, outmoded joke" but said Sharoni's complaint was "the latest exemplar in the academy of political correctness gone wild." She agreed with Lebow for calling the incident "a horrifying and chilling example of political correctness" and disagreed with Sharoni's response that invoking "political correctness" is a "blanket excuse by those who refuse to rethink and change their racist, sexist and homophobic beliefs and practices." Marcus concluded that Sharoni's complaint was "frivolous" and "counterproductive" and represented a "culture of eggshell fragility."[50] Journalist Conor Friedersdorf wrote in the *Atlantic* that Lebow's remark was "a joke," the ISA code a "gag order," and the request for an apology worse than a $5,000 fine. Friedersdorf asked, "Should *all* jokes with *any* sexual innuendo be banned from ISA conferences?"[51] Katherine Timpf, writing in the *National Review*, said Sharoni's complaint "threatens to end humor altogether."[52] The *Jewish Chronicle* in England opined: "she is being seriously ridiculous about a bad joke. In fact the whole business is a bad joke. . . . It's a small example of a sort of lunacy that is getting wilder and wilder and stronger and stronger and running out of control."[53] The point here is that these media responses declared that what Lebow said was acceptable, even when the ISA itself had deemed it a violation of its community standards and regulations.

---

50. We also note the ableist invocation of lameness as badness in her statement; again, not because it is the worst example of ableism, but rather because it gestures toward how assumptions about bodily normativity often appear together. See Marcus, "She Called His Elevator Joke Offensive."

51. Conor Friedersdorf, "Is a 'Ladies Lingerie' a Harmless Joke or Harassment?," *Atlantic*, May 9, 2018, https://www.theatlantic.com/politics/archive/2018/05/is-this-old-lingerie-joke-harmless-or-harassment/559760/.

52. Katherine Timpf, "Male Professor Faces Discipline for Telling a Female Professor a Joke," *National Review*, May 9, 2018, https://www.nationalreview.com/2018/05/richard-ned-lebow-joke-professor-simona-sharoni-discipline/.

53. David Robson, "Two Jews Got into a Lift and . . . ," *Jewish Chronicle*, May 17, 2018, https://www.thejc.com/lets-talk/all/two-jews-got-into-a-lift-and--1.464260.

Lebow wrote about the incident and the ISA's response in *Quillette* under the title "Warning: Telling a Lame Joke in an Elevator Can Endanger Your Career."[54] He, too, had "received endless emails and letters, all but two," he wrote, "expressing total support. The other two were friendly and urged me 'as a gentleman' to say I was sorry and let the matter pass."[55] For Lebow and his supporters, his comment was a joke and should never have elicited a complaint.

We note that jokes too can violate codes of conduct; they can promote racism, sexism, antisemitism, and other biases. In Lebow's lengthy rehearsal of the incident, he describes the ISA's response as a "warning" and suggests that his career and reputation were endangered—an odd claim, since he is the person who took the case to the media.[56]

In the US context, freedom of speech protects the speaker from arrest, but not from the personal or professional consequences of the words they say. A gag order prohibits people involved in a lawsuit or criminal investigation from talking to the public about those topics; it is not a gag order to instruct someone that saying sexist things will alienate their colleagues. Moreover, freedom of speech is cherished by liberal democracies, but democracies can still decide if certain speech is dangerous. In Germany, for example, antisemitic remarks, including jokes, can be grounds for arrest on charges of "Volksverhetzung" (incitement to hatred), a criminal offense.[57]

---

54. We note that this title is ableist too; it uses "lame" to invoke badness. Richard Ned Lebow, "Warning: Telling a Lame Joke in an Elevator Can Endanger Your Career," *Quillette*, November 23, 2018, https://quillette.com/2018/11/23/warning-telling-a-lame-joke-in-an-elevator-can-endanger-your-career/; and Richard Ned Lebow, "How My Lame Joke Saw Me Fall Foul of the Campus Zealots," *Spectator*, May 14, 2018, https://www.spectator.co.uk/article/how-my-lame-joke-saw-me-fall-foul-of-the-campus-zealots.

55. Lebow, "Warning."

56. Lebow.

57. The German Criminal Code prohibits incitement based on national, religious, or ethnic identity by defaming or calling for violence against members of those

Beyond state law, within any community there are shared codes of conduct that frown on disparaging language. Sharoni defines the issue in those terms: society is shifting, becoming multiethnic, multiracial, and accepting of sexual self-definition, with women taking prominent positions in the public square, and that requires changes in our speech and behavior:

> What most media outlets failed to consider is that in 2018, it is no longer acceptable to make comments with sexual, racist, homophobic or ableist references in public spaces. . . . This is not a result of "political correctness" or lack of cultural sensitivity but rather a sign of the changing times. Entitled white men can no longer get away with saying in a public space at an academic conference what they would in a bar, a locker room or an exclusively male boardroom. To work alongside others, in professional environments that are no longer as homogeneous as they used to be, we all have to change our behaviour, think before we speak and consider apologising when we offend someone. Codes of conduct are there neither to censor nor police speech but rather to help organisations and institutions adapt to the changing times by safeguarding mutual respect.[58]

Let us consider Lebow's comment in the elevator and why it prompted laughter from the young men who accompanied him. By invoking "ladies lingerie," Lebow was reminding his elevator audience that women wear lingerie and evoking images of women as seductive and alluring, an association that might be amusing, but not in an academic context. By responding to Sharoni's query, "which floor," with "ladies lingerie," Lebow removed her from the category of scholarly colleague, where he stood, into the category of "female." Lebow tried to justify his comment by claiming it was a reference to an earlier era, the 1940s and 1950s, when department

---

identities; see German Criminal Code, para. 130, sec. 1, accessed June 12, 2024, https://www.gesetze-im-internet.de/stgb/__130.html.

58. Sharoni, "Speaking Up in the Age of #MeToo," 146.

stores had elevator operators who announced what was sold on each floor. Once again, Lebow was shifting Sharoni into a different category, evoking, perhaps nostalgically, the era when women entered elevators not to participate in scholarship but simply as shoppers. As Sharoni points out, times have changed. While Lebow claimed his right to "free speech," he launched the attacks against Sharoni by insisting on his freedom *not* to speak, refusing to utter the two small words the ISA had requested: "I'm sorry."

Laughing with the other men in the elevator may have been a moment of male bonding via a sexist remark. Younger male colleagues may feel either pressure or aspiration to seem friendly and on the same page as their senior colleagues. Sharoni cites Emma Pitman, who writes, "Misogyny is, and always has been, collaborative. . . . Men who bond by denigrating women are intimidating and often dangerous."[59] This is not to say that every man in the elevator was a misogynist, but rather that they all, actively or passively, participated in a moment facilitated by a culture that permits misogyny and trivializes its harms.

Pitman writes, "We must resist the temptation to view misogyny as a spectrum. This is the wrong way to measure harm; it gives way to a complacency that says, 'it's just a joke, it's not like I actually touched her.' Misogyny isn't a sliding scale of harm where jokes are situated at one end and rape at the other. Rather, it functions like a human pyramid, where minor acts support major acts by providing, at best, a foundation of blithe indifference and, at worst, an atmosphere of amusement at the denigration of women."[60] Here the misogyny of the elevator remark is compounded by the media storm and the threats against Sharoni that followed.

Proclaiming his innocence, Lebow asserted that he had long supported women's rights and mentored women in his field. Yet our interviews taught us that a person could be a supportive mentor to

59. Emma Pitman, "Misogyny Is a Human Pyramid," *Meanjin*, January 15, 2018, https://meanjin.com.au/blog/misogyny-is-a-human-pyramid/.
60. Pitman.

women while also being someone who rarely cited women or who engaged in harassment. Lebow wrote in the *Spectator* that "increasingly on campuses where feminists and leftists have come to wield influence, they are abusing their power and behaving exactly like those they have long condemned."[61] The sentence is striking: Is a request for apology an abuse of power? Later, he wrote, "I am indeed sorry that Prof. Sharoni has received email threats; I certainly do not condone this kind of behavior. However, this attention is the product of an action that she began, not anything that I did."[62] With these statements, Lebow presented himself as the victim, appealing for sympathy from his readers and illustrating what Kate Manne has defined as "himpathy."[63] As Jilly Boyce Kaye and Sarah Banet-Wiser write, "When, in a himpathetic culture, victimhood is appropriated not by those who have historically suffered but by those in positions of patriarchal power . . . [that] maintains a hegemonic gender order."[64]

Far more dangerous than Lebow's joke was his decision to break confidentiality and set the media against Sharoni. With that decision he exercised his patriarchal power to transform his elevator remark into a verbal media assault against her, something that also occurred on a larger scale following the testimony of Christine Blasey Ford to the US Senate confirmation hearings for the appointment of Brett Kavanaugh to the US Supreme Court; after her testimony, death threats forced Ford and her family to go into hiding and to require twenty-four-hour security.[65] After reading

61. Lebow, "How My Lame Joke Saw Me Fall Foul of the Campus Zealots."

62. Lebow, "Warning."

63. See Kate Manne, *Down Girl: The Logic of Misogyny* (New York: Oxford University Press, 2017), 36.

64. Jilly Boyce Kaye and Sarah Banet-Wiser, "Feminist Anger and Feminist Respair," *Feminist Media Studies* 19, no. 4 (2019): 603–9, quote on 207.

65. Interview on National Public Radio March 19, 2024, https://www.npr.org/2024/03/19/1239378828/for-christine-blasey-ford-the-fallout-of-the-kavanaugh-hearing-is-ongoing.

Sharoni's account of the harassment Lebow launched against her, how many women would decide to file a complaint?

We have presented this case to illustrate one reason why some people are reluctant to report sexual harassment: filing a complaint may lead to backlash. In 2022, the *New York Times* reported that three women graduate students filed a complaint against a senior professor with Harvard University's Title IX office. As reported in the *New York Times*, one of the students filed a lawsuit against Harvard after the Title IX office obtained notes from her therapist without her consent and turned over those notes to the professor who was the object of her complaint.[66] Whether or not Harvard acted legally, that action was certainly unethical and sends a chilling message to anyone who has been harassed: privacy and protection are not guaranteed to those who file a complaint.

We also argue that, like the Harvard case, Sharoni's experience demonstrates the gendered issues in the larger culture of academia. The harm did not come from a single person alone; a wider culture supported the acceptability of harassing a woman who reported a violation of community standards. Moreover, there were other places where a different culture could have led to a different outcome. For example, if another man in the elevator had responded to Lebow's comment by saying, "That's not an appropriate joke," Sharoni likely would have felt differently. If Lebow had deferred to the rules of the ISA and apologized, the outcome would have been different. The expressions of hate directed toward Sharoni are frightening, and such treatment of a woman scholar can undermine the status of all women scholars, sending a message that women do not belong in the academy and reinforcing the burden felt by women that we constantly have to prove that we *do* belong.

66. Anemona Hartacollis, "After Sexual Harassment Lawsuit, Critics Attack Harvard's Release of Therapy Records," *New York Times*, February 15, 2022, https://www.nytimes.com/2022/02/15/us/harvard-kilburn-therapy-records.html?searchResultPosition=1.

Part III

4

Scholarship as
a Manly Enterprise

THE ORIGINS OF JEWISH STUDIES
IN NINETEENTH-CENTURY GERMANY

MOST OF US REMEMBER the thrill of being handed a diploma, a grand moment of celebration in the presence of fellow students, teachers, and family. At ceremonies at one Jewish institution, the male dean handed a PhD diploma to a female graduate, kissed her on the lips, and forced his tongue inside her mouth. Her moment of glory turned to disgust. She later learned that wasn't the first or the last time he had done that to a woman.

This scene would have shocked the earliest scholars in the academic field of Jewish studies, but the fact of a woman receiving a PhD diploma related to Jewish studies may well have scandalized them even more than the forced kiss. As part of our effort to understand gender biases in the field, we explore several of the sites and eras in which aspects of Jewish studies initially took shape. In this chapter, we look at the Wissenschaft des Judentums, which developed in nineteenth-century Germany, not to argue for a direct line of continuity, but to call attention to the male founders who defined scholarship as a masculine enterprise, leaving a legacy that resonates to this day.

While the nineteenth century may seem historically removed, its heritage still affects the field of Jewish studies. Some scholars working in Jewish studies, including Susannah, studied with refugee scholars from Germany whose teachers had been part of the first or second generation of the field. Those scholars developed the philological methods and set forth the key questions that continue to shape our scholarship, and their work remains required reading for everyone entering the field of Jewish studies. The Hebrew University in Jerusalem, founded in 1925, has long been called the "last German university" for its emphasis on philology and the many German Jewish émigré scholars who taught there and shaped its departments and areas of focus. And these are just the direct links. This chapter concentrates on the ways Wissenschaft culture has continued to affect Jewish studies.

We analyze the historical legacy of Jewish studies: the culture of our nineteenth-century forefathers. During its first century, Jewish studies was excluded from the universities of Europe. The first generation of Jewish studies scholars created the field—called Wissenschaft des Judentums—at a sophisticated academic level outside the universities and without the involvement of women scholars.[1] Scholarship in most fields was not just a men-only profession; it was a manly endeavor sometimes described in heterosexual metaphors. As Bonnie G. Smith writes, "Only men had the time to engage in the activities (archival research,

1. The German term is often translated as the "science of Judaism," which is not quite right in English; "Wissenschaft" might be better translated as "scholarship" in an inclusive sense, incorporating all the disciplines of the academy, including natural and social sciences and humanities, some of which first arose during the nineteenth century. At its outset, however, Wissenschaft des Judentums meant the historical study of Jews and Judaism, usually based on philological analyses of texts. The German term "Judentum" also has a significance different from that of the English "Judaism," as the German word can refer to the religion, Jews, or Jewishness—thus, the broad culture and religion of Jews.

teaching in universities) on which the founding of professional history depended."[2]

Is there a connection between sexual harassment and the male dominance in Jewish studies scholarship? We see uncomfortable links. Steven Cohen, for example, both admitted to assault and conducted research that painted women in reproductive roles, even as he worked with women colleagues. More than one scholar we interviewed noted that a male professor who collaborated almost exclusively with men also interacted with women inappropriately outside the classroom. Obviously, we are not drawing general conclusions about men who participate in male-only publications nor about men who work with women; rather, we are concerned that male dominance creates a cultural atmosphere that leaves women vulnerable to exclusion from scholarly projects and encourages men to dismiss, denigrate, or even prey on women.

Over time, images of professors emerged: a man wearing a tweed jacket, smoking a pipe, distracted or even absentminded, needing a wife to care for his children, cook his meals, run the household, and, at times, act as his secretary or research assistant while he was immersed in his work. The assumption of the male-bodied professor continues to today. One older male scholar mistook a female professor for the waitress; another mistook a scholar for his colleague's wife.

While I was socializing one night at the hotel restaurant [during a conference, a senior scholar in my field] waved me over to the table where he was sitting, and when I walked over to meet him, he asked if he could order.

During a lunch break at the AJS, I had one child on my arm and another next to me while talking with a male colleague. A male acquaintance of his came by and, seeing me, a woman with kids,

2. Bonnie G. Smith, *The Gender of History: Men, Women, and Historical Practice* (Cambridge, MA: Harvard University Press, 2000), 57–58.

immediately said excitedly: "Oh, so nice to meet you finally. So you are X's wife!"

Another of our interviewees noted that people of all genders often assumed she could not be the dean:

> *In the early 2000s, I was dean of graduate studies and research at a public university in southwestern Ontario. We had a large open office area, with individual offices around the perimeter. My admin assistant's office was outside mine, and when she was not at her desk, I kept my door open so as to welcome any staff, students, or profs to come in for a chat if they so wished. On numerous occasions, someone from outside our office would pop in, walk right past the sign that said "Dean" and ask me where the dean was or whether they could make an appointment to see the dean. Has the situation changed? Not much. People still expect admin assistants to be women and deans to be men, despite much evidence to the contrary.*

The field still retains assumptions that scholars are likely to be men, and that women play supporting roles. Scholarship requires solitary hours of study, but also collegial discussions, seminars, and lectures, as well as travel to archives, archeological sites, libraries, and manuscript collections that are privately held, usually by men wealthy enough to purchase them; access to some of these resources depends on close personal relationships and even friendship. In the nineteenth century, all of these were dominated by men. Many still are.

When it arose in the nineteenth century, historical critical scholarship was infused with modernity's confidence that it could conquer all problems as well as its concomitant claim to represent universal human experience. Yet in its focus and tools, historical study was a European male endeavor: "Seminars and archives were spaces reserved mostly for professional men, and it is in this context that the professional work of historical science can be seen as enmeshed in the development of masculinity in the nineteenth century."[3] Before women began to be admitted to universities toward the end of the nineteenth century, the physical spaces of scholarship were spaces in which men taught and studied. Male space was filled with books and papers and permeated with the atmosphere of self-importance, confidence, and grand projects. Professors delivered lectures with formality, sometimes as performances.[4] Students joined nationalist fraternities (which mostly excluded Jews), and professors became mandarins, members of a prestigious social class within Germany. European historians of the nineteenth century believed they were objectively narrating historical events, yet their publications reflected and served the nationalism of their country and lent implicit justification to its colonialist conquests with their own academic imperialism.[5]

Outside the realm of the Wissenschaft des Judentums, scholars were overwhelmingly white, Christian, European men who identified themselves as a universal human, while simultaneously constructing hierarchies of gender, race, language, social structure, religion, sexuality, and even definitions of human subjectivity, placing white, Christian, European men at the top. Even in contexts in which the study of Jewish texts would have enhanced scholarship, there was a lacuna; for instance, Hebrew was not included in the famed Oriental languages institute in Paris under the

3. Bonnie G. Smith, "Gender and the Practices of Scientific History: The Seminar and Archival Research in the Nineteenth Century," *American Historical Review* 100, no. 4 (1995): 1150–76, quote on 1153. On the archive as metaphor, see Allan Sekula, "The Body and the Archive," *October* 39 (Winter 1986): 3–64.

4. Heinrich Heine describes a lecture delivered in 1819 by August Schlegel at the University of Bonn in his book, *Die Romantische Schule*, book 2: "Beside him stood his servant in baronial livery, trimming the wax candles in the silver candelabra, which, together with a glass of sugared water, were placed on the professorial desk, in front of the distinguished personage. . . . What unprecedented adjuncts in the lectures of a German professor! This elegance dazzled us young people not a little." Heinrich Heine, *The Romantic School*, trans. S. L. Fleishman (New York: Henry Holt, 1882), 95.

5. Edward Said, *Orientalism* (New York: Vintage, 1978).

directorship of Antoine Sylvestre de Sacy, Judaism was not one of the religions included in the field of Oriental studies, and New Testament scholars were not trained to read rabbinic literature.[6] Only in the last decades of the twentieth century did academic structures begin to redefine themselves, both in Europe and in the United States.

The numerous state universities established in Germany in the nineteenth century where most Jewish scholars learned their craft were called "men's universities."[7] They were state funded and prepared students for professions of the state—in theology, law, medicine, and philosophy. Admission of Jews and women was tied to the question of whether they would be welcomed into the professions, and since many professions banned both women and Jewish men, these would-be scholars faced academic limitations. Women had been permitted to audit classes but were banned in 1879,[8] after which a sustained effort to admit women as students led to their formal admission, state by state, in Germany. By 1909 women were allowed to attend all twenty German universities, considered the finest research institutions in the world, and they were joined by growing numbers of women and Jews who came from other countries, though women could not add "BA" to their names until 1920.[9] Still, individual professors had the right to limit their lectures to men. In 1895 the renowned historian Heinrich von Treitschke "personally intervened to keep one woman from auditing courses at the University of Berlin," and that woman had to go to the University of Halle to receive her doctorate.[10] It was only at the turn of the twentieth century that the research universities of

6. Suzanne Marchand, *German Orientalism in an Age of Empire: Religion, Race, and Scholarship* (New York: Cambridge University Press, 2009).

7. Patricia Mazón, *Gender and the Modern Research University: The Admission of Women to German Higher Education, 1865–1914* (Stanford, CA: Stanford University Press, 2003), 2.

8. Mazón, 10.

9. Mazón, 14.

10. Mazón, 2.

Germany opened to women students seeking a degree. Even then, to be a student, let alone a professor, was thought to embody a masculinity that the university helped create.[11] To be a scholar was to enter a vocation that demanded self-sacrifice and hard work. Academic study was gendered male, characterizing aggressive acquisition of knowledge and objective judgment as manly pursuits.

Gendering and Sexualizing the Scholarly Act

Scholars often use rich metaphors to describe their work, and historians of the nineteenth century invariably used masculinist and heterosexual images. R. G. Collingwood wrote, "I study history to learn what it is to be a man," and Abraham Geiger said, "we became men and wanted manly fare, we wanted Wissenschaft."[12] Despite its claims to dispassionate objectivity, the very act of being a scholar was eroticized: archives and texts were to be penetrated to extract their secrets and produce knowledge, continuing an older tradition of masculinized hermeneutics, and women, household, and marriage provided the standard to distinguish the unimportant from the important.[13] The German historian Leopold von Ranke described archival documents as a "handsome Italian lady" with whom he was "in love," and as "so many fairy princesses living under a curse and waiting to be free."[14] He also spoke of an archive

---

11. Mazón, 29.

12. Collingwood quote from Bonnie G. Smith, "Historiography, Objectivity, and the Case of the Abusive Widow," in *Feminism and History*, ed. Joan Wallach Scott (New York: Oxford University Press, 1996), 551; letter from Abraham Geiger to Zunz, October 13, 1833, in Ludwig Geiger, "Aus Leopold Zunz' Nachlass," in *Zeitschrift für die Geschichte der Juden in Deutschland*, vol. 5 (Braunschweig: Schwetschke und Sohn, 1887), 248.

13. Smith, *Gender of History*, 71.

14. Leopold von Ranke, *Das Briefwerk von Leopold Von Ranke*, ed. Walther P. Fuchs (Hamburg: Hoffmann und Campe, 1949), cited in Falko Schnicke, "Princesses, Semen, and Separation: Masculinity and Body Politics in Nineteenth-Century German Historiography," *German Historical Institute London Bulletin* 40, no. 1 (2018): 26.

as a "virgin" waiting to be "entered" by him.[15] Such metaphors persist; Yii-Jan Lin calls attention to the erotic language used by scholars of New Testament text criticism from the eighteenth century to the present. In seeking the "original text," they describe texts as "adulterated" and "corrupted," as if they were unfaithful wives.[16]

The gender of Jewish scholarship reflected prevailing social attitudes. For example, while the historian Abraham Geiger devoted himself to integrating Jewish scholarship into the European academy, longed for a university professorship, and argued for women's rights in Judaism, he also wrote that the husband would "always remain master of the house" and "the husband will be the one who gives, the wife the one who receives."[17] While Geiger was a major advocate for liberal Judaism, he sounds like his Orthodox rabbinic opponent Samson Raphael Hirsch, who wrote, "This will-subordination of the wife to the husband is a necessary condition of the unity which man and wife should form together."[18]

Race, religion, and sexuality entwined in the rise of historicism. Jewish scholars were well aware of the anti-Jewish biases inherent in the scholarship of their Christian colleagues. Scholars of early Christianity were particularly egregious in their negative, denigrating depictions of early Judaism and rabbinic texts.[19] Edward Said writes, "Philology placed the scholar in the position of the European expert delivering to a European audience the exotic

15. Leopold von Ranke, *Neue Briefe*, ed. Hans Herzfeld (Hamburg: Hoffmann und Campe, 1949), 230; cited by Schnicke, "Princesses, Semen, and Separation," 43.

16. Yii-Jan Lin, *The Erotic Life of Manuscripts: New Testament Textual Criticism and the Biological Sciences* (New York: Oxford University Press, 2016), 3.

17. Abraham Geiger, *Jüdische Zeitschrift für Wissenschaft und Leben* (Breslau: H. Skutsch, 1870), 12, as cited in Michael A. Meyer, "German-Jewish Identity," in *Toward Modernity: The European Jewish Model*, ed. Jacob R. Katz (New Brunswick, NJ: Transaction Books, 1987), 260–61.

18. Samson R. Hirsch, *Judaism Eternal*, vol. 2 (London: Soncino, 1956), 58.

19. Susannah Heschel, *Abraham Geiger and the Jewish Jesus* (Chicago: University of Chicago Press, 1998).

fruits of foreign adventures," surveying "as if from a peculiarly suited vantage point the passive, seminal, feminine, even silent and supine East, then going on to articulate the East, making the Orient deliver up its secrets."[20] Philology took apart texts as if they were bodies, a "decarnalization, as the flesh of the text is organized into a corporate vessel of ideas, thoughts, and expression."[21] Doing philology might also be understood as a Christian act, an analysis of the meaning as spirit incarnate in the word, the classic distinction from the Pauline Epistles onward between Jewish carnality and Christian spirituality. In either case, as a (metaphorical) sexual act or an act of Christian belief, philology undertaken by Jews carried a valence of the transgressive.

With scholarly productivity described as procreation, the field of history "was sexualized to the exclusion of women, highlighting men's bodies and men's sexual capacities."[22] Not only because of their female bodies, but also because of their limited experience of the world, women, "even the most capable among them . . . will never be suitable as . . . historian[s]," wrote a German historian, Georg Busolt, in 1881.[23] At the same time, however, women were very much present in the imagination of men defining the maleness of their work. Excluded from the community of scholars, women were objects to be studied, and the conclusion was that women had a "corporeal inability to produce academic history."[24]

Among both Jewish and Christian scholars, masculinity was elevated as a force to protect not only the university but the whole society, and the male voice was viewed as universal and transcendent. In the words of Fustel de Coulanges, "It is not I who speak,

20. Said, *Orientalism*, 138.

21. John T. Hamilton, *Philology of the Flesh* (Chicago: University of Chicago Press, 2018), 6.

22. Schnicke, "Princesses, Semen, and Separation," 46.

23. Schnicke, 35.

24. Schnicke, 39.

Gentlemen, but History who speaks through me."[25] As Charlotte Witt writes, "patriarchal thinking attempts to achieve universality by repressing sexual difference."[26] Presenting their work in masculine terms was a tool scholars used not only to assert their power to speak for all people, but also to insert themselves as components of European imperialism. Treitschke, who famously wrote, "men make history," also excluded women from his university lectures and published one of the most notorious antisemitic screeds of his era in 1879.[27] The presence of both women and Jews at the university was widely imagined to pose dangers of social disintegration brought by modernity.

By the late nineteenth century, women were tolerated at many European universities as "guest students" outside of degree programs. Adolf von Harnack, an internationally renowned liberal Protestant professor of theology at the University of Berlin during the Second Reich, commented in 1911 on the entrance of women students:

> One day a lady presented herself [at the university], and this lady actually knew something, and consequently she came to be respected by those who were already there [i.e., the men]. Just two or three years earlier, the door had opened for a lady who was then noisily, unceremoniously kicked out. But that was long ago. Then came one lady after another, and I am convinced (you will certainly agree with me): we have had no lady who did not prove herself to be [as good as] a man, not a single one that I can remember. But I cannot readily claim the

25. Cited by Smith, "Historiography, Objectivity, and the Case of the Abusive Widow," 550.

26. Charlotte Witt, "Feminist History of Philosophy," in *Feminist Reflections on the History of Philosophy*, ed. Lilli Alanen and Charlotte Witt (Dordrecht: Kluwer Academic, 2004), 7.

27. Heinrich von Treitschke, *Deutsche Geschichte im Neunzehnten Jahrhundert*, vol. 1, *Bis zum zweiten Pariser Frieden* (Leipzig: n.p., 1879), 28; Heinrich von Treitschke, "Die Juden sind unser Unglück" (November 1879), in Treitschke, *Deutsche Geschichte im Neunzehnten Jahrhundert*, 1.

contrary [that the men were living up to their manliness]. In short, it went down well, we joined together as comrades, and soon it [the presence of women students] was entirely taken for granted, permanently established.[28]

Women, who had fought for years to earn degrees at the universities and had finally gained entry, were met with Harnack's condescending tone. He refers to them as "ladies" (*Damen*) rather than "women" (*Frauen*). Most importantly, men's achievement is the measure of women's success. It matters only if the women are as good as the men. And, it appears, women had to be excellent to be accepted, whereas men could just be men. University work remained a male domain, but a few women might enter—if they were as good as the men.

Given such attitudes toward women, it is not surprising that gender also colored scholarly analyses, including of religion. Some Jewish scholars treated piety, for example, with a gendered tone of eroticized denigration. They regarded apocalypticism, mysticism, and especially Hasidism as marginal or even foreign to Judaism and as eliciting effeminate emotions that emasculated men. Gershom Scholem, the distinguished twentieth-century scholar of Jewish mysticism, argued against the reputation of mysticism as feminine; Jewish mysticism, kabbalah, "is a masculine doctrine, made for men and by men."[29] In contrast to Christian mysticism, in which many women participated, kabbalah, he wrote, "lacks the element of feminine emotion which has played so large a part in the development

28. Adolf von Harnack, "Ansprachen in der Festsitzung des Kirchenhistorischen Seminars zur Feier des sechzigsten Geburtstages" (1911), in Axel von Harnack, *Aus der Werkstatt des Vollendeten: Als Abschluss seiner Reden und Aufsätze*, ed. Axel von Harnack (1930; Berlin: De Gruyter, 1991), 7–15; 11. Our thanks to Professor Christoph Markschies for the reference. See Christoph Markschies, "Dann kam eine Dame nach der anderen: Beobachtungen zu den ersten Studentinnen und Pfarrerinnen in Berlin-Brandenburg," in *Berolinensia: Beiträge zur Geschichte der Berliner Universität und ihrer Theologischen Fakultät* (Berlin: De Gruyter, 2021), 541–53, 542.

29. Gershom Scholem, *Major Trends in Jewish Mysticism* (Jerusalem: Schocken, 1941), 37.

of non-Jewish mysticism, but it also remained comparatively free from the dangers entailed by the tendency towards hysterical extravagance which followed in the wake of this influence."[30] The danger that Scholem identified was messianism, an impulse that could evade the control of the male rabbinic authorities, as happened in the Sabbatian heresy, and explode into sexual bacchanalia. In his schema, messianism was a kind of looming sexual threat. Making Jewish mysticism masculine also was important for Scholem in his justification for devoting his life to analyzing it: with his historiography, he could transform what might appear feminine—mysticism—into a masculinizing scientific undertaking.

In the field of history, even as Jewish scholars presented a lachrymose narrative of Jewish (feminine) suffering, they presented Jews as heroic (masculine) for withstanding persecution. In their descriptions of Judaism's relationship to Christianity and Islam, Judaism was not the rejected religion but was dominant as the progenitor and ethically superior religion. This, too, had a gendered valence: although Jewish scholars often used the mother-daughter metaphor, the underlying implication was that Judaism was the male religion that generated ideas, while Christianity and Islam were the receptive, feminine religions in whose soil those ideas were implanted. The historiography favored by the Wissenschaft scholars evolved into a popular theological presentation of Judaism as a masculine religion of ethical monotheism firmly rejecting nonrational dogma, paganism, and otherworldly mystical experience. Christianity, as Leo Baeck wrote, was a "romantic religion" suffused with feminine attributes of passivity: "it wants to be seized and inspired from above, embraced by a flood of grace which should descend upon it to consecrate it and possess it—a will-less instrument of the wondrous ways of God."[31]

30. Scholem, 37.

31. Leo Baeck, "Romantic Religion," in *Judaism and Christianity: Essays by Leo Baeck*, trans. and ed. Walter Kaufmann (Berlin 1922; Philadelphia: Jewish Publication Society, 1958), 192.

Modern Jewish scholars of that era, then, defended Judaism on multiple levels. On one hand, some denied women's inferiority so they could simultaneously reject the view of Judaism as an Oriental religion that had no place in the West. On the other hand, they claimed for Judaism a strong, manly character—even though presenting Judaism as a manly religion reaffirmed certain Christian prejudices against Judaism as patriarchal and despotic.

Women Entering the Academy

Despite the reigning associations of maleness and scholarship, women gradually entered Jewish studies. In this section, we discuss some examples of the gendered culture that made that process difficult, and we also discuss several examples of women who made their mark in the field of Jewish studies in spite of these obstacles. Yet, as earlier chapters showed, neither women's presence in the field nor their excellent scholarship has been enough to create a fully equitable field.

While seminars, archives, and publications were male spaces, the production of Jewish scholarship rested on a female foundation: the labor of the wives of male scholars, who kept house, cooked, and bore and cared for the children.[32] Before universities created professorships in Jewish studies, many Jewish scholars earned their living as rabbis or communal officials, doing their scholarship in their "free time," while their wives functioned in a public role as the "Rebbetzin" of the community, taking on the extra tasks associated with maintaining a kosher household, entertaining her husband's colleagues and students, and, in some cases, reading, copying, editing, and revising their husbands' manuscripts.[33]

32. Ismar Schorsch, "Wives and Wissenschaft: The Domestic Seedbed of Critical Scholarship," in *Gender and Jewish History*, ed. Marion A. Kaplan and Deborah Dash Moore (Bloomington: Indiana University Press, 2011), 27–43. See also Martha R. Fowlkes, *Behind Every Successful Man: Wives of Medicine and Academe* (New York: Columbia University Press, 1980).

33. Shuly Rubin Schwartz, *The Rabbi's Wife: The Rebbetzin in American Jewish Life* (New York: New York University Press, 2006).

How does a woman who is a receptive vessel, emotional, lacking will, and subordinate to men flourish in the world of scholarship? Was she thought to bring unacceptable emotion or even "hysterical extravagance" that would undermine the scientific legitimacy of scholarship? Who would support her vocation, how would she travel to archives and gain access to libraries, and where would she find the quiet privacy to read and write?

Although women were not welcomed into the guild of the nineteenth-century academy, nor of the Wissenschaft des Judentums, recent scholarship is bringing to light remarkable women whose intellectual engagements with Judaism flourished during those same years, but in very different circles. In her study of central European Jewish women intellectuals, Barbara Hahn has uncovered fascinating exchanges between Jewish women and some of the leading Christian intellectuals of the modern era, interactions that were conducted outside the framework of business relations.[34] Hahn's story of modern Judaism begins not with Moses Mendelssohn and Gotthold Lessing, a male-male, Jewish-Christian friendship hailed in Europe in its time and often said to mark the onset of the modern era, but with the forgotten story of Anna Constanze, Countess of Cosel, who, a generation earlier, had become a learned scholar of Judaism. After her death in 1765 the question was raised: Was she a Jew or a Christian? She had learned Hebrew and Yiddish and followed the dietary laws, but had this led to her conversion? Could one remain a Christian with such devotion to Judaism? Or was she in fact what a true Christian was intended to be, at least if the historical Jesus, a good Jew, served as the model? The puzzlement over her status stemmed, in part, from a category confusion: Christian Hebraists who were well disposed to Judaism were all men, as were Jews learned in Hebrew texts. Categories, in other words, may also create the disappearance of women.

---

34. Barbara Hahn, *The Jewess Pallas Athena: This, Too, a Theory of Modernity*, trans. James McFarland (Princeton, NJ: Princeton University Press, 2005).

We might wonder about those wives, daughters, and female friends who "assisted" male scholars with their work: How many of those women actually undertook the research and wrote up the findings of "male-authored" books and articles without receiving credit? Today scholars are recovering manuscripts by women and references to women's authorship in texts by men,[35] but the various canons of Jewish texts are almost exclusively male. We also wonder about canons: Why are so many women missing from collections of Jewish biographies and from anthologies of Jewish writings? Writing about the all-male canon of medieval English literature, Jennifer Summit argues that medieval women did write, but that their writings were "lost" as part of the process of producing a canon. She claims that the categories "woman writer" and "English literature" were "reciprocally formed" at selected historical junctures.[36] "Lost" writings do not simply disappear; "lost" is as much the result of structures, intentions, and ideological commitments intended not to preserve as canonized writings are the result of an intention to preserve. The absence of women in Jewish texts represents not an accidental void but the result of purposeful decisions made about what is significant and what is not. In Jewish studies, as scholars continue to discover evidence of women's learning and writings, we may come to understand that placing women outside the canons of rabbinic authority, philosophical literature, kabbalistic conventicles, and the historical surveys of

---

35. On occasion we have a rare glimpse: Paula Winkler Buber's collaborations with her husband, Martin Buber, on his collections of Hasidic stories and his Zionist writings that are not credited in the publications; Henrietta Szold, who edited and translated numerous important works of Jewish scholarship, including Louis Ginzberg's multivolume *Legends of the Jews* (from Hebrew), and her translation and condensation of Heinrich Graetz's eleven-volume *History of the Jews* (from German), among many other projects; and Martha Lewandowski Cohen, who curated the papers of her husband, the philosopher Hermann Cohen, after his death in 1918 and prior to her deportation and murder at Theresienstadt in 1942.

36. Jennifer Summit, *Lost Property: The Woman Writer and English Literary History, 1380–1589* (Chicago: University of Chicago Press, 2000), 8.

Jewish experience has resulted not only in the marginalization of women but also in men's distorted depiction of Judaism and their mistaken identification of their own maleness as normative. This understanding of maleness and femaleness, significance and insignificance, was as much a part of the Wissenschaft des Judentums community as it was of the academy writ large, and it continues to cast a shadow over the field.

The gendered cultures around Wissenschaft des Judentums had parallels in the United States. The entry of women into universities and the creation of women's colleges in the United States aroused heated debate not only over changes that education would bring to women's roles within society but also over the impact of higher education on women's bodies and dispositions and the image of "true womanhood."[37] In the United States, warnings came that as women's minds grew, their wombs would shrink; in Germany, women's journals warned that female students would become nervous, hysterical, and sexually disoriented (i.e., lesbian) and would degenerate into a "third gender," the same accusation often leveled against Jewish men in medieval times.[38] If circumcision allegedly caused Jewish men to lose their manhood, turning them into a third gender, a college education would allegedly do the same to women, rendering them neither female nor male. Even some early twentieth-century German feminist leaders, such as

37. On debates over women and higher education, see Mazón, *Gender and the Modern Research University*; and Carroll Smith-Rosenberg, *Disorderly Conduct: Visions of Gender in Victorian America* (New York: Knopf, 1985). On women's higher education in Germany, see Katharina von Ankum, "Motherhood and the 'New Woman': Vicki Baum's Stud. Chem. Helene Willfüer and Irmgard Keun's Gilgi—Eine von Uns," *Women in German Yearbook* 11 (1995): 171–88.

38. Calling women university students a "third gender" is illustrated in the 1901 novel by Aimee Duc, *Sind es Frauen? Roman über das dritte* (Are these women? A Novel concerning the third sex) (Berlin: Eckstein, 1901). The depiction of Jews as a third gender is discussed by Sander Gilman, *Freud, Race, and Gender* (Princeton, NJ: Princeton University Press, 1993); and Jay Geller, *On Freud's Jewish Body: Mitigating Circumcisions* (New York: Fordham University Press, 2007).

Helene Stöcker, saw an irreconcilable contradiction in women's higher education: "Spiritual motherhood, motherliness in its highest sense, is at the root of women's intellectual inferiority to men. But at the same time that she becomes aware of this dilemma, she realizes this painful conflict is in fact her most valuable asset."[39] She might contribute her "creative intuition" to science, though her sexuality and ability to mother would be damaged by her masochism and narcissism.[40] In those early decades of the feminist movement, educated women were thought to display "feminine masculinities."[41] Following World War I, the percentage of women students at German universities nearly doubled, but not their number in the professoriate. That so many women nonetheless flourished academically despite such prevalent attitudes is remarkable. Once graduated, however, women faced new difficulties as they sought professions or academic research positions. Political factors also intervened as post–World War I European national boundaries shifted, empires dissolved, immigration increased, dramatic monetary inflation affected investment in educational institutions, and the Nazi regime expelled Jewish faculty and students.

By the time women were admitted to European universities, few Jewish women had the opportunity to produce scholarly work before Hitler came to power, but some continued after the war. One example is Selma Stern-Täubler: born in 1890, she had no chance at a professorship but nonetheless produced highly significant works of scholarship, including an extraordinary multivolume

39. Helene Stöcker, "Mutterschaft und geistige Arbeit," in *Die Liebe und die Frauen* (Minden in Westf.: J.C.C. Bruns' Verlag, 1906), 88, cited by von Ankum, "Motherhood and the 'New Woman,'" 177.

40. Other examples of such arguments are brought by Katharina von Ankum and Ann Taylor Allen, *Feminism and Motherhood, 1800–1914* (New Brunswick, NJ: Rutgers University Press, 1992).

41. Claudia Breger, "Feminine Masculinities: Scientific and Literary Representations of 'Female Inversion' at the Turn of the Twentieth Century," *Journal of the History of Sexuality* 14, no. 1/2 (2005): 76–106.

study, *The Prussian State and the Jews*. Eva Reichmann, born in 1897, offers another example as a scholar who published pioneering studies of antisemitism but had no opportunity to hold a professorship. In other cases, women who collaborated with male professors were not always remembered for their contributions; Else Frenkel-Brunswik, Marie Jahoda, and Maria Hertz Levinson were among the Jewish women who helped shape the social sciences in central Europe even as Hitler came to power. And there are many others.

After 1933, Jewish refugee scholars from Hitler's Europe began arriving in the United States, Britain, Palestine, and elsewhere, bringing their German training and helping transform US universities into leading research centers. Yet the universities remained male domains. During the postwar years, women steadily entered the elite research universities as students and encountered the maleness of university life. Few women received professorships. In the United States, as Morton Keller and Phyllis Keller note, "Of the 321 respondents to a survey of the women who had received Radcliffe PhDs between 1902 and 1951, only 32 held full-time jobs."[42] Certain libraries were open only to men, and students and faculty sometimes socialized at private clubs restricted to men. Hanna Holborn Gray, a historian who ultimately became the first woman president of the University of Chicago, held a Fulbright Scholarship for a year at Oxford University in the early 1950s before earning a PhD at Harvard. At Oxford, she was assigned to St. Anne's College, one of the five women's colleges at that time. "I had not paid sufficient attention . . . to what Virginia Woolf had to say about women and Oxford. It was there (and afterward at Harvard) that I first really experienced what discrimination toward women in academic life could mean."[43] Later, as a young professor

42. Morton Keller and Phyllis Keller, *Making Harvard Modern: The Rise of America's University* (Oxford: Oxford University Press, 2001), cited in Hanna Holborn Gray, *An Academic Life: A Memoir* (Princeton, NJ: Princeton University Press, 2018), 158.

43. Gray, *Academic Life*, 115.

at the University of Chicago, Gray describes the male chair of her department reviewing her list of three possible candidates for an assistant professorship that included one woman and exclaiming, "Oh, Hanna, please don't appoint a woman; they make such difficult colleagues"—and then: "Oh, I never think of you as a woman!"[44] Gray is gentle in her memoir, writing that the "University of Chicago was a far more welcoming place for women than Harvard had been. . . . All libraries were open to women, and it was taken for granted that women should enter the Quadrangle Club through the front door," in contrast to Harvard's faculty club, which had a separate entrance for women until the 1970s.[45]

Scholarship has traditionally been less a job than a vocation, much like the vocation of a nun or monk. The life of a scholar was all-consuming, with little time for entertainment or vacation, let alone the needs of a wife and children; on the contrary, the male scholar's wife handled domestic affairs and, at times, functioned as his research assistant. As late as the 1980s, some women told us, they were in graduate school with men still shaped by this image, whose wives worked to earn the family income, shopped, cooked, kept house, typed the term papers, returned the library books, and functioned as assistants to their husbands. Of the Jewish studies women colleagues we spoke with who were graduate students in Jewish studies during the 1970s, 1980s, and 1990s, none knew of a woman with a male partner who undertook comparable supportive efforts, and few men had female partners who were also in graduate school. They felt their role was somewhere "between rebbetzin and student" rather than "budding scholar on par with their male colleagues." Even in those later decades of the twentieth century, women in the academy could still feel like oddities, violating the expectations of womanhood and the boundaries of male academic space. Often, we were told, they felt adrift, excluded from the intellectual exchanges of their fellow male students. This comes

44. Gray, 186.
45. Gray, 185.

out clearly in the following candid remarks of a senior scholar of Judaism, who reflected on her upbringing:

Growing up as the daughter of a European Jewish refugee scholar, I lived in a European sort of academic household. My father studied day and night, while my mother took care of the house and cooked the meals. All the colleagues of my father (all men) had the same arrangement. Occasionally, a wife was also well educated, but it was clear that the man's scholarly vocation took priority, and the daily tasks of shopping, cooking, and cleaning were her responsibility. With a mixture of sadness and horror, my mother used to tell me that the wife of one scholar demanded that he spend every Saturday night with her and away from his books. Had she not been so demanding, my mother said with some sadness and contempt, he might have become a great scholar. I shared her dismay until I discovered that he was a great scholar. I read his work in graduate school and was amazed. His wife's supposedly selfish requests for one evening of his attention each week certainly did not diminish his accomplishments, but she became a mythic figure of the demanding, destructive woman: the bad wife who undermines her scholar-husband. The lesson was clear: men were scholars, and women were their enablers at best and had to devote themselves to making possible their husbands' work with as little interference as possible; their needs were irrelevant and their relationship secondary. The few women scholars whom I knew, also refugees from Hitler's Europe, stood at the fringes of the academic circles, usually in fields that were considered marginal, such as art history, musicology, and ethnography. I still know male scholars with wives who handle everything for them, and I wonder, how can I compete, given that I have to shop, cook, clean, entertain, and mother my kids while they have full-time wives who do everything for them.

Memoirs of scholars and writers who emigrated from Europe to the *yishuv* (the Jewish settlements in Palestine prior to Israeli statehood) offer similar depictions of wives as enablers of their scholar-husbands. Amos Oz's memoir, for example, depicts a marital dynamic in the yishuv with the scholar-husband busy reading, writing, and meeting with colleagues, while the wife handles the household and disappears into the background.[46] Even as gender roles changed in other respects, these marital models represent significant continuity with the models in the Wissenschaft des Judentums.

Well into the 1970s, it was difficult for a woman in the United States to hold her own checking account and credit card if she was married, odd for a single woman to sit alone at a table in a restaurant, awkward to travel alone and stay alone at a hotel—all of which were necessary for scholars traveling to visit archives or libraries or to lecture at universities. Women professors appeared only rarely in novels and films, and when they did, they were often embroiled in some sort of sex scandal or love triangle, as in Gertrude Stein's short story, "Fernhurst: The History of Philip Redfern, a Student of the Nature of Women." Equally unappealing was the depiction in *The Small Room*, May Sarton's novel about a professor who lives a lonely and isolated life by herself in a small attic room, an unattractive future for a woman contemplating a life as a scholar. The 2021 Netflix series *The Chair* offered a glimpse of the complexities facing a contemporary Asian American woman chairing an English department, where she must handle an old guard of conservative white faculty while trying to retain a brilliant young Black female scholar on the faculty. While the series depicts the chair as smart and capable, it gives her a messy personal life as a single mother of a rebellious daughter and portrays her love life as comedic fodder. Images of women professors in popular culture often focus on the toll the profession can take on women's private lives without analyzing the larger context of the biases and difficulties women face. A European scholar told us that her male colleagues judged her by her appearance rather than her scholarship:

---

46. Amos Oz, *A Tale of Love and Darkness*, trans. Nicholas de Lange (Orlando, FL: Harcourt, 2004).

*My work [in Jewish history] was never taken seriously by my . . .
colleagues [all of whom were male]. When I came up for promotion,
one of them told me that my blue eyes were all that filled my research file.*

Second-wave feminism emerged in the 1960s and inspired Jewish women to seek access to educational and professional opportunities that had been reserved for men, including within Jewish
religious life. Women sought opportunities to study Talmud;
called for equality in communal worship; pursued ordination as
rabbis; developed bat mitzvah, Rosh Hodesh, and other rituals;
and demanded equal pay at equal rank within Jewish communal
organizations. Books, anthologies, articles, conferences, and journals shaped Jewish feminism in the 1970s and 1980s and stimulated
scholarship about women within the field of Jewish studies. In the
1970s and 1980s, few women held doctorates in Jewish studies, and
fewer held tenured professorships. During the 1980s and 1990s,
thanks in part to calls from students, feminist theory was becoming
an increasingly important tool of analysis in nearly all fields, raising
questions about gender and sexuality. Gender theory, especially
drawing from literary and cultural studies, emerged in Jewish studies during the 1980s and 1990s through the work of a group of
scholars who included many men, including Howard Eilberg-
Schwartz, Sander Gilman, David Biale, Elliot Wolfson, and Daniel
Boyarin, though their focus was more on constructions of masculinity than on women or gender as a category. Jane Gerber, Marion
Kaplan, and Paula Hyman were among the first women in the field
to hold tenured professorships and advocate scholarship on Jewish
women's history, while Rachel Adler, Judith Plaskow, Drorah
Setel, and Susannah Heschel were among the first to challenge
Jewish theological categories.

Initially, and not surprisingly, an apologetic tone permeated
early Jewish feminist historiography, with efforts to prove that Jewish women were even more devoted to Judaism than were Jewish
men. During the 1980s and 1990s, some Jewish feminist scholars

presented women as less inclined to assimilate than men, committed to maintaining Jewishness in the home and family, insistent on
keeping a kosher kitchen, and focused on transmitting Jewish
identity to their children, whereas men increasingly abandoned
their Jewish obligations: they stopped praying three times a day,
attending synagogue services, and studying rabbinic texts, and
they went to work on the Sabbath.[47] This scholarship presented
a different experience of modernity, one that insisted that women
were more faithful Jews than men.[48] Such apologetics has increasingly disappeared from feminist publications as scholars no longer
feel the need to present justifications for women as "better" Jews.

Yet the increasing inclusion of women as scholars has not fully
fixed the gendered issues in scholarship. An Israeli scholar explained that some scholars dismissed gender studies as not objective or scientific—an especially difficult dismissal to overcome
because of the association of objectivity with masculinity:

> I believe the problem is less the number of women [than] it is the
> gender perspective that feminist scholars bring. Critical gender theo-
> ries challenge the masculine orientation of scholarship, its gender
> biases, and the blindness of scholars who refuse to see the benefits
> men have accrued in a patriarchal system. Many see the critical
> tools of gender and feminist analyses as "political" and contaminat-
> ing the "objectivity" of research.

We are by now two centuries away from the beginnings of Jewish studies in nineteenth-century Germany, and the influence of
its founding assumptions is diminishing, though traces remain.
Our archives, seminars, and lecture halls are no longer populated

47. See, for example, Paula Hyman's article on Jewish women's boycott of kosher
butchers after prices were suddenly and dramatically raised: "Immigrant Women and
Social Protest: The New York City Kosher Meat Boycott of 1902," *American Jewish
History* 70, no. 1 (September 1980): 91–105.

48. Susannah Heschel, "The Impact of Feminist Theory on Jewish Studies," in
Modern Judaism and Historical Consciousness: Identities, Encounters, Perspectives,
ed. Andreas Gotzmann and Christian Wiese (Boston: Brill, 2007), 529–48.

exclusively by men, and scholarship today takes advantage of disciplines and methods not yet known to figures such as Ranke and Treitschke, let alone Abraham Geiger and Heinrich Graetz. Still, the shadow of previous generations looms. While it may be rare today to describe scholarly activity as "manly," we see in the too-frequent exclusion of women that the manly culture lingers, as the data we presented in chapter 1 demonstrated. In the next chapter, we examine another of the multiple origin stories of Jewish studies that continues to influence the field.

5

Insider and Outsider

NOSTALGIA JEWISH STUDIES AND
ITS IMPACT ON GENDER

I was presenting work on sexuality in Judaism at a conference aimed at bringing together scholarship on several religious traditions. I spoke about multiple interpretations of rabbinic texts in the past and the present, emphasizing the different lived experiences of Jews. There was one other scholar who worked on Judaism presenting at the conference: he was older, white, [and] bearded and wore a kippah. When it came time for the conversation after my panel, several of the other presenters and audience members asked the other scholar questions about the topic of my presentation: What are the textual rules about menstrual taboos, and what do they mean? What did rabbinic texts have to say about sex and purity—not how people today interpret them, but what do the texts really say? What is Judaism's philosophy about gender difference? He happily answered their questions as if nothing could be more natural. I have never felt more invisible.

What this scholar experienced conveys a taste of the complexities of being a female scholar in Jewish studies. Regardless of her sophisticated academic analysis, the audience turns to the man on the panel as the voice of authority: he was older, white, and bearded, and he wore a kippah. The experience is not unusual;

many women have had similar experiences in which their expertise is not accepted by their interlocutors, who turn for confirmation to a man, preferably one who is older, white, and bearded, and wears a kippah. But why? A pervasive conviction that "authentic" Jewish knowledge stems from the yeshiva learning of religious men undermines academic scholarship and the authority of women and creates a desire for traditional Jewish learning—focusing on what the text says rather than contextualizing it historically, questioning its authorship, situating it within a complex of intellectual debates, and analyzing its covert meanings. Experiences that marginalize women and non-Jews within the field of Jewish studies imply that only Jewish men, best if graying and bearded, truly understand Judaism "from the inside."

This substitution of imagined, "traditional" learning plays a dangerous role in academia, pulling us backward rather than impelling us forward. Within Jewish studies, this atmosphere easily creates outsiders, excluding those who do not belong to the past, including women, nonbinary, Black, Asian, and non-Jewish scholars. The patterns that denigrate or exclude women, people of color, nonbinary individuals, and non-Jews reinforce one another, drawing on stereotypes and buttressing biases, even unintentionally, through the power of nostalgia.

The creation of insider status in Jewish studies has roots in the type of learning that began in antiquity, when Jewish men created themselves as an elite by gathering to discuss religious texts and produce oral traditions. Sometimes meeting in small groups, and in later centuries in study houses, they created a tradition of male authority and of learning as a male practice. To paraphrase the feminist philosopher Mary Daly, who described how when God is male, the male is God: when men do the learning, learning is manly.[1] Recently, a senior university professor told his students, including women students, "You cannot understand

1. See Mary Daly, *Beyond God the Father: Toward a Philosophy of Women's Liberation* (Boston: Beacon Books, 1973).

Hasidism unless you have sat at a rebbe's *tisch*." Since only men can sit at a rebbe's tisch, he was actually announcing that women students had no hope of truly understanding the material.

The images of schools of men studying Torah remain powerful. Modes of study have changed over the millennia, but the exclusion of women from male houses of study has been reinforced by textual declarations such as the Mishnaic warning in the Mishnah of Rabbi Eliezer against teaching women: "If he teaches her Torah, he has taught her promiscuity" (Sotah 3:4). The famed medieval Sephardi rabbi Moses Maimonides concurred, saying that women's minds were generally not up to the task.

Yet such statements, sprinkled throughout the centuries, may not be apodictic prohibitions and seem to have concealed a very different reality. As Judith Hauptman, Tal Ilan, and others have demonstrated, rabbinic sources offer more evidence of women's participation in creating rabbinic culture than Rabbi Eliezer's pronouncement would lead us to believe.[2] Nonetheless, women's participation and creativity were not fully recorded as part of the written and oral traditions, and the engagement of Christian and Muslim scholars with Jewish texts was often omitted from Jewish tradition. Those omissions created a heritage that continues to influence contemporary sensibilities of insiders and outsiders in the field.

In classical Judaism, study is viewed as prayer, and just as men were obligated to pray three times a day, they were encouraged to study classical texts. Jewish men reached different levels of scholarly ability—until recently, only the elite were sent to yeshivot for advanced study of Talmud and commentaries—but even those with minimal education often gathered in the evenings to study. An old book in the library of the YIVO Institute for Jewish Research

---

2. Judith Hauptman, "A New View of Women and Torah Study in the Talmudic Period," *Jewish Studies, an Internet Journal* 9 (2010): 249–92, https://jewish-faculty .biu.ac.il/en/node/1055; Hauptman's article is available at https://jewish-faculty.biu .ac.il/sites/jewish-faculty/files/shared/hauptman.pdf.

bears a stamp, "The Society of Woodchoppers for the Study of Mishnah in Berdichev."[3] Some women studied, usually minimally and often thanks to a sympathetic father or brother who taught them, but not in Jewish schools. In the 1970s and 1980s, Modern Orthodoxy was still having this conversation ("May Women Be Taught Bible, Mishnah and Talmud?" asked one 1978 article in a prominent journal,[4] though today most Modern Orthodox women can and do study these texts). In most Haredi circles, women do not study these texts even today but, instead, learn Hebrew Bible, some commentaries, and ethical teachings. The tradition of Jewish study runs deep, nourishing many Jews but excluding others.

Most often, women learned Hebrew prayers and laws relevant to their household tasks from their parents. Both women and men learned how to live as Jews through family life and experience in Jewish societies, by observing and imbibing not only words and deeds but also beliefs and ways of being in the world. Women's knowledge and commitment to observing the laws of kashrut, niddah, Shabbat, and festivals is essential for passing down Jewish practices. Women teach women, mothers teach daughters; according to an old saying, "A *yiddishe bale-boste* takes instruction from her mother only."[5]

Today it is still true that men—specifically Jewish men—are the most likely to have been raised with the languages and reading skills required for the study of ancient texts. They are also the most likely to have been exposed to Talmudic and other traditional Jewish sources, usually in the context of confessional religious learning, not academic scholarship. One scholar explained: "When

3. Abraham J. Heschel, *The Earth Is the Lord's: The Inner World of the Jew in East Europe* (New York: Abelard-Schuman, 1964).

4. Arthur M. Silver, "May Women Be Taught Bible, Mishnah and Talmud?," *Tradition: A Journal of Orthodox Jewish Thought* 17, no. 3 (1978): 74–85.

5. Haym Soloveitchik, "Rupture and Reconstruction," in *Rupture and Reconstruction: The Transformation of Contemporary Orthodoxy* (London: Littman Library of Jewish Civilization, in association with Liverpool University Press, 2021), 100n18.

I was first exposed to Talmud as an eleven-year-old in an Orthodox day school, all I knew is that this was what Jewish boys did."[6] Many Jews, especially observant Jews, see this kind of religious textual study as a male domain. Although Orthodox Jewish communities have, for the past few decades, developed seminaries and adult education centers for women, institutions for boys and men still outnumber them.

With the rise of modern academic scholarship, a new path to studying classical Jewish texts developed, along with new approaches drawn from the social sciences, including historicist approaches that contextualize Judaism in ways that classical text study never did. In recent decades, new opportunities have opened for women to engage in the kinds of religious text study that used to be limited to men. Today women can and do study these same texts in both religious and academic contexts; people of all genders and religious commitments discuss their interpretations of Jewish texts. And in the academic framework, scholars need not be Jewish to make important contributions.

Yet some of the ancient patterns that developed over the centuries continue not only to structure how religious Jews learn today but also to cast a spell over today's academic Jewish studies. In spite of the vibrancy of both women's scholarship and scholarship about gender, as we demonstrated in chapter 1, this scholarship does not occupy the center of the field of Jewish studies. Despite their important contributions, women scholars are cited less often, and sometimes ignored.

Exclusion of women, embodied experiences, different ways of knowing: these are not necessary consequences of studying these texts, as many excellent scholars demonstrate. Moreover, topics *of* study and methods *for* studying are often deeply related, a correlation exemplified by scholars who employ poststructuralist, feminist, and other methods. In 1992, Judith Romney Wegner led the way

6. Benjamin Barer, "The Way of Talmud: Exploring Talmud Study as a Spiritual Practice" (PhD diss., Hebrew College, 2018), 3.

when she published *Chattel or Person?*, a study of how the male-authored Mishnah constructs women, their rights, and their relationships to men.[7] Since then, the field of rabbinics has become a vibrant site for a range of feminist analyses, including the work of Rachel Adler, Judith Hauptman, Charlotte Fonrobert, Michal Bar-Asher Siegel, Vered Noam, and Tal Ilan, among many others. Scholars such as Daniel Boyarin have used gendered analysis to offer readings of masculinity in rabbinic texts. Strikingly, women, nonbinary, and queer scholars have also reshaped the field of rabbinics more broadly, bringing both literary tools to analyze rabbinic texts and historical tools to place those texts in a broader cultural context. Max Strassfeld has explored the centrality of gendered bodies for understanding rabbinic legal modes of reasoning, while Noam Sienna has published an anthology of queer texts from biblical times to the present, including rabbinic texts.[8] Gail Labovitz, Julia Watts Belser, and Rafael Rachel Neis have each demonstrated the importance of attending not only to gender but also to embodied experiences, including disability, when reading rabbinic texts.[9] These scholars, and others like them, recognize that the bodies described by rabbinic texts, as well as the bodies of those who read them, play central roles in interpretation. But the methods of attending to these issues, and those who are attend to them, are not (yet) the norm.

7. Judith Romney Wegner, *Chattel or Person?* (New York: Oxford University Press, 1992).

8. Max Strassfeld, "Translating the Human: The Androginos in Tosefta Bikurim," *Transgender Studies Quarterly* 3, nos. 3–4 (2016): 587–604; and Noam Sienna, ed., *A Rainbow Thread: An Anthology of Queer Jewish Texts from the First Century to 1969* (Philadelphia: Print-O-Craft, 2019).

9. Julia Watts Belser, *Rabbinic Tales of Destruction: Gender, Sex, and Disability in the Ruins of Jerusalem* (New York: Oxford University Press, 2017); Julia Watts Belser, *Loving Our Own Bones: Disability Wisdom and the Spiritual Subversiveness of Knowing Ourselves Whole* (Boston: Beacon, 2023); Rachel Rafe Neis, *The Sense of Sight in Rabbinic Culture: Jewish Ways of Seeing in Late Antiquity* (New York: Cambridge University Press, 2013); and Gail Susan Labovitz, *Marriage and Metaphor: Constructions of Gender in Rabbinic Literature* (New York: Rowman and Littlefield, 2009).

To clarify, traditional modes of study continue to serve a function. Yeshiva study of Talmud produces knowledge of texts that can inspire Jewish piety. Within the academy, the approach is different. Scholars learn ancient languages that are crucial to the study of ancient Jews and Judaism, and intertextual readings can be fascinating. Philology, the study of manuscript variations, and source criticism have led to crucial insights into canonical rabbinic texts and some members of the communities who created them. So have cognate fields of study, including archeological investigations and studies of Akkadian, Greek, and Persian languages and cultures that resonate in rabbinic texts. The study of Talmud and midrash also became central to nineteenth-century Jewish scholars demonstrating parallels between rabbinic texts and the Qur'an and the New Testament.[10]

Traditional religious approaches to classical Jewish texts continue to inform academic scholarship, though the two approaches raise different sorts of questions. Religious study looks for meaning and guidance in leading a religious life, and at times it shuns historical-critical methods of analyzing biblical and rabbinic texts, believing the texts to be timeless and divinely authored. In an academic context, the authors are historical figures, and the goal may be trying to determine when and in what context the text was written and transmitted, and under what influences. Boundaries between religious and academic learning are often crossed in helpful ways, such as when religious Jews decide to train as academic scholars, or Christian and Jewish scholars study at each other's theological seminaries, or academics raised without religious backgrounds study at religious seminaries. Such interactions can stimulate new ways of thinking and broaden our scholarly contextualization. Still, given the gender separations that exist in some Jewish religious communities, our concern is that religious assumptions about women's roles in classical study continue to

10. Susannah Heschel, *Abraham Geiger and the Jewish Jesus* (Chicago: University of Chicago Press, 1998).

affect some of our academic work. We also see important intersections with the marginalization of non-Jewish scholars.

The valorization of studying rabbinic texts has affected the academy so much that the ideal Jewish studies scholar is expected to possess an encyclopedic knowledge of biblical and rabbinic Hebrew texts. The technical inquiries and claims of philology, the study of the history and details of language, rank high as expertise in Jewish studies, far higher than, for example, the study of Yiddish literature or the anthropology of Los Angeles Jews or the history of Jews in Argentina. Yet too often the measure of the "authentic" scholar of Judaism is correlated to the traditional, learned Jewish man.

Novel readings of classical texts, especially if they follow traditional methods of interpretation, also garner praise, whereas scholars who demonstrate external influences on those texts—Christian motifs in the Haggadah or how Islamic law shaped Jewish law—often encounter resistance. That is, sometimes what counts as good interpretation in the scholarly realm is far too similar to what counts as good interpretation in the religious realm. "Only five people in the world will be capable of understanding the book I am writing on midrash," boasted a scholar two generations ago; he and many of his listeners assumed obscurantism was the mark of high scholarship. Today, broad influence, a wide readership, and numerous citations are taken as markers of important scholarship. Religious study emphasizes close reading, intertextuality (reading one verse alongside a seemingly unconnected one from a different part of the corpus), and disputation among classical interpreters to make sense of the text. Today, graduate seminars in Jewish studies often focus similarly on close readings of classical texts—going very slowly, word by word, and teasing out all the possible implications and questions. Some classes are even structured like religious modes of study, having students prepare for class in pairs, a classical Jewish mode of (male) study called *hevruta*. Students can react quite differently to hevruta study. At one graduate program in Jewish studies, the male students welcomed hevruta study enthusiastically, feeling that it empowered them as if they were yeshiva scholars. The women in the program reacted quite differently: some felt they were being asked to participate in a male project that had excluded them for millennia; were they now to imitate men? Other women have embraced the formerly male method as their own.

Their reactions suggest that Jewish men may be more socialized to these forms of learning—of reading and of knowledge production through hevruta study—than women or non-Jews. It can also mean that Jews from Orthodox backgrounds, which increasingly includes women, fit into the field more naturally than those who are not. There is no simple hierarchy; male scholars are more likely to "fit in" than women, Orthodox more than nonreligious or "less" religious (in itself a pejorative term for Reform, Conservative, and other Jews), and Jewish more than non-Jewish.

While the ability to read biblical and rabbinic texts in Hebrew and Aramaic—the languages in which those texts were read by most Jews in yeshivot through the centuries—offers far greater insight than reading the texts in translation, those readings are ultimately fixated on male authors writing from men's perspectives. That kind of focus can perpetuate the sense that the Bible, Talmud, and ancient male interpreters and their texts are the *real* center of Judaism, whereas the lives of women and nonelites are peripheral or less important. When readers concentrate solely on a close reading of the text, examining each word philologically, they can end up replicating the text in their scholarly methods, producing academic conversations that erase women, which is then reflected in the textbooks that present Judaism and Jewish religious practice as an entirely male endeavor, as we demonstrated in chapter 1.

The continuities between yeshiva learning and scholarship, as well as academic nostalgia for traditional learning, established processes of scholarship that canonized assumptions that (1) some kinds of knowledge are more important than others and (2) some kinds of bodies are the default bodies of the scholar. Textual knowledge, particularly the interpretation of canonical religious literature, ranks as paramount. The default image of the scholar of Judaism is male, cisgender, white, and Jewish. When we say "default," we mean this: the image most people picture unless told otherwise. A male default is why some people may refer to a woman as a "female professor" and a man as just a "professor."

One of the reasons that a man is the default image of a Jewish studies scholar has little to do with Jewish studies specifically. It is true for scholars in general, as we discussed in chapter 1. Even though women now earn about half of research-based doctoral degrees in the United States and Canada, the dominant image of professors remains male. Male academics are also often imagined as having more expertise than female academics: recent studies have found that students tend to see male college instructors as more educated and qualified and female college instructors as less educated and qualified than they actually are.[11] African American professor Willie James Jennings describes the image of the professor that prevailed in the minds of a hiring committee at an Ivy League university in which he participated. Even though the committee interviewed several different types of candidates, including a Black woman, they ultimately selected a white man. Jennings described him as follows: He was "a tall, dark-haired, baritone-voiced, perfectly groomed bearded man dressed like a professor in the middle of a celebrated career. He had 1.5 years of study in Germany, knowledge of German language, theology, biblical languages, seminars, blue suit, brown wingtip shoes, slow speech, legs crossed, quiet confident comportment."[12] Jennings writes, "I had learned to love an intellectual form that performed

11. JoAnn Miller and Marilyn Chamberlin, "Women Are Teachers, Men Are Professors: A Study of Student Perceptions," *Teaching Sociology* 28, no. 4 (2000): 283–98.

12. James T. Keane, "Willie James Jennings Exposes One of Academia's Greatest Problems: Non-white Students Don't Feel Like They Belong," *America: The Jesuit Review*, November 9, 2021, https://www.americamagazine.org/arts-culture/2021/11/09/willie-james-jennings-theology-cbc-241798.

white masculinist self-sufficiency."[13] The man's linguistic knowledge as well as his body and voice signaled professorial authority. Too often, women scholars feel that they do not fit the image of a scholar, that they do not belong, that they are somehow frauds. Thus, even for scholars who do not fit this image, the idea of a professor is often still synonymous with a tall, white, cisgender man with certain kinds of linguistic and textual knowledge.

The issue of elevating male modes of textual study also exists beyond Jewish studies. Ilyse Morgenstein Fuerst has shown how Islamic studies elevates textuality, philology, and one particular language: "Stated hiring preferences, including teaching obligations, entrench an 'essence' of Islam or Islamic studies at odds with scholarly discourse about Islam, Islamic studies, and religious studies that may be summarized as a simple, troubling equation: Islam = Middle East + Arabic + Texts."[14] She points out that Islamic studies positions tend to assume that the essence or center of knowledge about Islam comes from the Arabic language, the Middle East, and texts, rather than, say, anthropology. This is similar to the role of gender in studies of rabbinics and Hebrew Bible: excellence in Hebrew and Aramaic and texts occupy central space.[15] As in Jewish studies, traditional gender roles in Islam leak into scholarship. Tamiya R. Zaman argues that Shahab Ahmed's widely read 2016 book *What Is Islam? The Importance of Being*

13. Willie James Jennings, *After Whiteness: An Education in Belonging* (Grand Rapids, MI: Eerdmans, 2020), 39.

14. Ilyse Morgenstein Fuerst, "Job Ads Don't Add Up: Arabic + Middle East + Text ≠ Islam," *Journal of the American Academy of Religion* 88, no. 4 (December 2020): 915–46, quote on 915.

15. Morgenstein Fuerst also uses job ads to show that the conflation of philological, textual, and linguistic expertise extends across subfields in Islamic studies, where it is much more confined to subfields in ancient Judaism. Moreover, Judaism and Islam have been painted with similar brushes in the history of scholarship, as Morgenstein Fuerst notes: they "share a classificatory history, having been labeled as Semitic, racial-linguistically defined religions that are inherently legalistic, monolithic, and regionally situated." Morgenstein Fuerst, "Jobs Don't Add Up," 939.

Islamic analyzes male scholarship on male-authored texts in the field of Islamic studies to create a normative male Muslim subject as it "willfully ignores a growing body of female and feminist scholarship" in its 632 pages.[16] There is a long list of books in Jewish studies that also ignore women and draw little on scholarship by women. Although the historical particulars are different, Muslims and Jews have shared some historical cultures, including the fact that in most Islamic cultures, men have been assumed to be the textual experts. The fields of Jewish studies and Islamic studies also share a lack of gender parity and demonstrate interesting parallels between their feminist approaches to Islam and Judaism and to the challenges of modernity that claimed to offer universal rights yet limited those rights to men.[17] When the feminist movement arose in the Middle East and North Africa during the Nahda (the Arab renaissance), Jews and non-Jewish Arabs collaborated in formulating their arguments and faced gendered political and economic challenges.[18]

Outsider status and gendered assumptions are not identical in all academic fields, however. Even within Jewish studies, sexism, discrimination, and outsider status work differently within different subfields. In this chapter, we look at several of these subfields to explore women's representation and experience, as well as the gender norms. In these, we see echoes of the nostalgia for yeshiva environments of the past.

16. Taymiya R. Zaman, "An Islam of One's Own," *Comparative Studies of South Asia, Africa and the Middle East* 40, no. 1 (May 2020): 214–19, quote on 217. See also Kecia Ali, "The Omnipresent Male Scholar," *Critical Muslim* 8 (2015): 61–73; and Shahab Ahmed, *What Is Islam? The Importance of Being Islamic* (Princeton, NJ: Princeton University Press, 2016).

17. Beth Wenger and Firoozeh Kashani-Sabet, eds., *Gender in Judaism and Islam: Common Lives, Uncommon Heritage* (New York: New York University Press, 2014). Kristian Petersen has established a crowdsourced database of women scholars who work on Muslims and Islam, "Women and Nonbinary Scholars of Islamic Studies," accessed June 12, 2024, https://drkristianpetersen.com/women-of-islamic-studies/.

18. For examples of feminist arguments, see the material collected by Tarek el-Ariss, ed., *The Arab Renaissance: A Bilingual Anthology of the Nahda* (New York: Modern Language Association of America, 2018).

While we consider the yeshiva as an origin story for Jewish studies and trace its relationship to certain subfields today, we are not aiming at comprehensiveness. Here, we concentrate on subfields that focus on premodern material because we think the links to nostalgia for Jewish learning can be seen more clearly there, not because we somehow judge these subfields as worse. We invite our readers to consider the many additional subfields, including Jewish philosophy, modern Jewish thought, Hebrew and Yiddish literatures, the study of antisemitism, anthropology, sociology, and Jewish history. We might ask about the status of certain fields associated with women, such as Jewish art and music. We want to call attention to recent studies, such as the critiques of Jewish religious thought by Mara Benjamin and Andrea Cooper, and we want to point out the presence of women scholars in relatively newer fields, such as the study of Jews in Islamic cultures.[19] We are also aware that some senior male scholars in certain fields have been particularly supportive of women and nonbinary students and colleagues, demonstrating the importance of individual commitment to inclusion in the field. Yet we also worry about a pyramid shape within certain fields, with male scholars dominating, earning the grants, and setting the agenda, while female and nonbinary scholars are subsumed in the lower ranks. By pointing to problems in a few specific subfields, we hope to encourage change.

Archaeology

"Biblical archaeology" or archaeology of the "ancient Near East"[20] might at first glance seem to avoid some of the issues associated with the male, Protestant dominance of biblical scholarship.

---

19. Andrea D. Cooper, *Gendering Modern Jewish Thought* (Bloomington: Indiana University Press, 2021); and Mara H. Benjamin, *The Obligated Self: Maternal Subjectivity and Jewish Thought* (Bloomington: Indiana University Press, 2018).

20. Like its kin "Middle East," this a problematic term for its Eurocentrism— "near" to what? East of what? Yet it is still the most widely recognized label, so we use it here.

Archeology focuses on material objects, spaces, and structures far more than on texts. The perceived Jewishness or level of religious observance of the scholar matters less in archaeological scholarship about the Bible than it does in textual scholarship. But the field of archaeology has its own significant problems with respect to gender and power, having emerged during an era of imperialism, colonialism, Orientalism, and racism, as white European and North American men dominated the field in the nineteenth and early twentieth centuries.[21]

Archaeology has long held gendered assumptions about who is fit for what kind of work. Archaeologists have observed a "man in the field, woman in the lab" dichotomy, with men as the imagined (strong, athletic) workers on archeological digs, and women doing the (safer) laboratory work with the artifacts.[22] Archaeologist Diane Bolger talks about "the traditional image of the male archaeologist as hunter/conqueror/adventurer," which remains a prominent image, even though women have been active contributors since the early days of archaeology.[23] Maybe you have seen the Indiana Jones films. Even if an artifact never vaporizes anyone in real life, the films' ideas about swashbuckling masculinity reflect cultural assumptions about archaeological research. Especially for women, pregnancy and parenting are still often seen as disqualifiers

21. For a wider perspective on this history, see Margarita Díaz-Andreu García, *A World History of Nineteenth-Century Archaeology: Nationalism, Colonialism, and the Past* (New York: Oxford University Press, 2007).

22. Patty Jo Watson with Michael Rathje and Michael Shanks, "Patty Jo Watson," in *Archaeology in the Making: Conversations through a Discipline*, ed. William L. Rathje, Michael Shanks, and Christopher Witmore (New York: Routledge, 2013), 47–67.

23. Diane Bolger, "Gendered Fields in Near Eastern Archaeology: Past, Present, Future," in *Gender through Time in the Ancient Near East*, ed. Diane Bolger (Lanham, MD: AltaMira, 2008), 351. On women's participation, see Jennie Ebeling, "Archaeological Views: Missing from the Picture," *Biblical Archaeology Society*, September 30, 2019, https://www.biblicalarchaeology.org/daily/archaeological-views-missing-from-the-picture/#171001.

for fieldwork.[24] Dig directors and other scholars have used even the possibility of pregnancy or caretaking responsibilities as reasons to discount women from serious fieldwork. Because of these assumptions, male dig directors may also fare better in courting philanthropic support.

This is not just about images; it is also about numbers. A decade ago, fewer than a third of digs in Israel had a woman director or codirector.[25] Today, among active digs in Israel, only 36 percent are directed or codirected by women.[26] Women form the majority of dig volunteers and graduate students, but men are the substantial majority of dig directors. Though women rank among the top archaeologists more prominently than in the past, one Mediterranean archaeologist notes, "The field is also dominated by men. And it's traditional. Fieldwork tends to be very hierarchical and directors have enormous latitude and authority."[27]

This last observation—about the authority structures on digs—points to the prevalence of gender-based harassment and even sexual assault. (We discussed harassment and assault in depth in chapter 2.) Archaeologist Beth Alpert Nakhai reported on gender-based discrimination and assault in the field: "Sexual violations [harassment or assault] were tolerated at 20 percent of digs, while alcohol and drugs were rampant at a great many; physical assault, racial or religious harassment, theft, and vandalism

---

24. Beth Alpert Nakhai, "Archaeology/History," in *Women and the Society of Biblical Literature*, ed. Nicole L. Tilford (Atlanta: Society of Biblical Literature, 2019), 116; and Beth Alpert Nakhai, "Cleaning Up the Field: A Conversation about Harassment in Mediterranean Archaeology," *Eidolon*, December 26, 2017, https://eidolon.pub /cleaning-up-the-field-f7c4c15a2f08.

25. Jennie Ebeling, "Where Are the Female Dig Directors in Israel?," *Bible and Interpretation*, May 2011, https://bibleinterp.arizona.edu/opeds/ebeling358011.

26. The *Biblical Archaeology Review* maintains a list at https://www.biblicalar chaeology.org/digs/. We accessed the site on July 5, 2022. Out of thirty-six active digs, sixteen had female directors or codirectors. We chose this method of gathering data because it is similar to Ebeling's method.

27. Nakhai, "Cleaning Up the Field."

occurred at approximately 25 percent. Violations of professional integrity, including discrimination in field and postfield opportunities and assignments, were also common."[28]

These problems occur on archeological expeditions across the globe, so these issues are not particular to the Jewish studies corners of archaeology. But an archaeological dig is a particular kind of place with its own culture and relationship to the surrounding country. Digs can facilitate sexual harassment and assault in a number of ways: The prevalence of alcohol and the pressure to drink to fit in, and the intimacy with which one lives with others, often twenty-four hours a day in close quarters, all create opportunities for harassment and assault. Further, to victims, reporting it can seem like an insurmountable challenge: people travel from far away, they may be unable to protect themselves from intimidation or harassment, and they may not know the local laws or know how to report incidents. That same feeling of being far away from society and its regulations may encourage participants to feel that the social strictures of home do not apply.

Jennie Ebeling asked archaeologists who had directed digs in Israel/Palestine about gender bias in the field. They identified both academic and cultural biases, including the attrition of women from graduate school before finishing a PhD, men's almost exclusive leadership in the highest positions on digs and in professional organizations, and everyday sexism, especially assumptions about childbearing and parenting. They also noted that women are better represented in so-called early (prehistoric) and late (classical and Islamic) periods—and less represented in biblical eras. Ebeling explains: "This may carry over from the early days of archaeology in Palestine/Israel in the late 19th and early 20th centuries, when

28. Beth Alpert Nakhai, "How to Avoid Gender-Based Hostility in Fieldwork," *Chronicle of Higher Education,* July 15, 2018, https://www.chronicle.com/article/how-to-avoid-gender-based-hostility-during-fieldwork/; and Beth Alpert Nakhai, "The Harvey Weinstein in Your Industry," *Game Plan,* podcast, October 25, 2017, hosted by Rebecca Greenfield and Francesca Levy, https://www.bloomberg.com/news/articles/2017-10-25/the-harvey-weinstein-in-your-industry-j9742fly.

many archaeological projects were run by male scholars trained in biblical studies and focused on prominent *tell* [mound] sites with biblical significance."[29] Thus, archaeology related to the Bible may share the same set of gendered assumptions about authority and expertise on biblical interpretation as we saw in textual biblical studies. We might also add that it has historically featured mostly white, European men coming to the Middle East, excavating ancient sites (and destroying much in the process), and then proclaiming knowledge. These images of white, male experts have lost much of their cachet, but they have not fully lost their influence.

When Ebeling asked these scholars, "Do you think that the situation has improved in the past 25 years?" and "Do you think it will improve in the future?," a significant number answered "no."[30] Professional archaeology has more women than it used to, but in spite of greater gender parity in graduate programs, the dig directors, holders of prominent university positions, and even PhD graduates are still far more likely to be men.

Although archaeology differs from other subfields dealing with ancient Jewish texts and cultures, the necessity of living together in close quarters does not mean that gender problems are intractable. Increasing women's presence in leadership roles, especially as directors, can increase safety. Each field site should institute a formal complaint process and follow up on those complaints. In 2018, Nakhai found that only half of digs had protocols for appropriate and ethical conduct, and even those were not always well publicized. For reasons of safety as well as to create a working culture that discourages harassment, digs need such protocols, as well as clearly defined and enacted consequences for violating those protocols.

People of all genders, sexualities, and races should be welcomed to work as scholars in archeology, especially of the ancient Near East and on matters related to biblical studies. Ethically and

---

29. Ebeling, "Where Are the Female Dig Directors in Israel?"
30. Ebeling.

intellectually, this is better than a homogeneous field. Important new methods of interpreting the Bible have been developed, including from feminist theory and disabilities studies, as have studies that try to reconstruct the practices of women in ancient Israelite religion. Nevertheless, Jewish studies–related archaeology continues to be haunted by its history of seeing white, male scholars as the true experts.

Rabbinics

The subfield of rabbinic literature even more clearly dramatizes our suggestion about how the appeal of "traditional" learning continues to shape the gendered dynamics of Jewish studies. To begin to think about the study of rabbinic literature, we must first acknowledge that, to most people who live in the twenty-first century, these texts seem unusual. They do not follow genre conventions we regularly encounter elsewhere. To understand them—even in translation—an aspiring scholar needs to learn how to read them, often with someone who has had training and practice. As the editors of *The Cambridge Companion to the Talmud and Rabbinic Literature* write, "The language, rhetoric, hermeneutic, and logic is often highly encoded and requires a significant amount of training—linguistic, philological, and historical—for one to acquire the skill of decoding them in any meaningful way."[31] Rabbinic texts are not particularly accessible, even if they are translated. Then again, many of the other literary genres and historical documents that academics study are also strange at first encounter. When scholars describe rabbinic texts as difficult and requiring years of training, however, they reinforce the very concept of such material as elite, important, rarified, and hard to

---

31. Charlotte Elisheva Fonrobert and Martin S. Jaffee, eds., *The Cambridge Companion to the Talmud and Rabbinic Literature* (New York: Cambridge University Press, 2007), 20.

understand for outsiders, which in turn can reinforce the idea that the study of rabbinics should be limited to Jewish men.

Starting in late antiquity, learning often happened within study houses or "academies," where teachers were men, and all the students were men. Moreover, the texts in this corpus were overwhelmingly authored by a small group of elite men—or, more accurately, the texts we have are the redacted oral traditions of a small group of elite men. Their intended audiences were likewise other small groups of elite men. Methods of interpretation changed over time, but the system of learning still remains, with men learning with and from men: these men were Jewish, free (not enslaved), presenting as gender conforming (not intersex, not gender nonbinary), and often but not exclusively able bodied (an example of the exception is Rav Sheshet, often quoted in the Talmud, who was blind). Though a few of these men may not have conformed to wider cultural norms of masculinity of their times, they were still men.[32] There are a few examples of learned Jewish women whom rabbinic sources portray as participating in rabbinic discussions and contributing to the transmission of rabbinic traditions,[33] but none within the structures of these academies, learning pairs, or other authoritative spaces.

In this ancient context, religious authority was overwhelmingly based in biblical texts and oral traditions (which would later be written down) about those texts. Not only was textual interpretation done by men; the activity itself was seen as a crucial part of expressing and cultivating manliness. Michael Satlow explains: "The rabbinic evidence repeatedly returns to a consistent construction of manhood, which is portrayed as directly in opposition to the construction of womanhood in these texts. For the rabbis,

---

32. Daniel Boyarin, *Unheroic Conduct: The Rise of Heterosexuality and the Invention of the Jewish Man* (Berkeley: University of California Press, 1997); and Yakir Englander, *The Male Body in Ultra-Orthodox Jewish Theology* (Eugene, OR: Pickwick, 2021).

33. Tal Ilan, "The Quest for the Historical Beruriah, Rachel, and Imma Shalom," *AJS Review* 22, no. 1 (1997): 1–17.

being a man means using that uniquely male trait, self-restraint, in the pursuit of the divine through Torah study."[34] This vision promoted self-mastery, which centered on religious learning and downplayed corporeality, and it associated women with self-indulgence and corporeality. The authors and readers of these traditions, then, saw textual study as a masculine activity.

The content of these texts varies widely, from economics to theology to social relations. Women very rarely appear in these texts as participants in these discussions, but they do appear as the objects of discussion. Tractates about menstrual impurity and sexual relations are written by male rabbis, not women, and they discuss women's bodies at length; indeed, women's reproductive organs are among the most frequently discussed body parts in rabbinic literature. While the central concern is regulating when during the month a woman's body is available for intercourse with her husband, the discussions tell us much about the underlying sexual concerns of the male rabbis. Men construct their maleness through their discussions of women: the fascination with women's sexual organs and their functions, secretions, and (im)purities becomes a discursively constructed appropriation by men of a woman's body.[35]

Rabbinic discussions of women's bodies also intersect with other bodies on the margins. For example, Menachot 93a includes the following instruction about bringing an animal offering: "Everyone places their hands upon its head, except for a deaf person, a *shoteh* [a person with mental illness or intellectual disability], a minor, a blind person, a non-Jew, a Canaanite slave, the agent who brings the offering on its owner's behalf, and a woman." "Everyone," then, is often a rabbinic category for adult, non-disabled

34. Michael L. Satlow, "'Try to Be a Man': The Rabbinic Construction of Masculinity," *Harvard Theological Review* 89, no. 1 (1996): 19–40, quote on 20.

35. Susannah Heschel, "Sind Juden Männer? Können Frauen jüdisch sein? Die gesellschaftliche Definition des männlichen/weiblichen Körpers," in *Der Schejne Jid: Das Bild des "jüdischen Körpers" in Mythos und Ritual*, ed. Sander L. Gilman, Robert Jütte, and Gabriele Kohlbauer-Fritz (Vienna: Picus Verlag, 1998), 86–96.

Jewish men, especially in the case of rituals. In other places, the categories of the *tumtum* and the *androginos* also represent sex or gender difference; these too are seen as part of the community but not its central voices. Adult Jewish men were the primary writers and intended audience; we rarely hear the voices of others, but that does not mean there is nothing for scholars to learn about them.

Scholars recognize the study of rabbinic literature as one of the central subfields of Jewish studies. It claims a significant number of faculty members in academic departments in North America, Israel, and Europe, and it ranks as one of the top four or five sub-fields that members of the Association for Jewish Studies (AJS) identify as their primary interest.[36] Thus, exploring its gendered dynamic provides a useful window into the field more generally.

Jane Kanarek asks, "What does it mean to study Talmud as a woman? What does it mean to study this literature which contains the names of so few women? What would it mean to immerse myself in a literature which can matter-of-factly discuss the status of a three-year-old's virginity or how a woman is acquired in marriage? Most basically, I consider what it means to study a literature that was not written for me—and often even forbidden to me."[37] Today's academic Jewish subfields do not ostentatiously exclude women or non-Jews—either as scholars or as topics of study. But in some ways, the traditions of textual interpretation and of who the assumed interpreters are still live on.

36. The 2018 AJS member survey listed "Social Science" at 13 percent; "Modern Jewish History in Europe, Asia, Israel, and Other Communities" at 12.2 percent; "Modern Jewish History in the Americas" at 9.3 percent; "Bible and History of Biblical Interpretation" at 8.6 percent; and "Rabbinic Literature and Culture" at 8.2 percent. *Association for Jewish Studies: 50th Anniversary Survey Report*, October 5, 2018, https://www.associationforjewishstudies.org/docs/default-source/surveys-of-the-profession/2018-ajs-survey-report-(1).pdf?sfvrsn=2.

37. Jane Kanarek, "Ancient Voices," in *Why Study Talmud in the Twenty-First Century? The Relevance of the Ancient Jewish Text to Our World*, ed. Paul Socken (Lanham, MD: Lexington Books, 2009), 42.

Sometimes rabbinics scholars don't realize that when the text is talking about women, it is constructing masculinity and male power that is reinforced by asserting the solo voice of men—and when the texts talk about men, it is constructing women as absence, void, silence.

I registered for a class in graduate school, taught by a visiting instructor who specialized in Talmud. The first day, I walked in, and I was nervous: the other students were four guys in yarmulkes. They must know the Talmud better than me, I thought. But, it became clear during the first meeting, that my Hebrew was actually better than theirs, and I was more skilled at reading the Aramaic and Hebrew texts. Halfway through the semester, something weird finally dawned on me. We would start each class on a new page, seemingly having skipped a daf *[page] and a half. I discovered that the other four students and the professor were reading together at the synagogue. They were all getting together and reading the same text there. No one invited me—or even bothered to tell me it was happening.*

A professor who completed her doctorate in the early 2000s reported to us that she was quite talkative in her graduate seminars except in the classes she took on rabbinic texts that were taught by a male, Jewish professor:

I'm not sure I know exactly why I couldn't speak up in his classes; I was well prepared and knew the material. Somehow there was a bonding that took place between him [the professor] and the other students, who were all men, that left me feeling I had no right to be in the room. No one ever said anything, and I just don't know if I felt inhibited because of my own feelings or if I was picking up on some silent message they were sending me that I didn't belong.

Another woman told us that on the first day of her graduate seminar in Talmud at an Israeli university, the professor asked only the women students for their background in rabbinics. The condescension toward women continued until most of the women in the program, feeling alienated, transferred to other departments. Some women felt intimidated by their professors, viewing them as authority figures, like male rabbis, who could not be challenged.

Reading rabbinic literature requires languages, rabbinic Hebrew and Aramaic, that take significant time to learn. For much of Jewish history, Hebrew was seen as a masculine language.[38] Women might read the Bible and even say many prayers in vernacular languages, while men used Hebrew in religious contexts. Today, Orthodox boys are taught Hebrew and Aramaic, while Orthodox girls are taught only Hebrew. Within the Orthodox context, young women and men study in separate institutions for the most part; in Haredi communities there are even fewer options for women to study, and Talmud is generally not taught to women. Some Orthodox institutions have begun to encourage women's scholarship, and the graduates of Maharat, a modern Orthodox seminary that ordains women rabbis, have become important voices of Jewish learning.[39] But even today, male Jewish scholars are more likely to enter graduate school with more necessary language skills than their female or non-Jewish counterparts. Once they arrive, they may all find that there is a shared assumption that male, yarmulke-wearing scholars are experts, or at least experts-in-the-making, even if women students are just as well trained as men.

Echoing the description by Jennings of the ideal scholar, a colleague told us: "There is an image of who is the scholar in rabbinics: a white, Jewish, cis man who went through yeshiva. And the less you can approximate that, the harder it is for you in the field." This is not to say that the field is full of individual people keeping others out because of their deep-seated sexism or transphobia. Rather, there is an underlying assumption that expertise goes

38. Naomi Seidman, *A Marriage Made in Heaven: The Sexual Politics of Hebrew and Yiddish* (Berkeley: University of California Press, 1997).

39. Beth Kissileff, "Orthodox Women Scholars' Growing Authority Is Recognized in Push to Publish," *Religion News Service*, March 29, 2022, https://religionnews.com /2022/03/29/orthodox-jewish-women-scholars-growing-authority-is-recognized -in-push-to-publish/.

along with certain kinds of bodies and not others. This assumption can be shared by scholars of all genders; as in the story above, women scholars might begin an encounter assuming that male scholars are more authoritative. Happily, those assumptions can be overcome, but overcoming them is not simple, and it can begin only when we recognize them.

From antiquity to the present, then, male Jews have been associated with textual expertise and authority. We also see continuities in the way knowledge is produced and what questions are deemed central, with a line of continuity from the earliest biblical and rabbinic texts to the work of contemporary scholars: an assumption that men's lives, men's concerns, and men's questions are normative. Who a man wants for a wife and how he takes a wife, treats a wife, and divorces a wife are key rabbinic questions in which women function as objects, not subjects, a pattern that some contemporary textbooks and history books and works of theology repeat.

Predictably, the field of rabbinics shares some practical obstacles with other studies of the ancient world. Sources can be scarce, and sources explicitly pertaining to women are even more scarce. For much of the history of scholarship on rabbinics, the study of women and gender has been deemed an ancillary topic, or a special interest. Tal Ilan recalls that when some scholars turned their attention to women, their scholarship began with "a rather naïve attempt to encompass the entire historical perspective of Jewish women in Palestine, under the assumption that knowledge of all the sources will inevitably produce a complete history."[40]

But just because we can never know a complete history does not mean that all meaningful histories are impossible, or that all histories equally fail to give insight into women and gender in the past. Nor do incomplete sources give us license to relegate the study of women to special interests. Formerly, Tal Ilan explains,

---

40. Tal Ilan, *Mine and Yours Are Hers: Retrieving Women's History from Rabbinic Literature* (Leiden: Brill, 1997), xi.

the field "subconsciously maintained that women's history can be subsumed under traditional headings such as marriage, family, sex, child-rearing, cooking, and housework," but now serious scholars should "no longer view any historical event as devoid of women's presence and significance."[41] We must look for women's presence and roles, even when the sources do not foreground them.

Women pioneers in the field of rabbinics, including Rachel Adler, Judith Hauptman, Judith Wegner, and Miriam Peskowitz, were inspired by the Jewish feminist movement of the 1970s and 1980s to investigate the treatment of women in Talmudic and midrashic literature. All the more exciting is the growing number of women in the fields of Second Temple Judaism and rabbinics. Thanks to their work, many scholars now view women and gender as foundational: Charlotte Fonrobert looked for "women's spaces" in her study of rabbinic texts related to menstruation; Cynthia Baker examined evidence about gender and sexuality in material sources alongside texts; Rafael Rachel Neis and Julia Watts Belser analyzed how rabbinic science categorizes human bodies and their material products.[42] The field has come a long way, though even now scholarship on women, gender, and sexuality can run the risk of being seen as a special-interest topic.

History is not the only methodological option for knowing more about women and Judaism. Rabbinic texts remain the largest sources for knowledge about women and nonbinary people in this historical period. Yet scholars need not hunt for historical kernels of truth only in those texts. Many other methods, including literary readings of rabbinic sources, religious studies approaches,

41. Ilan, xi.

42. Charlotte Elisheva Fonrobert, *Menstrual Purity: Rabbinic and Christian Reconstructions of Biblical Gender* (Stanford, CA: Stanford University Press, 2000), 129; Cynthia Baker, "How Do Ancient Jews and Gender Matter?," *Gender and Social Norms in Ancient Israel, Early Judaism and Early Christianity: Texts and Material Culture* 28 (2019) 257–68; Rachel Rafael Neis, "Fetus, Flesh, Food: Generating Bodies of Knowledge in Rabbinic Science," *Journal of Ancient Judaism* 10, no. 2 (2019): 181–210; Belser, *Rabbinic Tales of Destruction.*

rhetorical analyses, and contemporary approaches in the fields of theology and ethics all offer ways to know more about women and gender.

As in many academic corners, some rabbinics scholars still operate under the assumption that issues of gender are special interest or secondary. Books on gender may not appear on graduate exam lists, and when they appear on undergraduate syllabi, it may be during a single week. The omission or marginalization of gender in university courses and required reading for doctoral programs is odd. After all, rabbinic literature is the most powerful and foundational source for institutionalizing gender and sexuality in Jewish life, and the production of gender roles and regulating sexual identities and behaviors is one of the primary tasks of rabbinic literature. Although gender studies has become much more visible than it was a generation ago, with scholarly publications presenting original and exciting results, scholars who work on gender, sexuality, or trans studies can still hear that their work is too niche to be considered for this journal or that job. One scholar who works in queer and trans studies told us:

> There is this image of who is the scholar in rabbinics: he went through yeshiva, he is male, he is Jewish. The less you can approximate that, the harder it is for you in the field. I didn't experience much overt harassment, but I had a tough time finding a job in rabbinics, even though my adviser was really supportive and wrote letters and even picked up the phone. My work didn't quite fit traditional ideas of what rabbinics is.

Scholars in North America and Israel dominate the study of rabbinics (though Europe is also growing as a center), but the gender dynamics of the field differ with geography. Some women rabbinics scholars argue that the gender gap in the field of rabbinics in Israel is partially because people assume that only men can be sufficiently trained because only they can come from the "right" background of a yeshiva. At an AJS panel, rabbinics scholar Sara Ronis agreed, but she explained, "the problem goes beyond that.

People who just focus on technical elements of the Talmud miss huge structural issues with how it constructs gender and ethnicity in ways that I think are essential to modern conversations about the text."[43] One woman who works on medieval Hebrew texts and is now on the faculty of a major research university told us that her graduate school experience in rabbinics seminars involved

> *not so much the harassment as a feeling that you don't have a place at the table because you are a woman, you are young, didn't go to yeshiva—an alienation also because I didn't come from a religious home.*

As this scholar suggests, the scholarly practices of these methods often follow male norms of behavior. Rabbinic philology, for example, often insists on expertise even at the expense of breadth, punishes any missteps, and pursues a model of competitive, individualized work.[44] Exclusiveness can be worn as a badge: necessary language training as well as intricate knowledge of particular texts serve as the only legitimate way to enter the scholarly conversation. In its most intense moments, this kind of elitism can create atmospheres that feel "judgmental" and "exclusive," as scholars told us. While it may not explicitly exclude people who

43. Sara Ronis, "Different Approaches to Rabbinics Research: Between the United States and Israel," panel, AJS Annual Conference, Boston, December 2018.

44. There is a vast literature on the ways that such behaviors and norms are coded male. For example, see Muriel Niederle and Lise Vesterlund, "Gender Differences in Competition," *Negotiation Journal* 24, no. 4 (2008): 447–63; Maria De Paola, Francesca Gioia, and Vincenzo Scoppa, *Teamwork, Leadership and Gender*, IZA Institute of Labor Economics (University of Bonn), Discussion Paper Series 11861, September 2018, https://papers.ssrn.com/sol3/papers.cfm?abstract_id=4193376; Christian N. Thoroughgood, Katina B. Sawyer, and Samuel T. Hunter, "Real Men Don't Make Mistakes: Investigating the Effects of Leader Gender, Error Type, and the Occupational Context on Leader Error Perceptions," *Journal of Business and Psychology* 28, no. 1 (2013): 31–48; and Melissa C. Thomas-Hunt and Katherine W. Phillips, "When What You Know Is Not Enough: Expertise and Gender Dynamics in Task Groups," *Personality and Social Psychology Bulletin* 30, no. 12 (2004): 1585–98.

are not Jewish men, it rewards people who are socialized into these behaviors.

Rabbinics scholars who attend to gender and sexuality have noted the way that these masculine norms discourage participation and stifle innovation and risk taking and can even enable bullying.[45] One scholar told us:

> *The field doesn't observe the niceties of not picking on grad students. I've watched people be unconstructively mean. You worry that if you don't have all the manuscript variations at your fingertips, you'll be humiliated. The overall effect, whether it happens to you or not, is that it creates a conservative field. The effect of the conservatism is so stifling that it affects what we say in advance.*

Another scholar described her experiences in graduate school as evidence of what we might now call toxic masculinity: "nothing explicitly sexual or gender related was said by male professors, but the nastiness, the aggression, was clearly intended to bolster their macho identity." Scholars may wonder why they should take a chance on something new or radical when they could be spending their time crafting a bulletproof philological point with extensive manuscript comparison that would not expose them to criticism. They might choose deepening language skills over engaging in broad, theoretical, or comparative scholarship. This mode of philological practice is so central to the field of rabbinics that it sets the tone for what is expected at conferences, in job interviews, and in peer-reviewed publications.

But, you might say, philology is important. Expertise in ancient languages and manuscripts creates knowledge about the world of the past. We agree. Given this, we might ask, are there different ways to do philology that would be more inclusive and better encourage innovation and wide-ranging thinking? Rabbinics scholar

---

45. A prominent instance of this conversation happened at the 2018 AJS Annual Conference: "What Is the Place of Philology and Source Criticism in Talmudic Studies? Yesterday, Today, and Tomorrow."

Beth Berkowitz told us that the field would move toward new approaches if it would "shift the way philology works and how we understand what philology is for." What if, she wonders, "philology were more like rhetoric? We can attend to the way words are used for certain things in certain contexts. Attentiveness to word choice, for example, can serve as a way to understand the speech and its role in making meaning." Rabbinic texts open themselves to similar kinds of analyses. "The end point isn't just technical history," Berkowitz says. She notes that this approach "seems more in line with feminist work, especially the kind that is more typical in the humanities."[46] For Berkowitz, philology and literary theory coexist, informing different aspects of her scholarship. Another scholar told us she noted a difference between the training she received in the United States and that in Israel: "In America I learned about different ways literature scholars read texts. Postcolonial theory opened my eyes to new ways of reading the Talmud, but in Israel such approaches were unknown to my Talmud professors." Turning to newer methods of textual analysis was necessary, a Talmudist told us, because her male professors and fellow students conveyed the impression to her that philology was a male domain and she was unwanted.

Rabbinics, then, carries over many of the gendered assumptions about the gender of textual experts and what modes of textual interpretation are most important. But those assumptions need not continue to structure the field: scholars can make changes regarding scholarly training and faculty positions, and which methods of learning and interpretation are prized and what questions are addressed.

Hebrew Bible

The field of Hebrew Bible is sometimes called "Hebrew Bible/Old Testament." Even this name hints at some of its questions, methods, and issues: competing religious contexts, multiple theological approaches, and the prominence of later Christian texts in the interpretation of older biblical materials. Although they both centrally investigate ancient and canonical religious texts, then, some of the foundational issues in the study of the Hebrew Bible differ from those of rabbinic literature. In addition, the wider field of biblical studies often groups together Hebrew Bible and New Testament scholarship. Most prominently, the field is dominated by non-Jewish scholars, a significant number of whom were trained in, write from, or teach in confessional Christian contexts; after all, there are far more Christian seminaries and colleges than Jewish ones.

Nevertheless, the Jewish corners of the study of the Hebrew Bible and rabbinics share structural and intellectual features that matter when we think about gender: they privilege language and philology, have a significant group of male scholars who received their language training as youngsters in religious environments, and often focus on source or textual criticism.

Institutional context matters. For the field of Hebrew Bible, many of those institutions are Christian colleges, universities, and even seminaries. Some scholars receive education in one or more of these contexts, and many also hold faculty positions in them. A significant number of these faculty positions require the professor to sign a statement of Christian faith. More than a quarter of the members of the Society of Biblical Literature (SBL), the main scholarly organization for Bible scholars in North America, identify their department as "Biblical Studies," a department name that is almost exclusively used in Christian institutions. Another 14 percent identify their department as "Theology," another Christian institutional departmental name in North America (in European institutions, where faculties of theology are either Protestant or Catholic, the term *theology* often denotes a broader set of inquiries). Only 3.5 percent say they work in a Jewish studies department.[46] A few Jewish institutions train and employ Hebrew Bible scholars— Hebrew Union College, the Jewish Theological Seminary, Yeshiva

---

46. *2019 SBL Membership Data*, Society of Biblical Literature, January 2019, 14, https://www.sbl-site.org/assets/pdfs/sblMemberProfile2019.pdf.

University, and Brandeis University are the largest—but they are far outnumbered by the many Christian colleges and seminaries. A significant amount of scholarship comes from those trained and working at secular and unaffiliated universities too, such as Harvard University and the University of Chicago, but Christian numerical dominance in the field is undeniable.

But why should this make a difference for gender in the field? In some of the more conservative Christian environments, many administrators, students, and faculty believe that women should not teach biblical studies at all.[47] Using 2 Timothy as a prooftext, many see women Bible professors as violating the injunction for women not to teach in church. For example, a theology professor at the evangelical Phoenix Seminary explained, "Mixed-gender theology classes should be taught by men. It is illogical to say a woman should train men to be Bible teachers and pastors when she shouldn't be one herself. If women shouldn't be pastors or elders in churches, then they should also not have that role in other contexts."[48] Even for Christian institutional environments that do not explicitly forbid women's teaching, religious gender norms often favor men as intellectual leaders.[49] This both affects and is affected by the demographics of these institutions: men often outnumber women at both the graduate student and the faculty levels.

Moreover, as biblical studies scholar Sarah Shectman observes, "seminaries are major feeders to PhD programs in biblical studies,

---

47. To see a debate about whether women can and should teach biblical studies at colleges and universities, see "Should Christian Colleges Let Female Faculty Teach Men the Bible?," *Christianity Today* 58, no. 4 (May 2014). Moody Bible Institute, for example, follows complementarian theology in which men are the proper religious leaders and teachers. Moody Bible Institute, "Moody Believes," accessed December 17, 2023, https://www.moodybible.org/beliefs/.

48. "Should Christian Colleges Let Female Faculty Teach Men the Bible?," 21.

49. For one example, see Sarah Pulliam Bailey, "Leadership Changes at Cedarville University Point to Conservative Direction," *Religion News Service*, December 13, 2013, https://religionnews.com/2013/12/13/reports-conservative-shakeup-ohio -christian-university-hits-women/.

and those seminaries are generally dominated by white, Christian males."[50] Some Christian denominations, such as the Roman Catholic Church, the Churches of Christ, the Church of Jesus Christ of Latter-Day Saints, and the Southern Baptist Convention, ordain or recognize only men as clergy, which means that men are overrepresented in faculty positions.[51] It also means that those denominations are likely to encourage men more than others to pursue higher education. When it comes to race, the landscape of denominational seminaries reflects a legacy of enslavement and racism in which Black churches tend to be affiliated with a separate set of institutions. The mostly white seminaries tend to be better connected and have a longer history of cooperation with more prestigious PhD-granting institutions, and so they are better at recruiting graduate students and placing faculty. And, as a recent sociological study of US Christians found, "Basically, if you believe that a white man rules the heavens, you are more likely to believe that white men should rule on Earth."[52] These problems characterize some Christian institutions more than others, and they are not *only* Christian ones—many Jewish institutions train more male scholars and very few scholars of color—but they are certainly ones with Christian inflection given the makeup of the field.

50. Sarah Shectman, "Contingency and the Future of Women in the Society of Biblical Literature," in *Women and the Society of Biblical Literature*, ed. Nicole L. Tilford (Atlanta: Society of Biblical Literature Press, 2019), 341–42.

51. Although Catholic sisters often pursue educational missions, they far more often teach in primary and secondary schools.

52. Quotation from Melissa de White, "Who People Believe Rules Heaven Influences Their Beliefs about Who Rules on Earth," *Stanford News*, January 31, 2020, https://news.stanford.edu/2020/01/31/consequences-perceiving-god-white-man/?fbclid=IwAR32BF48Pb54kZPtq03ZJY8fMCGZ_4Eh_0A3ardCkGmALj1JjlHvq OF3fJc. The original study is available in Steven O. Roberts et al., "God as a White Man: A Psychological Barrier to Conceptualizing Black People and Women as Leadership Worthy," *Journal of Personality and Social Psychology* 119, no. 6 (2020): 1290–315.

In the most recent SBL surveys, published in 2019, women made up about 24 percent and men 76 percent of the membership.[53] Those percentages have been steady in the most recent past, but there are more women now than there were in earlier decades. Senior scholar Carol Newsom writes that early in her career, she encountered many (male) scholars who "couldn't put together the two terms 'woman' and 'serious scholar.'"[54] Women scholars were fewer, and they also faced marginalization and underestimation. Those obstacles have decreased, but they have not disappeared.

Moreover, the study of women and gender did not constitute the kind of scholarship at the center of the field. Athalya Brenner-Idan recounts: "I lost my appointment at Haifa University because of my feminist criticism of biblical literature. University committees considered my book *Israelite Woman* . . . as non-research and a nonstarter."[55] Although feminist methods and research about gender are now more widely considered legitimate research, they are still often viewed as special interests rather than essential knowledge.

Women have also taken on visible leadership roles in the field: between 2011 and 2020, six of the ten SBL presidents were women. Brenner-Idan served as SBL president, an election that suggests the broader acceptance of research about women and gender as real scholarship—a major shift from earlier in her career. But, as Brenner-Idan points out, "To be a president of the Society of

---

53. The choices offered were male, female, and transgender, so it did not count other genders or sexes. It is also entirely possible that it undercounted transgender members, as people who identify as trans also often identify as male or female, but participants could mark only one choice. See *2019 SBL Membership Data*, 8. The report also did not break down its membership by gender and field, so we do not have data for how Hebrew Bible, Second Temple, rabbinics, or New Testament scholars break down by gender.

54. Carol Newsom, "Becoming a Biblical Scholar: A Misfit's Search for Models and Mentors," in Tilford, *Women and the Society of Biblical Literature*, 71.

55. Athalya Brenner-Idan, "Having Been, 2015: Some Reflections," in Tilford, *Women and the Society of Biblical Literature*, 92.

Biblical Literature is to function as a figurehead. This is largely an honorary position."[56] We should not see her election, or those of the other women presidents, as a sign that the field has overcome sexism.

In biblical studies broadly construed, men still outnumber women three to one, and many of the institutions that make up the pipeline for training new scholars continue to encourage (and reward) white men. Nonetheless, Christian feminist scholars around the world have produced a strong and vibrant body of literature of feminist commentaries, analyses, and debates about the Hebrew Bible, as well as some reconstructions of Israelite women's religious practice and roles in society.[57] Given the numerical dominance of Christian institutions and scholars, as well as the theological issue with women teaching in some Christian contexts, it is clear that any conversation about gender in biblical studies will have to consider the relationship of the field to Christian institutions.

Beyond its institutional weight in biblical studies, Christianity also has a deep relationship to methods. "As a field, Jewish Studies has a problem with the Bible," biblical studies scholar Rebecca Scharbach Wollenberg recently wrote.[58] Other scholars have also noticed that the study of the Hebrew Bible has been something of an awkward fit at the AJS conference. The issue is that biblical studies, as the field currently stands, centers on a history of Christian interpretation. One 2016 panel, cheekily titled "Who Let the Bible into AJS?," highlighted how the Hebrew Bible is a central Jewish studies topic in one sense, but because of the history of scholarship—which has been primarily in conversation with Christian institutions—it has never been a seamless fit for Jewish studies spaces.

Even though it is not always explicit, this Christian history of interpretation affects methodology. Bible scholar James Kugel

---

56. Brenner-Idan, "Having Been," 94.

57. These include Susan Ackerman, Mieke Bal, and Rhianna Graybill.

58. Rebecca Scharbach Wollenberg, "Torah Study, Jewishly," *AJS Perspectives*, Fall 2018, 17–18.

uses the word "fateful" to describe "the great alliance between Protestantism and modern Biblical scholarship."[59] That fate is not necessarily a dire one, but it has set much of the path of biblical studies. Tammi J. Schneider explains: "Much of modern scholarship on the Hebrew Bible is rooted in historical-critical considerations of the text which, to some extent, grow from notions about the Hebrew Bible rooted directly in Luther's relationship with that text. What this means for women and feminist studies is that regardless of how data driven or grounded in modern methodology our research is, until recently, they [women and feminist studies] were still sidelined and not incorporated into more mainstream commentaries and discussions of the texts."[60] This is not to say that all biblical scholars read and internalize Luther. But the dominant scholarly methods and practices are part of a history of interpretation that goes back to early Protestantism.

These are not fringe issues: historical-critical methods form the center of biblical studies. The most frequently selected methods and approaches of SBL members were "philology of Greek" and "philology of Hebrew," and the most frequently selected interpretive approach was "historical criticism."[61] Historical criticism includes philology, and many of the same gendered issues in the field of rabbinics arise in very similar ways in biblical studies: these methods emphasize the learning of ancient languages, they encourage individual work and competitive behaviors, and they are less collaborative.

These gendered norms are reflected in the gender of the scholars who research in these fields. In our conversations, several scholars observed that within the SBL conference, the more "historical-critical" a unit is, the worse the representation of

59. James L. Kugel, *How to Read the Bible: A Guide to Scripture, Then and Now* (New York: Simon and Schuster, 2007), 28.

60. Tammi J. Schneider, "Scholarship of Promise," in Tilford, *Women and the Society of Biblical Literature*, 133.

61. The raw numbers are "philology of Greek" at 2,627 members and "philology of Hebrew" at 2,456 members. See *2019 SBL Membership Data*, 8.

women is. Units that used other methods or theories, such as material studies, ethics, or literary methods, reflected the greater gender diversity in those fields. The gendering of method affects who receives graduate training and how. Former SBL president Gale Yee recalls: "As a graduate student, I still did not consider myself a feminist. This was probably due to my thorough training by men in the historical-critical method, where I had to sink or swim in a male and Eurocentric vortex."[62] Feminist research methods and questions were viewed as special interests at best, and poor scholarship at worst, and, Yee notes, they were also connected to the imagined history of white Europe.

Biblical scholarship has also been subject to criticism for its Eurocentrism, whiteness, and Protestant theological commitments.[63] Biblical studies was infused with the imperialism that was the key project of European nation-states during the era in which the field took shape. That imperialism made use of racial theory that was coming to prominence in the nineteenth century to justify its colonialism and the atrocities that accompanied it. New interpretations of the Bible—such as the claim of polygenesis, the idea that God created human races in several separate acts of creation—were developed in support of racism and imperialism. Dominated by Protestants, biblical scholarship offered little room for Jewish or non-European scholars to participate. The exclusion of Jewish scholars, the rise of neo-Marcionism among German Protestants, and the frequent Protestant denigration of Israelite religion (many also sought to sever it from Judaism) led some Jews to label "higher biblical criticism" as "the higher antisemitism."[64] Ultimately, many scholars in biblical

62. Gale Yee, "Negotiating Shifts in Life's Paradigms," in Tilford, *Women and the Society of Biblical Literature*, 104.

63. See, for example, Denise Kimber Buell, "Anachronistic Whiteness and the Ethics of Interpretation," in *Ethnicity, Race, Religion: Identities and Ideologies in Early Jewish and Christian Texts, and in Modern Biblical Interpretation*, ed. Katherine M. Hockey and David G. Horrell (New York: T&T Clark, 2018), 149–67.

64. See, for example, Solomon Schechter, "Higher Criticism—Higher Antisemitism," in *Seminary Addresses and Other Papers* (Cincinnati: Ark, 1915), 35–39.

studies, a field centered in Protestant theological faculties at German universities, developed antisemitic approaches to the Bible in accord with the Third Reich. Some of the scholars from that era continued to influence the study of the Bible in the postwar years as well. This history has created an academic culture in which interpreters from colonized regions rarely find their insights accepted, or even heard. As Madipoane Masenya observes, in biblical studies, "one becomes an insider as one is being trained as a student, an insider to the theologies which are foreign to oneself, an insider as one trains African students in Western-oriented studies of the Bible, an insider as one does research. If the research conducted is not played according to the rules inside the game, it will not earn this 'insider/outsider' accreditation to the Western academic status quo, which itself remains basically an outsider to the African status quo."[65] In certain ways, Jewish biblical scholarship began as a response to the domination of white male Protestants of the field, sometimes in mimicry, sometimes in apologetics. Rather than seeking integration into the Protestant models of scholarship, biblical studies scholars coming from Jewish studies can form intellectual alliances with those developing a new kind of biblical scholarship.

Second Temple Judaism and Late Antiquity

There is an in-betweenness to the field of "Second Temple Judaism." As a subfield, Second Temple Judaism exists at the intersection of Jewish and Christian communities (both in their formative stages); it includes the time when the biblical canon was still somewhat in flux; and it includes communities from diverse geographic regions, empires, and cultures. Many of its most important texts, written by Jews in Greek, were preserved by Christians and forgotten within Judaism, as the Greek texts, though written by

---

65. Madipoane Masenya (ngwana' Mphahlele), "Teaching Western-Oriented Old Testament Studies to African Students: An Exercise in Wisdom or in Folly?," *Old Testament Essays* 17 (2004): 455–69, quote on 460.

Jews, were viewed by Jewish scholars as noncanonical and irrelevant to an imagined normative Judaism, especially when they present ideas and practices that deviate from rabbinic Judaism. For a long time, Second Temple texts were appropriated by Christian scholars for comparison with the New Testament and early Christianity. More recently within Jewish studies, the Second Temple era is treated as an extension of Hebrew Bible studies, and the split between studies of early Judaism and early Christianity is eroding.

The in-betweenness of the field as part of Judaism or Christianity affects the identity of scholars as well. Hindy Najman recalls: "I was told once, if you behave like a male and a Protestant your seminar presentation would be far better received. I did neither. It is important to state that I did not see all of this clearly as a graduate student. Much of this is retrospective reflection and critique."[66] This advice reflects the scholarly norms that reward the same kinds of behavior into which white men are socialized in everyday life: assertiveness, competitiveness, and leadership rather than collaboration. But the idea of behaving like a white Protestant— presumably, engaging in biblical interpretation that hews closely to historical-critical methods—also points to the field's distinctive methodological assumptions that male, Protestant modes of scholarship are the most valuable ones.

Second Temple Judaism also suffers from a problem common to many subfields—that women and gender are seen as niche and therefore safely ignorable. Sara Parks argues that the inclusion of women scholars in the field has not fully solved the problem of making inquiries about women and gender central to the field: "Although at least half of the scholars entering the field may now be women, and although scholarship on ancient women, on biblical and apocryphal female characters, and on the construction of femininity and masculinity in antiquity is now thriving," Parks still

66. Hindy Najman, "Community and Solidarity: The Place of Women in Hebrew Bible and Ancient Judaism," in Tilford, *Women and the Society of Biblical Literature*, 137.

sees "an impermeable conceptual wall between them and what is perceived as 'regular' scholarship."[67]

She also describes a pattern, "the Brooten Phenomenon," when sexist lenses lead scholars to overlook, misinterpret, and fail to recognize the significance of evidence, which they distort to conform to entrenched conventions, to the larger detriment of our understanding of early Judaism and Christianity. In 1982, Bernadette Brooten analyzed archeological remains and inscriptions to demonstrate that, contrary to scholarly assumptions, ancient Judaism had female leaders in the synagogue. Archeologists excavated synagogues in ancient Israel that included pillars, which they assumed held up the balcony where women sat. Brooten demonstrated that the pillars were decorative; there was no evidence of a women's balcony. Similarly, she argued that inscriptions naming women as leaders of ancient synagogues, interpreted by prior (male) scholars as indications that these women were wives of male synagogue leaders, should be taken at face value, indicating that women in antiquity served as leaders. Prior scholars had projected their own experience of Orthodox synagogues, where women sit separately from men (and often in a balcony), and only men are leaders.

Parks asks why the scholarly response to Brooten was so slow and resistant. The "Brooten Phenomenon" indicates how easily we may be misled by our preconceptions. Scholars are always eager for discoveries, yet the reception of Brooten's work demonstrates an odd reluctance. Sometimes scholars do not look for evidence about women, and sometimes we look at evidence from the past and misread it through the lens of today. Brooten herself points to entrenched suppositions that distort scholarship: "The assumption is usually that the Hellenistic world was more progressive and the Jewish world more conservative with respect to women,

---

67. Sara Parks, "'The Brooten Phenomenon': Moving Women from the Margins in Second-Temple and New Testament Scholarship," *Bible and Critical Theory* 15, no. 1 (2019): 47.

so that when one discovers progressive elements in Judaism [such as mixed seating and women leaders], the tendency is to attribute these to Hellenistic influence." Brooten's work has opened a host of new questions. If women were leaders and sat together with men in synagogues, when and why did gender separation begin? How do we reconcile the prescriptive rabbinic texts that claim the authority of divine revelation with the historical evidence that contradicts its laws regarding worship? Do Jewish women now have a "usable past"?

Yet while they acknowledged these ongoing problems, several scholars told us that Second Temple Judaism today is actively moving away from some of the most entrenched gender norms and religious biases. Perhaps aided by its existence at the intersections of communities, geographies, and methods, this area of study might have better gender parity, in part because it is less bound by confessional, theological scholarship in institutional contexts. In addition, like biblical studies this subfield is also shaped by Christianity, but not always to the same extent as, say, studies of the Pentateuch. One scholar summarized: "Because the sources are outside of the canon, the people who study the sources also can be."

The subfield of Second Temple Judaism is not a feminist utopia, but it helps illustrate the links between canonicity, Christianity, and gender issues in the scholarly realms of ancient Judaism.

I had a very different graduate school experience than a lot of other people because I had teachers who were largely women. The experience of having an all-female dissertation committee was really formative in a way that I didn't figure out until much later. Initially, I thought the field was a meritocracy, rewarding the best work, but then I saw the way that wasn't true, especially for women. And I also notice that it related to the quality of the work in the field: I realized how boring and hidebound scholarship was when it was the product of scholars in a male lineage field staring at the Pentateuch. I saw some women trying to convince those guys that they should be let in.

But now, I don't feel like trying to convince these men to take me and other female scholars seriously. I don't feel like trying to reform them, or make them more interesting, or more open to people's ideas. That's their own responsibility. There is much more exciting scholarship going on beyond these narrow conversations with a narrow group of scholars. I'm also convinced that's not where the future is. Someday they're just going to realize that they're sitting alone in a dark basement, and somebody shut the power off. The party is elsewhere now.

This scholar explains how her graduate education showed her the contrasting norms between certain kinds of biblical studies and others. The exclusivist impulses she saw in some corners of biblical studies went hand in hand with unimaginative scholarship.

She also makes a compelling prediction: scholarship that excludes and does not innovate will not create an interesting conversation. It will not be the center of excitement or new ways of thinking. That is not just because the scholarship is written by men, but also because of the exclusiveness of their conversations. Another scholar in the field emphasized the way that male-exclusive conversations produced inferior scholarship:

Part of what I find interesting about my experiences with sexism in Jewish studies, in comparison with other fields, is the degree to which it functions to foster male mediocrity at the expense of meritocracy. There are fields in which one sees all-male panels, etc., and might feel left out as a woman who has not been invited to participate. At least in my corners of Jewish studies, I have never seen a manel, manthology, etc., that is not so middling in quality that I wouldn't want even my name associated with it, let alone my time. All-male networks, in other words, permit the flourishing of scholars who could not otherwise make it—in my view, to the detriment of the field of Jewish studies at large and especially its academic reputation in the broader scholarly world. Women in Jewish studies play by the rules of meritocracy; their male counterparts quite often do not,

*especially but not only if they so happen to come from more tradi-
tional backgrounds.*

Both of these scholars emphasize a crucial point: scholarly conversation that includes only insiders is not only ethically problematic; it is also less productive intellectually. Indulging in a nostalgia
for Jewish learning will thus hold back the field from innovation,
creativity, and interesting scholarship; most important, nostalgic
scholarship, with its promotion of a patriarchal Jewish past, leaves
Jewish women trapped in what is often a useless or frozen past.

Conclusion

To be their best, fields of premodern Jewish studies need to cultivate a variety of scholarship and scholars, including women, gender
nonbinary people, and non-Jewish scholars who have not been socialized in the ways of learning in religious contexts. Changes in
Jewish communal life, such as the movements to educate Orthodox
women in Talmud, may be good for Judaism, but they alone will not
solve the problem within Jewish studies. In fact, they can feed the
issue of making those outside the observant Jewish community,
including non-Jews, feel like outsiders in the field of Jewish studies.
They let a few more people in, but they allow the fundamental dynamic to continue. As our interviewees observed, opening the field
to new approaches and methods, and, above all, to a variety of
people, creates more exciting scholarship.

From its inception, Jewish studies raised concern among Jews
that historical study would shatter the divinely revealed status of
religious texts. Approaching the Bible through methods of philology and archeology would challenge religious faith and practice.
Nostalgic belief that all Jews had been pious and observant of Jewish
law until the modern era was certainly shattered by historical discoveries and new methods of analysis, as were convictions that Jews
had endured a lachrymose history. The grip of nostalgia also affected the image of the scholar, imagined after the model of the

rabbi as a wise, learned man who spoke of the greatness of Judaism and exhorted Jews to greater piety, and certainly not a critical feminist, a woman, a trans person, a lesbian, or a scholar who at times overturns our cherished nostalgic myths but who also offers us historical accuracy and complicating interpretations.

6

Jewish Studies in the University

CONVERSATION PARTNERS AND INSTITUTIONAL STRUCTURES

YET ANOTHER ORIGIN STORY of academic Jewish studies in the United States begins in the 1960s and 1970s. During these years, Jewish studies course offerings increased dramatically at colleges and universities across the United States, academic programs opened, and students enrolled. The moment also marked the founding of many other interdisciplinary programs, including those often referred to as "ethnic studies," as well as women's studies. These often shared a reasoning behind creating a whole program, rather than just individual faculty positions in other departments: they were intrinsically interdisciplinary, and they were unlikely to receive sufficient institutional support from departments that often viewed them as marginal at best.[1]

The moment was optimistic for US universities, which had achieved a new importance and expansion following World War II. The GI Bill brought two million veterans to colleges, providing

---

1. Judith Baskin, "Jewish Studies in North American Colleges and Universities: Yesterday, Today, and Tomorrow," *Shofar* 32, no. 4 (2014): 11; and Marc Dollinger, *Black Power, Jewish Politics: Reinventing the Alliance in the 1960s* (Waltham, MA: Brandeis University Press, 2018). Dollinger credits Black studies with spurring the creation of Jewish studies programs.

upward economic mobility and (somewhat) greater racial diversity, and universities began to expand, with faculty increasing from 246,722 members in 1949, to 450,000 in 1969, and 675,000 at the end of the 1970s,[2] and student enrollments increasing from 3.6 million in 1959 to 8 million in 1969.[3] During the 1960s and 1970s, the number of institutions of higher education increased, and the total size of the student body tripled.[4] The baby boomer generation sent more Jews to college than had any previous generation. Jewish studies entered many US universities as McCarthyism diminished and requirements that faculty sign a loyalty oath ended, and campus support for the nascent civil rights movement grew.

The late 1960s and 1970s were also a moment when Jews in the United States identified more with their Jewishness. The Six-Day War in 1967 and the Yom Kippur War in 1973 brought Israel to the forefront of many American Jewish communal discussions. Increased discussion of the Holocaust permeated both academic and communal spaces. In US culture more broadly, groups like Irish and Italian Americans began to highlight their own distinctiveness as white ethnic groups, and Jews did too.[5] In 1972 Congress passed the Ethnic Heritage Act, which provided funding to elementary and secondary schools to learn about white ethnic groups. In this environment, Jewish students, Jewish parents, and Jewish donors saw value in a curriculum in Jewish studies.

In these years, the "postwar race for prestige" among the universities also led to preferential hiring of men.[6] Jobs were plentiful, but, for example, "female scientists who did find work rarely made it onto the tenure track or else were shunted off into minor

2. Ellen Schrecker, *The Lost Promise: American Universities in the 1960s* (Chicago: University of Chicago Press, 2021), 19.

3. Schrecker, 13.

4. Schrecker, 13.

5. Matthew Frye Jacobson, *Roots Too: White Ethnic Revival in Post–Civil Rights America* (Cambridge, MA: Harvard University Press, 2006).

6. Schrecker, *Lost Promise*, 21.

fields and inferior positions."[7] Jews were better represented on faculties than they had been in the past, but some also encountered overt discrimination when applying for faculty positions.[8] Many colleges began offering Jewish studies courses by hiring a local male rabbi (women were just beginning to be ordained to be rabbis in the 1970s and 1980s) to teach a class on Judaism.

As it grew, Jewish studies had to reinvent itself as a profession suitable to the US academy. In the fall of 1969, the Association for Jewish Studies (AJS) was founded by a small group of forty-seven academics who sought to promote and professionalize the field. Their effort marked a generational break with older scholars and with the American Academy for Jewish Research, which had been founded in 1919.[9] Within the AJS, fissures emerged over concerns that echo to this day: should professors of Jewish studies be practicing Jews; should a doctorate in the field or a rabbinical ordination qualify a scholar; should academic teaching reflect a "Jewish" or "Zionist" point of view; what questions and topics should govern the field; and how much—if at all—should Jewish studies engage theoretical debates of neighboring academic disciplines.

In the 1960s and 1970s, it also became clear that not all efforts for inclusion were necessarily aligned. The 1975 UN Decade for Women conference in Mexico City in 1975 called for "the elimination of colonialism and neo-colonialism, foreign occupation, Zionism, apartheid, [and] racial discrimination in all its forms," which many understood to be an accusation of racism against all Zionists.[10] Many Jewish feminists felt betrayed by feminist

7. Schrecker, 21.

8. Schrecker, 20.

9. Kristen Loveland, "The Association for Jewish Studies: A Brief History," Association for Jewish Studies, 40th Annual Conference, December 2008, 2–3, https://www.associationforjewishstudies.org/docs/default-source/ajs-history/ajs-history.pdf?sfvrsn=2.

10. For a retrospective analysis that includes Jewish perspectives, see Ellen Cantarow, "Zionism, Anti-Semitism and Jewish Identity in the Women's Movement," *Middle East Report*, no. 154 (September 1988): 38–50.

movements and forced to choose between elements of their identity. Many Jewish studies scholars became suspicious that women's studies scholars and programs harbored antisemitism, and many women's studies scholars felt that support of Israel was supporting oppression of Palestinians.

These tensions continued to shape the field for years to come. The first conference on women and the Holocaust was held at Yeshiva University's Stern College in 1983, organized by Joan Ringelheim, a pioneering scholar on women in the ghettos. Scholarly papers were delivered, and the audience responded with questions and personal testimony, often very emotional. Among the speakers and audience members were women survivors and children of survivors asking about the specific conditions and problems faced by women in ghettos and camps. In some ghettos, for instance, women and the elderly were selected first by the Jewish Councils for deportation. At some concentration camps, pregnant women and women with small children were sent by the SS to gas chambers rather than hard labor, giving men a greater chance of survival. Some scholars argued, based on diaries and memoirs, that Jewish women in concentration camps more easily established bonds of friendship and care that helped them survive the horrific conditions. Yet the research had barely begun before attacks began. Writing in *Commentary* magazine, one of the editors claimed that "feminist scholarship on the Holocaust is intended explicitly to serve the purposes of consciousness-raising—i.e., propaganda . . . validating feminist theory" aiming "to sever Jewish women, in their own minds, from their families as well as from the larger Jewish community" by "painting the Nazis less as antisemites than as 'sexists.'"[11]

The hostility toward the very question of Jewish women's unique experiences diminished over time, and scholarship on

11. Gabriel Schoenfeld, "Auschwitz and the Professors," *Commentary* 105, no. 6 (June 1998): 45.

Jewish women during the Holocaust has grown, but that moment remains a reminder of the hostility toward new modes of inquiry that do not center on white, Ashkenazic, cis heterosexual men. One Holocaust studies scholar explains:

> I think when I started in Holocaust studies it was a far more male-dominated field but [it] has rapidly had a lot more women involved in the field. As a result it has gotten a lot better. [About a decade] ago I wrote an article on rape of Jewish women during the Holocaust. I had great reviews of the piece, but the older male editor of the most important journal in Holocaust studies rejected the article because, despite the reviewer feedback and my scholarship, he simply refused to believe that Jewish women were raped during the Holocaust. The article was finally published (with no revisions from the one that was rejected), and the idea that Jewish women experienced rape during the Holocaust has become so mainstream as to seem ridiculous to younger scholars that this was a controversial issue. Gender studies in Holocaust studies was so much later to arrive than in other segments of European or world history. Questions about women's role in history coincided with second-wave feminism. By the mid-1980s when Holocaust scholars pushed for examining women's experiences during the Holocaust, they got the kind of pushback that scholars of women had experienced over a decade before in mainstream history. It wasn't until the late 1990s that we really saw any production of such scholarship in Holocaust studies beyond the smallest trickle of works. For a field with as much output as Holocaust studies, that is ridiculous.

A woman who organized a conference on women and holocaust theology at a European university told us that while rabbinics, philology, history, and the social sciences were "masculine" fields, theology was disparaged by her male colleagues as a "feminine" field.

As this scholar suggests, a host of factors matter for when and where women's and gender studies scholarship earns respect and its rightful place in Jewish studies.

Today, even as tenure-track positions increasingly are eliminated in favor of adjunct teaching at many colleges and universities, Jewish studies remains a field that offers new faculty positions, from postdoctoral fellowships for newly minted PhDs to endowed professorships for seasoned scholars (nearly all of whom were men in the first decades, though there is more gender diversity in these positions now). When the funding came from donors, rather than the university's own budget, new dilemmas emerged: Were the professors appointed to meet the academic needs of students and colleagues or the political interests and gender preferences of the Jewish community? Moreover, was the university administration's primary allegiance to its faculty or its donors?

Such questions continue to be debated: Should Jewish studies as a field engage the concerns of the academy or promote Jewish identity and communal concerns? Gender helped to configure that debate. By the 1980s and 1990s, the Jewish feminist movement was bringing major changes to Jewish religious practices and increased access of classical Jewish texts to women, and those changes affected Jewish studies as well. The early annual meetings of the AJS were intended to cultivate Jewish studies as a serious research field whose presence at the university was essential to its academic mission. Still, at the annual conference banquet, AJS members recited together the grace after meals, *birkat hamazon,* over the protests of those who thought religious expression should remain private at an academic meeting. The public prayers continued until one year when Professor Jane Gerber, the first woman to serve as AJS president (1979–81), stood up to lead the prayers. The practice of public prayer quickly ended, likely because those who advocated public prayers were also those who opposed a woman leading the prayers.[12] In 1986, the Women's Caucus was founded within the AJS, and the proportion of women members of the AJS has risen from 10 percent in the 1970s to over 50 percent today.

---

12. Loveland, "Association for Jewish Studies," 7.

During the 1980s, the number of Jewish studies scholars grew, and the field attracted some scholars whose training was not necessarily in the study of Jewish history or texts yet who nonetheless saw the study of Jews as a creative way to think with new theoretical approaches in literary theory, cultural studies, and gender. In 1985, the AJS became a constituent member of the American Council of Learned Societies. That acceptance, after several unsuccessful applications, served as a final validation, with the larger academic world recognizing Jewish studies as "an important and well-populated field of study" with a "unique intellectual focus and interdisciplinary concerns."[13]

The field was becoming intellectually vibrant and stood at the forefront of new methods and ideas. Jewish studies expanded quickly; by the 1990s, the AJS counted over four thousand courses offered nationwide, excluding those of rabbinical schools. In the 1970s, applicants for teaching positions were vetted by the senior AJS leadership. Graduate students were required "to fill out a form listing universities attended, Jewish training, knowledge of Hebrew and Yiddish, their major academic interest and thesis topics, and to provide the signature of a Regular AJS Member."[14] That sort of private vetting by an old boys' club allowed the mostly male senior scholars of the AJS to select and promote certain graduate students for academic positions. Objections from graduate students in the 1980s ultimately led to an open listing of available academic positions. Nonetheless, nearly all the senior full professorships in Jewish studies were occupied by men well into the 1990s.

Despite the growing presence of Jewish studies programs at US universities, and Jewish scholars working within women's studies and other interdisciplinary fields, faculty in Jewish studies often found themselves excluded (or excluded themselves) from the multicultural agenda that was beginning to shape the curriculum

13. Baskin, "Jewish Studies in North American Colleges and Universities," 12.
14. Loveland, "Association for Jewish Studies," 9.

in the 1990s. The conservative nature of Jewish studies made it anachronistic to multiculturalism, and its exclusion kept it from exploring the methods and theories promoted by the newer theoretical modalities of multiculturalism.

At a roundtable discussion, "Does the English Department Have a Jewish Problem," held at the 2009 annual meeting of the Modern Language Association, panelists noted the absence of a concentration in Jewish American literature from the ten most important American doctoral programs in English, despite the impact of Jewish literature and culture in the United States.[15] The discussion continued in a special issue of the journal *Melus*, published in 2012, where Jonathan Freedman articulated the problem: "ethnic" literature was defined in multicultural categorization as nonwhite, whereas Jews were defined as white, and American Jewish literary output was thus excluded from the category of ethnic. At stake was not "ethnicity" but the subaltern position held by a particular group, and Jews were defined on the side of power.[16]

Yet the discussion ignored gender. Do all Jews hold the power of "whiteness"? Are Jewish women "Jews" or "women"? Do women lose their status as "women" if they are defined as Jews? Many women, even the subaltern, may have access to a limited degree of patriarchal privilege thanks to fathers, brothers, and male partners and friends, but not all Jewish women are white, wealthy, or powerful, including within the Jewish community: ask an *agunah*. Today 10 to 15 percent of Jews are people of color. White Jewish women may experience the privilege of whiteness while suffering from the discrimination and denigration of sexism. Investigating the relationship of research on Jews to a multicultural agenda, Bryan Cheyette argues that postcolonial theorists align "the Jews" with white European imperialism rather than

15. The presentations were published in the Summer 2012 issue of *Melus* 37, no. 2.

16. Jonathan Freedman, "Do American and Ethnic American Studies Have a Jewish Problem; or, When Is an Ethnic Not an Ethnic, and What Should We Do about It?," *Melus* 37, no. 2 (2012): 19–40.

recognizing the many Jews among those colonized or targeted for destruction. Jews, he claims, constitute a "repressed Jewish other" within postcolonial ideology, which excludes Jews from the category of insurgents fighting against imperialism and betrays "the common wretchedness of different men, the common enslavement of extensive social groups," Cheyette writes, using Frantz Fanon's formulation.[17] Contemporary theorists, under postcolonial influence, often ignore women's particularity and stumble over the complexity of Jews, which mirrors that of women: women can be found among the most powerful and among the most impoverished, and Jews have been both beneficiaries of imperial power and among its greatest victims, as Melanie Kaye-Kantrowitz has pointed out.[18]

Male, female, and nonbinary Jews both fit multicultural paradigms and do not fit at all. Jews of all genders were among the murdered victims within Europe in the Holocaust and yet were also among its most accomplished economic and intellectual citizens; they were targets of antisemitism yet achieved great success in assimilation. Jewish studies confounds categories of multiculturalism because Jews are both the colonized of Europe and European colonizers, examples of Michael Hardt and Antonio Negri's global "ontological empire" as well as the ultimate "other";[19] Jews are the objects of Edward Said's European Orientalist discourse and the cocreators of European Islamic studies.[20] But gender, sexuality, misogyny, and patriarchy configure each of these

17. Frantz Fanon, "Racism and Culture," quoted in Bryan Cheyette, *Diasporas of the Mind: Jewish and Postcolonial Writing and the Nightmare of History* (New Haven, CT: Yale University Press, 2018), 59.

18. Melanie Kaye-Kantrowitz, *The Colors of Jews: Racial Politics and Radical Diasporism* (Bloomington: Indiana University Press, 2007); see also the recent collection edited by Maud Mandel, Lisa Leff, and Ethan Katz: *Colonialism and the Jews* (Bloomington: Indiana University Press, 2017).

19. Michael Hardt and Antonio Negri, *Empire* (Cambridge, MA: Harvard University Press, 2000), 354.

20. See Edward Said, *Orientalism* (New York: Vintage, 1978).

experiences in complex ways. Unfortunately, even some theorists within Jewish studies fail to consider gender in their work, while Jewish feminist theorists sometimes fail to draw the connections between women and Jews and the usefulness of feminist theory to illuminate Jewish experience. The most sophisticated conceptual categories of the academy, especially within feminist scholarship, illuminate Jewish experience. Like women, Jews, too, experience Eve Sedgwick's "definitional crisis" and Judith Butler's "constitutive ambiguity."[21] Jews do not possess Jewish identity but perform it, creating Jewishness through the dynamics of citationality, much as gender is created and performed through similar dynamics. Yet without considering the specific regime of gender within a given location, social stratum, economic status, and political and religious regime, understanding of Jewish experiences remains narrowly defined around a percentage of male-identified Jews. The complexities of Jewishness potentially make Jewish studies one of the most exciting fields and one that benefits from theoretical modalities that complicate rather than simplify our analyses.

Those who rethink Jews through the lenses of theory, however, are at times treated as outliers within Jewish studies, and feminist scholarship is often at the margins of the field, an "add-on," as we demonstrated in chapter 1. Moreover, multicultural explorations within Jewish studies are sometimes treated similarly. Scholars of Sephardic Jews, for example, have long found their work marginal to Jewish history, which has centered on Europe. The history of Zionism is told as a European story, with Mizrahi and African Jews as latecomers to the State of Israel. Models of Jewish modernity are nearly always male and Eurocentric, ignoring the vastly different experiences of Jews in North Africa and the Middle East, including Jewish women, who participated in the Nahda (Arab

21. Judith Butler, "Against Proper Objects: Introduction," *Differences: A Journal of Feminist Cultural Studies* 6, no. 2 (1994): 6; Eve Kosofsky Sedgwick, *Epistemology of the Closet* (Berkeley: University of California Press, 2008), 20.

renaissance), and whose political conditions under colonialism were far different from those of European Jews coping with the quest for emancipation. Jewish involvement in colonialism, both as colonizers and as colonized, is a recently introduced topic, as is study of Jewish-owned slave plantations in the Caribbean. Yet it is often these new areas of study that not only reveal neglected aspects of Jewish history, especially of women, but also give us insights into particular Jewish religious and political entanglements in aspects of modernity that bring Jewish studies into conversation with the issues raised by critical attention to race, including enslavement of Africans. The historian Natalie Zemon Davis, for example, asks how Jews in Suriname reconciled their Passover celebration of freedom from enslavement when they enslaved people on their plantations.[22] Philosophers might consider how the transatlantic slave trade, so important to the economy of Amsterdam, affected Spinoza's understanding of freedom.

Is Jewish studies *at* the university or *of* the university? The question continues to be debated and bears implications for gender within the field. If Jewish studies is a branch of the Jewish community on campus, women and nonbinary scholars in the field may reflect the marginal position of women and nonbinary leaders in some sectors of the larger Jewish community. If Jewish studies is truly integral to the university, the field will have to accord the same respect for women and nonbinary scholars and for the scholarship on women and gender that is integral to university culture and academic scholarship. Several factors affect the answers to these questions, including the often marginal status of Jewish studies, the state of interdisciplinary and multicultural networks, and the impact of philanthropy on Jewish studies.

22. Natalie Zemon Davis, "Regaining Jerusalem: Eschatology and Slavery in Jewish Colonization in Seventeenth-Century Suriname," *Cambridge Journal of Postcolonial Literary Inquiry* 3, no. 1 (January 2016): 11–38; see also Aviva Ben-Ur, *Jewish Autonomy in a Slave Society: Suriname in the Atlantic World, 1651–1825* (Philadelphia: University of Pennsylvania Press, 2020).

Jewish Studies beyond the United States

While this book is focused on women in the field of Jewish studies in the United States, we want to give voice to women and nonbinary colleagues overseas with a few brief examples of their experiences and the structures of Jewish studies programs. Most Jewish studies scholars work on topics outside the United States and spend time studying and researching abroad; thus they have to cope with the academic and cultural disparities and biases particular to those locales that invariably affect women and nonbinary scholars.

At some British universities, for example, Jewish studies is affiliated most closely with units of theology or divinity. Jewish studies in the Netherlands has a long history of Christian Hebraism, and Italy, too, has a long and rich history of Jewish scholarship. The large Jewish community in pre–World War II Poland also had a remarkable community of Jewish scholars, and Polish universities today are encouraging scholarship on Jews and Judaism. Faculty in Jewish studies can be found at universities in other parts of Europe as well, including France, Belgium, Serbia, Ukraine, and the Scandinavian countries. Some of the leading scholars in Europe are women, and gender theory has played an important role in their work.

The largest number of Jewish studies programs in Europe are at German universities, which have established professorships and institutes in a range of subfields and produce an enormous number of publications each year. Scholars pay significant attention to the study of antisemitism and the Holocaust and its aftermath; German Jewish philosophers; images of Jews in German literature; and the history of Jews in the Holy Roman Empire and in Germany. In addition, archival sources pertaining to Jews have led to historical discoveries; perhaps most interesting are the medieval *genizot* discovered in the attics of former synagogues and the accidental Jewish archeological finds of Jewish material culture uncovered by chance during excavations for building projects.

While women have made important advances in all fields at German universities, problems remain—but so do opportunities. Some of the most interesting and important work on German antisemitism comes from women scholars whose initial field was gender and German literature. Their training in feminist analysis gave them a deeper awareness of the cultural production of anti-Jewish stereotypes in German culture. Yet women in the German academy told us of significant incidents of gender discrimination, as did American women who studied there or taught as visiting professors in Germany. The specifics may differ, but the underlying problems are familiar. One of our colleagues told us of her experience:

> I worked at a respected German institution, where the president of an important research foundation arrived at a reception, sat next to me, showed me the invitation letter, and remarked in a friendly way: "Just to let you know: my name is spelled incorrectly here." I let him know in my most charming manner that I was not the secretary—and at least he felt a bit ashamed.

Male professors directing endowed institutes often invite male colleagues to deliver lectures or serve as visiting professors, which makes it difficult for women students and faculty to receive recognition and respect for their research projects, our interviewees told us. Given what we explained about scholarly networks in chapter 1, this should not be a surprise, but we hope it is a situation that can be changed.

Elsewhere, such as in Poland, a new enthusiasm for Jewish history is reflected in the growing number of professors of Jewish studies at the universities. Scholarship on Jews in Poland has led to a host of archival discoveries, including about the rise of Hasidism and Jewish social history. The Jewish Historical Institute in Warsaw has long been a repository of important documents, including the Ringelblum archives from the Warsaw ghetto. As in so many other countries now run by authoritarian regimes, with antisemitism on the rise, Jewish studies is a field that falls under political pressure, while at the same time offering the possibility of resistance to antisemitic politics and ideologies and support for a future democratic regime. Some European scholars are working actively to elevate the status of women faculty and the study of gender and sexuality within Jewish studies. They see both problems and reasons for hope. One Polish colleague told us:

> In Jewish studies and related fields, it is almost exclusively women and queer men who work on gender studies issues. The best you can hope for as far as straight, male allies is researchers who will add a gender component to their research [in hopes of that improving the likelihood they will receive a grant]. "Gender history" is still focused on women, and it is still dealing with issues like "giving agency" to women in history and telling women's stories. It also addresses intersections with class, though, so perhaps this will help open the space for Jewish histories that engage gender critically.

She recalled a moment when a speaker addressed "our (male) colleagues" (since Polish is a gendered language, it was clear the speaker was addressing men). "Oh, this is not for me!" our interviewee thought. This was for men. Men were the important audience. "There is an awful lot of work to be done on this level," she concluded.

Sexual harassment, too, can happen in any country. There are no internationally recognized standards of appropriate behavior, which can make interactions confusing or uncomfortable. Differences in culture can also make people second-guess whether something was really inappropriate. Yet while there may be cultural confusion over whether two kisses is an appropriate greeting for a colleague, things like ignoring women during academic events or making explicitly sexual comments clearly are not appropriate. We heard problems of gender discrimination and harassment from colleagues working across the globe. A senior woman professor from the United States told us about the varieties of sexism she experienced from European and Israeli male colleagues while spending a year at a European research center:

The French and Italian men made explicit sexual overtures, the British men were condescending, and the Israeli and German men simply ignored me and whatever any of the women said at our seminars. I'm not making a blanket statement about these cultures. I realized that women have to adjust to different gender cultures when our research takes us to other countries, but what annoyed me was that the men didn't seem to think they had to change their behavior. They made comments even in public settings about women and about feminist scholarship that shocked me.

Sexist behavior toward women students and faculty can be especially damaging given the small size of European countries, the lack of diversity among faculty, and the outsized role played by doctoral advisers in their students' future careers.

These examples are not meant to be exhaustive; there is so much scholarship on Jews and Judaism conducted around the world that we would need several books to describe its many institutional histories, contexts, finances, and scholarly productivity. But these examples suggest that national histories and cultures of higher education play a substantial role in determining who studies, what they study, the methods they use to study, and who has the opportunities to present their scholarship in the international forum of ideas.

Philanthropy, Gender, and Politics

Jewish studies in the United States has benefited enormously from generous philanthropy, often from Jewish donors who have established university professorships, but the field has also been vulnerable to a changing and increasingly polarized political landscape. The complexities of women's roles and gender attitudes have affected both donors and recipients. During the 1980s and 1990s, Jewish concerns about intermarriage spurred donations to Jewish studies courses in hopes of strengthening the Jewish identity of students. In more recent years, however, Jewish philanthropy has shifted to concern over political attitudes toward Israel, Zionism, and antisemitism among faculty and students on campuses.

Jewish studies, of course, also sits in a wider context of higher education, and the economics of higher education have changed significantly in the past decades. Universities and colleges are supported by tuition, the return on their endowment investments, government support, grants from foundations, and private philanthropic gifts. Additional amounts can be generated by sports events, grants earned by faculty, rental of facilities, and other "branding" efforts. Although we might reasonably discuss the ethics or implications for Jewish studies of any of these sources, our concern here is with philanthropy, the major source of funding for Jewish studies programs in the United States, and its impact on women.

Philanthropic support for colleges and universities in the United States stems primarily from individuals, often as channeled through their charitable foundations, and it is on the rise, having increased to about $58 billion in 2023.[23] Unfortunately, more and more often gifts are restricted donations to an institution—that is, donors specify a program or cause rather than donating for unrestricted use by the university. Philanthropy—which Alison Bernstein, a former vice president of the Ford Foundation, has called the "closest cousin" of higher education—has always had a social agenda.[24] "Since the late 1960s, a few key philanthropies— Ford, Rockefeller, Carnegie, and Mellon—encouraged scholars to take a fresh look at the curriculum in terms of gender, especially in the social sciences and humanities," Bernstein writes.[25] Private philanthropy also played a crucial role in providing education for women, establishing Black colleges, and developing particular

23. Council for Advancement and Support of Education, "Giving to U.S. College and Universities at $58 Billion in Fiscal Year 23," February 21, 2024, https://www.case.org/resources/giving-us-college-and-universities-58-billion-fiscal-year-2023.

24. Alison R. Bernstein, *Funding the Future: Philanthropy's Influence on American Higher Education* (New York: Rowman and Littlefield, 2014), xxi.

25. Bernstein, 5.

fields. Philanthropy also targeted reforms in business and legal education, most notably during the Cold War of the 1950s, when the Carnegie and Ford Foundations shaped the emergence of Latin American, African, and Asian studies.[26] Such philanthropy "played an indispensable role in making American higher education quantitatively and qualitatively different from any other higher education sector in the world."[27] Some private philanthropists also sought to reform universities and make them more accessible to students from poor and working-class backgrounds. Jewish philanthropists have donated unrestricted funds to universities and have also been indispensable in establishing Jewish studies programs.

During the 1980s and 1990s, Bernstein notes, conservative philanthropists increasingly shifted from responding to universities' liberal agendas to creating agendas of their own. Small conservative foundations, whose money generally comes from private individuals, created research centers promoting libertarian economics and conservative politics on campuses where liberal and progressive political views have dominated. As Nancy MacLean has argued in her study of the radical right, targeting educational institutions was part of a national Republican Party strategy in the United States to influence public policy.[28] Claiming that universities lean left, with predominantly left-wing faculty teaching a left-wing curriculum, conservative foundations use their financial clout to influence academia.

Jewish philanthropy to universities has followed a similar trajectory, shifting from unrestricted support for Jewish studies to targeted political causes, including regarding the State of Israel. Over the past two decades, professorships and programs in

26. Ellen Condiffe Lagemann, *The Politics of Knowledge: The Carnegie Corporation, Philanthropy, and Public Policy* (Chicago: University of Chicago Press, 1992).

27. Bernstein, *Funding the Future*, xxvi.

28. Nancy MacLean, *Democracy in Chains: The Deep History of the Radical Right's Stealth Plan for America* (New York: Viking / Penguin Random House, 2017).

Israel studies have been funded around the United States, and while they are intended to be scholarly, they are also intended to promote support for Israel on campus. Some Jewish donors view universities as a battleground, where combatants seek influence over American attitudes toward Israel. Whereas many donors once supported Jewish studies in an effort to enhance Jewish knowledge and encourage the commitment of Jewish students, many have shifted their goals in recent years away from influencing Jewish students to addressing academia's critics of Israel. (In truth, the notion that professors' political views influence students on the Israel/Palestine issue has little support. As one recent study summarized, "Contrary to much commentary, but consonant with a significant stream of scholarship, campus effects are weak to nonexistent" in creating "anti-Israel" attitudes.)[29]

One prominent donor priority of the past fifty years has been to respond to the dire predictions of rising assimilation and intermarriage and a declining Jewish birthrate. Studies by the sociologist Steven M. Cohen, discussed in chapter 3, were funded by large-scale donors and—not surprisingly—provided the justification for their philanthropic decisions. Cohen raised the alarm that non-Orthodox Jews were not having enough children to maintain their numbers, and the majority were intermarrying and had little connection to the Jewish community. At this rate, he argued, non-Orthodox Jews would disappear. How to maintain continuity? Cohen's answer was to encourage endogamy and increase fertility. (In chapter 3 we discussed how this research agenda intersected with his sexual harassment and assault of women scholars.) Jewish studies donors' commitments reflected other Jewish communal projects that were often visible on campus. Birthright Israel, for example, became a tool to encourage young Jews to

29. Rachel Shenhav-Goldberg and Jeffrey S. Kopstein, "Antisemitism on a California Campus: Perceptions and Views among Students," *Contemporary Jewry* 40, no. 2 (June 2020): 237.

marry one another, and funding of Jewish studies at many universities sought to stimulate the Jewish identity of Jewish students.

Philanthropy at universities is triangulated: donors, recipients, and professional fund-raisers. Where does gender fit in? Philanthropists are powerful figures essential to universities, many of which have large administrative units devoted to "advancement" or "development" and cultivating donors, an effort that is often gendered in troubling ways. Advancement departments tend to be filled with a high percentage of women at the lower ranks, and most of the donors who are approached are men, primarily middle-aged or older alumni whose college experience occurred forty, fifty, or sixty years earlier, in an era in which the vast majority of professors and administrators were male. Women's studies and Jewish studies barely existed, and few women students pursued graduate degrees. For women faculty hoping to raise funding for their programs, relations with both development administrators and donors can be fraught.

One woman who holds a leadership position in Jewish studies at her institution told us:

> Fund-raising is one of the things that most deeply concerns me about Jewish studies. The role of philanthropy and wealthy people in our society has so many implications. As opposed to, say, universities funded primarily by taxing, you have donors deciding what's important to them. I also think it has implications for gender. The previous [professor in my role] was very buddy-buddy with the donor. That is not how I would describe my relationship with him. If you have rich Jewish male donors, is there a certain kind of synergy that gets created with certain kinds of male professors?

Fund-raising for Jewish studies is affected by men's dominance in positions of leadership in the Jewish community and by the role of Jewish philanthropists and organizations in financing academic positions. As a 2021 report prepared by a Jewish nonprofit leadership initiative notes, "Most people working at Jewish nonprofits are women. But most CEOs of Jewish nonprofits—especially at the largest organizations—are men."[30] Many Jewish communities, and even some Jewish studies scholars, insist that faculty serve as representatives of the Jewish community on campus. Individual donors and local organizations such as Jewish Federations often provide financial support for lectures, conferences, and even professorships in the field, and some not only participate in raising the funds to establish a Jewish studies professorship or program but also occasionally participate in the selection of the professor who will hold that position.[31] This raises concerns about donors steering the ship in terms of what is studied as well as who is hired. As Judith Baskin, a former president of the AJS, has written, "Dependence on donor generosity has also raised challenging issues of academic objectivity versus parochial communal agendas; questions of undue emphasis placed on donors' particular interests and propensities; and concern over the increasing amount of faculty time and effort devoted to fundraising activities."[32] Major controversies have broken out over publications by some scholars. In 1996, Howard Eilberg-Schwartz, a pioneer in gender analysis of Jewish texts, "made the decision to leave the academy because he could not reconcile the competing requirements of his academic freedom and those of the community that funded his academic position."[33]

30. Leading Edge, "The Gender Gap in Jewish Non-profit Leadership: An Eco-system View," 2021, https://leading-edge.cdn.prismic.io/leading-edge/aacd0b8e -5a8a-4c4b-b62a-d0ae6dd3333e_The+Gender+Gap+in+Jewish+Nonprofit+Lead ership+%E2%80%94+An+Ecosystem+View-2021-10-21.pdf.

31. Liam Adams, "Anxieties over a Donor's Role in a Faculty Search Boil Over at Case Western," *Chronicle of Higher Education*, October 12, 2017, https://www .chronicle.com/article/anxieties-over-a-donors-role-in-a-faculty-search-boil-over-at -case-western/; and Aaron W. Hughes, "Jewish Studies and Local Communities," JewSchool, blogpost, May 4, 2016, https://jewschool.com/jewish-studies-and-local -communities-76638.

32. Baskin, "Jewish Studies in North American Colleges and Universities," 19.

33. Laurie L. Patton, *Who Owns Religion? Scholars and Their Publics in the Late Twentieth Century* (Chicago: University of Chicago Press, 2019), 201.

Major Jewish donors to universities are often guided by Jewish communal priorities and politics, and by executive directors of local Jewish Federations, who are more likely to be men;[34] this can affect women and nonbinary scholars' success in leadership positions. A recent study by the Hewlett Foundation demonstrates that philanthropy is guided by peers.[35] When the Jewish studies program chair is a man, male Jewish communal leaders, heads of foundations, and alumni may see him and relate to him differently than they would to a woman. When donors viewing the gendered hierarchy of university development offices see men at the top and women at lower levels, that, too, affects their perceptions of the status of women scholars within the university.

While most job descriptions in Jewish studies do not require membership in a religious community or participation in the local Jewish community, "an increasing number of positions funded by communities or deeply connected to local communities do indeed come with that expectation. The meeting points between the two, and the necessary rules of engagement in public discourse, may not overlap at all."[36] One professor who spoke with us expressed worry that successful fund-raising for Jewish studies affects other academic units' perceptions of Jewish studies programs and faculty:

> The rich Jewish donor to Jewish studies creates all kinds of problems for faculty. I think it creates a perceptual problem within colleges and universities—this impression that it's an implant. How does that shape the way our peers and students see what we do? So many students taking Jewish studies courses, for example, come in

34. Rosenfeld reports that women run 43 percent of Jewish Federations in North America, but only two of the top twenty according to size. Arno Rosenfeld, "Who Runs the Largest Jewish Federations? Not Women," *Forward*, September 8, 2022, https://forward.com/news/517128/women-jewish-federations-north-america/.

35. William and Flora Hewlett Foundation, "Peer to Peer: At the Heart of Influencing More Effective Philanthropy," February 13, 2017, https://hewlett.org/peer-to-peer-at-the-heart-of-influencing-more-effective-philanthropy/.

36. Patton, *Who Owns Religion?*, 221.

thinking it's some kind of advocacy. Some donors want it to be too. These assumptions create a lot of misunderstanding.

Blurry lines between Jewish studies, donors, and Jewish communal interests are not distinctive to Jewish studies; they are mirrored in other fields as well, such as the studies of Hinduism, Islam, and Christianity.[37] Scholars in those fields have also encountered difficulties with communal leaders who sometimes object quite vociferously to the ways in which scholars study their religions, including gender analyses. Scholars struggle with the complexity of having donors with a particular set of interests who want to promote a certain worldview or set of political positions. Donors have withdrawn their gifts, refused to fulfill their pledges, and ended their contributions because they have objected to political comments made by professors. Two of the most widely reported cases involved senior women scholars in Israel studies.[38] At times donors have used their financial clout to undermine faculty and actively prevent the hiring of people. Sometimes university administrators have bowed to that pressure, and sometimes they have protected the independence of the institution and the academic freedom of faculty. For women, the task is even more complex. Women in leadership must produce scholarship, run programming, and navigate obligations to the university administration, while cultivating donors who are often older men.

37. For a few examples, see Elizabeth Redden, "Return to Sender," *Inside Higher Ed*, February 21, 2016, https://www.insidehighered.com/news/2016/02/22/uc -irvine-moves-reject-endowed-chair-gifts-donor-strong-opinions-about-study; Elizabeth Redden, "A Donor's Demands, a Revoked Chair," *Inside Higher Ed*, May 24, 2019, https://www.insidehighered.com/news/2019/05/24/professor-says-au-cairo -wronged-him-canceling-his-chair-after-he-resisted-donors; and Elizabeth Redden, "Grant for Islamic Studies Put on Indefinite Hold," *Inside Higher Ed*, January 8, 2008, https://www.insidehighered.com/news/2008/01/08/grant-islamic-studies-put -indefinite-hold.

38. Francie Diep, "'It's Outrageous': 2 Donor Conflicts Reveal Tensions for Jewish-Studies Scholars," *Chronicle of Higher Education*, March 10, 2022, https://www .chronicle.com/article/its-outrageous-2-donor-conflicts-reveal-fraught-tensions-for -jewish-studies-scholars.

Women in Jewish studies have told us about difficulties navigating donor relationships. Some women told us that their universities preferred to showcase male faculty to donors in hopes of creating a male-male bond. Quite a few women described inappropriate hugs or sexually provocative remarks from male donors. Should a woman scholar endanger a potential donation of millions to her program by not tolerating a man who makes inappropriate comments or touching? Several women have told us that they faced precisely that dilemma. The pressure to please the mostly male cohort of donors is fierce, and expressing a complaint of harassment would likely end the donation. At one large Jewish studies program in Europe, female graduate students, postdoctoral fellows, and junior faculty were asked to "mingle" with a group of older male donors. One woman from that program told us that she and the other women felt "treated like escorts." One man sat next to her, started touching her, and suggested they go dancing. She extricated herself and complained to the director of the program, a woman, who told her, "I can't do anything about that" and continued to demand that she attend receptions with the donors. She refused. At a different institute, a woman who complained to her female supervisor about a male donor who had harassed her was told, "these are weak men" and "he was in love with you." Program directors like these should protect women from harassment and assault, not enable the men's harassment, acting, as one woman remarked, "like pimps or whorehouse madams." Male donors, in a position of power thanks to the wealth they could choose to bestow (or not), felt free to exercise their power over the young women scholars who, in turn, were beholden to their supervisors for financial support for their research projects. Ultimately, everyone involved knew that money would create strengths in the Jewish studies program—additional faculty, stipends for graduate students, funding for conferences and lectures—that would bring opportunities and prestige all around.[39]

39. For a discussion of a few of the Jewish philanthropists who have been exposed for sexual harassment, see Keren McGinity, *#UsToo: How Jewish, Muslim, and Christian Women Changed Our Communities* (London: Routledge, 2023), 26–31.

To be successful in fund-raising, a scholar needs support from colleagues and from the community; as Baskin writes, local rabbis are "often a source of endowment funding from wealthy members of the Jewish community."[40] Like almost everyone in the field of Jewish studies, we have observed colleagues cultivating potential donors with flattery but also with ideological commitments. We also know colleagues who have suffered because donors do not approve of their area of scholarship or the arguments in their publications. Jewish donors often have an image of Judaism that is drawn from synagogues or communal organizations and do not realize that scholars take a different, critical approach in their work. Sexism on campus—from faculty, administrators, and students—can damage a woman scholar's reputation in the community or convince her university that her position or research would not be a good recipient of support from a donor. One woman told us that she was the first woman appointed to teach Jewish studies at a small university. She arrived on campus only to be shunned by her Jewish male colleagues, who would not even greet her when they passed on campus, let alone work with her as part of a team in the program. They ultimately succeeded in spreading negative rumors about her within the local Jewish community, shattering that possible source of fund-raising: she left the university, unwilling to work in a hostile environment.

We are not the first to notice the distinctive role of donors in Jewish studies and how this dynamic affects women. As Jennifer Thompson points out, in Jewish studies, "philanthropic influence can affect women differently than men, both because of an expectation that women will tolerate sexual harassment by philanthropists in order to secure their program's future and because of funding priorities that can be understood as sexist."[41] Of these funding priorities, "Jewish continuity"—the bearing and raising of Jewish children—clearly puts a more significant onus on

40. Baskin, "Jewish Studies in North American Colleges and Universities," 20.

41. Jennifer Thompson, "The Birdcage: Gender Inequity in Academic Jewish Studies," *Contemporary Jewry* 39, no. 3 (2019): 427–46, quote on 429.

women, given social assumptions about who is responsible for children. As Lila Corwin Berman, Kate Rosenblatt, and Ronit Stahl show, both historically and in the present, "American Jewish continuity discourse was embedded within patriarchal and misogynistic structures."[42] And that discourse often matters to donors.

Although women's colleges in the United States have been highly successful in receiving donations from their all-female alumnae, women are often neglected as potential donors at other universities. But even when women are donors, they can be a problem. One holder of an endowed chair told us about her relationship with the donor for that chair:

> My position was funded by a local woman who doesn't have an academic background. It used to be that we didn't have much to talk about. Sometimes it was awkward. I had a baby, and it really improved my relationship with her. When I see her now, she just wants to see photos of my kid, and she's not interested [in my academic work]. I also had experience with another woman [who disagreed with me politically]: when I had a kid, all was forgiven. These women in the community of donors can be very invested in Jewish continuity.

Sexual harassment by donors became a public issue in 2018 when the vice president of Hillel International, Sheila Katz, accused the billionaire donor Michael Steinhardt of harassment: "It wasn't funny the first time prominent philanthropist Michael Steinhardt asked me to have sex with him. It wasn't funny the second time, either. It wasn't funny the third time, or the fourth time in that meeting. It wasn't funny when he attempted to auction me off to two men in his office for $1 million. It wasn't funny when, before I left, he told me it was an 'abomination' that I was

---

42. Lila Corwin Berman, Kate Rosenblatt, and Ronit Y. Stahl, "Continuity Crisis: The History and Sexual Politics of an American Jewish Communal Project," *American Jewish History* 104, no. 2 (2020): 167–94.

unmarried and childless, and that he would not fund my work because of that fact."[43] Katz reported the harassment to Eric Fingerhut, the CEO of Hillel, who told her she would not have to meet with Steinhardt in the future. Yet that response also undermined Katz's authority in the organization and left Steinhardt in a position to harass other women in the Hillel organization. Meanwhile, Hillel continued to accept donations from Steinhardt, who has also funded other Jewish organizations, including Birthright Israel, which takes Jewish youths on free trips to Israel; Steinhardt reportedly harassed women working for Birthright as well. In another case, Rabbi Rachel Sabath Beit-Halachmi reported that Steinhardt suggested that she become his concubine while he was funding her first rabbinical position in the mid-1990s.[44] Ultimately, it took four years for Hillel International to investigate and remove Steinhardt from its board. One outcome of its investigation was that Hillel finally instituted a formal procedure for filing complaints of harassment.

In the newspaper reports about Steinhardt, some male Jewish communal leaders stated that they had long observed Steinhardt's harassment of women and had rebuked him privately but not shunned his money. Other men, such as Charles Bronfman, defended Steinhardt and called the accusations "downright outrageous!"[45]

This event reinforced the observation that harassment is not just the issue of one bad apple; it has consequences beyond the

43. Sheila Katz, "Michael Steinhardt Sexually Harassed Me. I Spent the Next 4 Years Trying to Hold Him Accountable," *Jewish Telegraphic Agency*, March 26, 2019, https://www.jta.org/2019/03/26/opinion/michael-steinhardt-sexually-harassed -me-i-spent-the-next-4-years-trying-to-hold-him-accountable.

44. Hannah Dreyfus and Sharon Otterman, "Women Who Worked with Billionaire Philanthropist Michael Steinhardt Say He Asked for Sex," *Pro Publica*, March 21, 2019, https://www.propublica.org/article/women-who-worked-with -billionaire-philanthropist-michael-steinhardt-say-he-repeatedly-asked-for-and -about-sex. This item also appeared in the *New York Times* on the same day.

45. Dreyfus and Otterman.

event itself. To avoid being harassed, how many women lost the opportunity to request philanthropic support from Steinhardt—and from other male donors? How many women were not considered for top leadership positions of Jewish organizations because the hiring committees knew they would not be able to meet with Steinhardt or would refuse to do so?

Funding for academic Jewish studies programs is a very small part of Jewish philanthropy, but it has been affected by major shifts in recent decades. Lila Corwin Berman, in her studies of Jewish philanthropy, has pointed to three important changes in the long history of Jewish charitable giving: a shift from support of social welfare projects (hospitals, for instance) to support for endowments; from projects for alleviating Jewish poverty to projects promoting Jewish identity; and from small but regular donations to communal funds from nearly every Jew to much larger donations from megadonors.[46] As a result, a small group of wealthy Jews control the institutions and programs that serve the masses of Jews, determining which will be funded and for what purposes. Many individual annual donations have been replaced by family foundations, taking the funding decisions from Jewish communal consensus to a small number of wealthy Jews and the trustees of their legacies. Through their money, megadonors could increasingly influence the political, cultural, and gender commitments of American Jews and gain prestige, power, and also a "safety net"—for example, against accusations of sexual harassment.

While Steinhardt was not a major donor to Jewish studies programs or to the AJS or other professional academic societies, archives, or research grants, he was a longtime, powerful leader of the Jewish megadonor community that included donors to university Jewish studies programs, and his behavior is a window into the culture and politics of that community. How do women professors negotiate with donors whose community is dominated by

---

46. Lila Corwin Berman, *The American Jewish Philanthropic Complex: The History of a Multibillion-Dollar Institution* (Princeton, NJ: Princeton University Press, 2022).

men whose money can provide a safety net against accusations of harassment?

Fund-raising for Jewish studies can sometimes conflict with other Jewish student institutions on campus, particularly Hillel and Chabad, both of which operate independently of the auspices of university advancement departments. Some university advancement offices prefer to reserve Jewish donors for other purposes, such as constructing a new engineering building or supporting the business school. While Hillel and Chabad are not constrained by those policies, faculty are required to abide by them. One colleague told us that the campus Chabad sent out fund-raising letters asking parents to support Jewish life on campus. More than one parent told her they had already given to Jewish studies because they thought that's where their money was going. As these parents' mistake suggests, the lines between fund-raising for Jewish studies and fund-raising for Jewish communal organizations can look blurry to all but the most vigilant.

Israel Studies, Gender, and Philanthropy

That private philanthropy may both endow a university program and attempt to destroy it became clear in 2022 when the funding for a chair in Israel studies, donated to the University of Washington by a member of the Seattle Jewish community and held by the highly respected scholar of Palestine under the British Mandate Liora Halperin, was withdrawn from the university by the donor.[47] The withdrawal of the gift by Becky Benaroya stemmed from a clash between the political interests of the donor and her discomfort with academic approaches to the study of the State of Israel, including the standard terminology and modes of interpretation developed within the academy. Recognized as a highly accomplished, brilliant

---

47. Mari Cohen, "The Fight for the Future of Israel Studies," *Jewish Currents*, Summer 2022, https://jewishcurrents.org/the-fight-for-the-future-of-israel -studies.

scholar, Halperin regained a chair and research funds when the university agreed to restore funding from its general budget.

Such clashes involving donors, whether motivated by politics or misunderstanding of academic approach, are not infrequent within the field of Jewish studies and, especially, within the newer field of Israel studies, a field that has been the target of numerous controversies.[48] Within months after being hired for a tenure-track position in Jewish studies, a junior scholar was told by the provost that

> *college donors were upset I was hired rather than a senior scholar, and the provost named a few older Israeli men. He went on to say that an Israeli scholar "could be a real spokesperson for Israel on campus, so now I have a problem and I have to figure out what to tell the donors."*

Indeed, a fundamental question is whether the study of Israel belongs to Jewish studies or to Middle Eastern studies. Institutionally, many universities place Israel studies with Jewish studies (Northwestern's Crown Family Center for Jewish and Israel Studies and Columbia's Institute for Israel and Jewish Studies, for example) or under its aegis (like Indiana University's Olamot Center). Like Jewish studies, Israel studies is an interdisciplinary field, ranging from political science to literature and beyond, and most faculty who consider themselves part of Israel studies are also in other departments. Today, there are twenty-seven centers for Israel studies at public and private universities around the world, and twenty-three Israel studies endowed professorships in the United States. Additional professorships in the field exist in Canada, Europe, Australia, and India.

As expected from its location in the social sciences and humanities, as well as its adjacency to Jewish studies, Israel studies faces similar issues about women scholars and gender equity in the

---

48. Jonathan Mahler, "Uprooting the Past: Israel's New Historians Take a Hard Look at Their Nation's Past," *Lingua Franca*, August 1997, 25–32.

field. But it also has distinctive issues with the presence of non-Jewish students and scholars in general and Palestinian scholars in particular. One scholar at a large university told us that colleagues were suspicious that a non-Jewish Asian woman was pursuing a study of Israel in her graduate program as part of a comparative program, as if Israel could be studied only by whites and Jews.

Women scholars are underrepresented in some strains of Israel studies, especially the quantitative and political sciences. If we count in a very narrow way who, exactly, qualifies as a scholar of Israel studies, it is possible to say that there are barely any female senior scholars of Israel studies in North America. If, instead, we paint the field of Israel studies with a broader brush, you would count many scholars of Hebrew literature, anthropology, or Middle Eastern studies as part of the field of Israel studies. *The Oxford Handbook of Israeli Politics and Society*, published in 2021, had four male editors, and thirty-six of its forty-six contributors were male.[49] Whatever way you count, however, it is clear that the field has not reached gender parity.

There is an irony here: the State of Israel is often imagined to be born of a more egalitarian ethos, but the field of Israel studies does not always reflect that. The mythology of the State of Israel includes the assertion of its gender egalitarianism. The nationalism that shaped it called for self-determination, and so did many of its politically active women. Women could vote from the state's founding in 1948. Today, women do mandatory military service. Yet there has never been true gender equity. Pay gaps, glass ceilings, and other inequalities persist. Margalit Shilo called her final chapter about women's suffrage on the eve of the creation of Israel "Victory and Defeat."[50]

49. Reuven Y. Hazan, Alan Dowty, and Menachem Hofnung, eds., *The Oxford Handbook of Israeli Politics and Society* (New York: Oxford University Press, 2021).

50. Margalit Shilo, *Girls of Liberty: The Struggle for Suffrage in Mandatory Palestine*, trans. Haim Watzman (Lebanon, NH: Brandeis University Press, 2016), 135–44.

Israel studies also suffers from the same kinds of banal assumptions about women's roles that occur in other fields. One Israel studies scholar told us:

> We hosted some scholars from Israel on a big panel a couple of years ago, and everybody in the group from the host institution was assigned a task. My male colleagues were assigned the tasks of being the hosts, introducing them to donors, and other tasks that facilitated interaction with them. I was disappointed that the postdoc and I were assigned the tasks of cleaning up after dinner.

Perhaps, we might think, this kind of assignment is merely one more example of structures wherein the women are expected to do domestic tasks while men do intellectual ones. But it also connects to some of the specific characteristics of the field of Israel studies.

One Israel studies scholar noted a male-dominated academic ethos in Israel but also explained that this did not necessarily mean that male colleagues were sexist or exclusionary in general. She contrasted her early-career experiences with her more recent ones:

> When I think of the eight of us [scholars in close conversation in her earlier career stages], I am the only woman. Until I found my way into Jewish studies, all my collaborators, coauthors, people to go out to dinner with at conferences were all men. . . . In Israel, again, all my close colleagues are men. With my colleagues who are my age and stage, I feel appreciated and respected. It could be that older generations are less respectful, but I don't get that from my peers.

As this scholar hints, Israeli culture itself may pose some hurdles because much research and scholarly interaction takes place in Israel, and a large number of scholars are Israeli. The Israeli academic environment differs from that of North America, and the scholars we talked to told us the environment in Israel is still more male dominated. Twenty years ago it would be common to walk down the hall and see all male faculty members plus a woman secretary. Those demographics are changing now, but its history means that many of the older generation of more esteemed scholars are male.

Many of these older men also share a military background. Israel has mandatory service for men and women, but more men serve, both because more women request exemptions (such as for marriage and child rearing) and because more men choose the military as a career path. A significant number of prominent Israel studies scholars have a military- or defense-related background, so that shapes the way they see society, power, and organization and encourages them to pursue security studies, a field that is both dominated by men and coded as masculine. That atmosphere makes it less attractive to women scholars. Some also seem to believe that one must be Israeli to understand the politics or military history of Israel. Several colleagues described a widespread mentality that values the scholarship and opinions of Israeli scholars over scholars from elsewhere. When colleagues are older men, it can be difficult to determine whether their seeming preference for association with and for scholarship by other older male scholars is about gender roles or about bias in favor of Israeli scholarship.

One scholar told us:

My training was in Hebrew literature with a focus on Israeli literature. Since my work has always been interdisciplinary, I consider myself to be in both Jewish and Israel studies. If Jewish studies is usually benevolently patriarchal, stemming from a traditional Jewish worldview of women as wives and mothers, then Israel studies is aggressively patriarchal—a world in which women are usable commodities. I have been in rooms with male academics where they would literally turn in on a circle and talk only to other men in the room—and exclude women both physically and intellectually from the conversation. The "bro" culture extends beyond those who are Israeli (and have a military frame of reference) to men more generally in the field. There are barely any senior women in the field; the men behave appallingly, often shouting at speakers on panels or talking over them. There are many cases of sexual harassment and

*indecent proposals, and yet here too I have found wonderful
mentors—both men and women.*

Even within the field, some topics and methods seem to be gendered male. As in many social science fields, in Israel studies,
quantitative, political, military, and global issues are often deemed
more important, whereas qualitative, cultural, domestic, literary,
and educational issues are deemed "softer" and more feminine.
Underrepresentation (or lack of visibility) in geopolitical areas of
study isn't wholly different from what happens in other related
fields in the United States. Mira Sucharov, a Canadian political
scientist in Israel studies, told us that when she worked on her
PhD at Georgetown, "the women's washroom near the political
science department was spotless" because it was rarely used. There
were very few women faculty members, and many students had
all-male dissertation committees. The numbers are changing, but
even in the best of moments, there can be a lingering sense that
the men who research political trends and military conflict are
doing the "real" research. By contrast, many of the women in the
field study Israeli popular culture, literature, film, or art or focus
on peacemaking efforts.

In Israel studies, gender represents one axis for thinking about
inclusion and exclusion. Analyses of gender and sexuality in the
rhetoric of early Zionist discourse, in the *yishuv* and the state, help
to clarify the relationship between Jewish and Zionist identities,
racial fantasies, and political decision making. Examining fantasies
regarding sexuality illuminates attitudes toward Jewish, non-
Jewish, and Palestinian identities.[51] Rather than being relegated

51. A relatively new movement seeks to accommodate Haredi students by offering
gender-segregated educational space in institutions of higher learning. Male students
are guaranteed an all-male learning environment with all-male professors. The initiatives are mainly aimed at having men enter the labor market, and so many of the
courses are in economics, business, and other "secular" subjects. Groups of professors
have spoken out against this plan, noting that it funnels more resources to men and
allows the exclusion of women authorities. See "Segregated Campuses," accessed

to academic silos, such studies should be integral to those of the political scientists and social historians. Knowledge and academic spaces can be easier to access if a researcher is Jewish, such as with the archival and ethnographic experiences, during which, scholars told us, their own Jewishness opened doors. Haredi students and faculty, especially men but also some women, present another axis of inclusion and exclusion as they enter the university. Some academic doors are harder to open if a scholar is not Jewish, and if a scholar is a non-Jewish Arab or Palestinian, doors may be closed altogether. One scholar shared her experiences doing research in Israel, pointing to the ways that her gender mattered—and her Jewishness mattered even more. She gave two examples that both begin with riding in cars:

> "Oh, how are you getting back to Tel Aviv? Okay, let me give you a ride," someone at the archives would say. I've gotten a lot of rides, primarily from men, often who were also working at the archives. They would express concern for me, and try to look out for me [since they knew I was not Israeli]. They would often ask if I have family in Israel. . . . It matters quite a lot that I'm Jewish. I'm a woman, I'm a foreigner, but I'm Jewish. I use connections (family), and they can provide me materials in a way that might not be as accessible to people who are not Jewish. And scholars who are Arab or Muslim might not feel comfortable doing that research in the first place. . . .
>
> There are female researchers in a lot of fields. It can be difficult, being on one's own, without a social support network, relying on strangers. . . . I've had some, well, not terrible, but still really unpleasant sexual harassment in taxi cabs. For me, it's very connected to the research because when I'm relying on those kinds of transport, I'm not as self-sufficient.

December 20, 2023, https://haredimedu.wordpress.com/english/, a website maintained by "a small group of professors" who organized in 2013 "to accommodate ultra-Orthodox students without institutionalizing extreme sex segregation."

Our bodies—and others' perceptions of them—shape our experience, and as this scholar shows, they also create and foreclose research opportunities. As a woman, she was seen as nonthreatening to the men who gave her rides; as a Jew, she was seen as sharing experience with Jewish Israelis and, perhaps, as worth protecting. Had she been a man, she would have been less likely to experience harassment from a taxi driver. Had she been a Palestinian woman, she might have been subject to a different kind of harassment. Would she have been offered a ride home from the archives by a Jewish researcher? Would she even have had access to the same archives and archival materials? For those who conduct research in Israel, these identities often have a different salience and prominence than they do in, say, the United States or Europe.

A conference one of us attended at an American university brought together Israeli Jews and Palestinians for a workshop on the history of Zionism and Israel. The scholars noted that such a gathering was unlikely to occur within Israel. For a Palestinian living in the West Bank or Gaza, gaining permission to enter a major city within Israel is extremely difficult, often impossible, and a conference on Zionism at an Israeli university would not include Palestinian speakers challenging Zionist narratives and would not permit a discussion of terms such as "colonialism." Conferences on Israeli political issues that include Palestinians or scholars with strongly left-wing political views are more easily held at universities in the United States.

Conclusion

That universities serve as a platform for research and teaching on particular topics of concern to the general public is neither new nor surprising. Donors often come with a sense of entitlement, assuming their own commitments should be reflected in the classroom. Students, too, come with expectations and requests to study particular topics in a certain way, and sometimes students will refuse to read an assignment because it conflicts with their beliefs.

Yet the academic curriculum is established by the faculty, generally overseen by departments, committees, and deans, with acknowledgment of the standards of a field. Their oversight does not always work perfectly; some courses can become out of date if the instructor does not keep up with the field, and some can lose academic credibility if they are heavily politicized. Donors, too, can potentially distort a curriculum through financial support for courses or publications that present a particular political position or omit relevant points of debate or fail to contextualize a topic. These might include, for example, funding for journals that have editorial boards dominated by men or conferences with few or no women presenting papers; indeed, these are areas in which donors can play a significant role in affecting the playing field for women and nonbinary scholars. In some ways, we are confronted with cultural and generational conflicts over gender and sexism. The issues with philanthropic support of Jewish studies include gender but also go well beyond it. We do not have easy answers.

In recent decades, the model of a four-year undergraduate education in the liberal arts has increasingly become training for a well-paying job, and colleges market themselves as routes to career success. Well into the 1970s, a college education was supposed to bring women a "Mrs." degree as well, and few women pursued graduate or professional training after college; the percentage who did rose significantly in the 1970s, largely thanks to the women's movement. The sharp increase in tuition that began in the 1980s turned students and parents into consumers, expecting not only an education but a "college experience" as well as a route to securing them a good job, wealth, and success. Roger L. Geiger writes, "Heightened competition for able students has brought some improvements to undergraduate education, but it has also greatly furthered student consumerism, thus weakening university control over student learning."[52] That, in turn, has changed the

---

52. Roger L. Geiger, *Knowledge and Money: Research Universities and the Paradox of the Marketplace* (Stanford, CA: Stanford University Press, 2004), 5.

structure of the university, with increasing numbers of administrative management, and with faculty as employees serving the educational desires of students. University costs were lowered by reducing the number of tenure-track faculty and increasing the number of contingent faculty, but that diminishes the quantity and quality of academic research as well as the governing role of faculty within the university.

The field of Jewish studies is also affected by a related downturn in the student market for humanities and social science majors. Students are often urged to concentrate on STEM, government, and economics as paths to financial security, fields that tend to be dominated by male faculty, whereas the humanities, whose faculties have greater gender parity, are shrinking. Jewish studies, usually located within the humanities or social sciences, has been affected at some institutions by falling student majors or enrollment. College administrators penalize low course enrollments by withdrawing resources or even closing departments.

Yet there are reasons to be hopeful. As Baskin notes and as we have experienced, "increasingly in the twenty-first century, more and more students who take courses and choose undergraduate majors and graduate training in Jewish Studies are non-Jews who have come to the field out of intellectual curiosity, not out of interest in their own religious or ethnic heritage."[53] Non-Jews may find that studying Jews and Judaism mirrors their own experiences, even when quite different, and their presence in the classroom and within the professoriate provides different perspectives. For Jewish students and faculty, the academic field of Jewish studies offers new ways to understand Judaism and Jewish historical experience that differ from the narratives provided by synagogues and communal institutions.

Jewish studies is a field undergoing change in its students, leadership, and intellectual impact. The growing participation of women faculty and students in the field is contributing to its

---

53. Baskin, "Jewish Studies in North American Colleges and Universities," 22.

transformation into a vibrant presence on the academic landscape by their engagement with the varieties of multicultural
questions and theoretical modalities. Difficulties remain, including serious conflicts on college campuses that at times shift from
political debate into antisemitic, racist, and misogynist demoniza-
tion. Recognizing and supporting the vibrancy of Jewish studies
as well as the struggles it faces on campuses is a challenge to scholars, students, administrators, and donors.

Conclusion

MOVING TOWARD GENDER EQUITY

WE WROTE THIS BOOK to promote change in the field of Jewish studies and to give voice to our many colleagues who have experienced bias, discrimination, and assault and cannot tolerate the status quo. We have contended throughout that bias is embedded in academic culture, including within our field. We have demonstrated the extent of the discrimination with our quantitative data; we have examined the rise of Jewish studies, which, like most academic fields, took shape in an era in which women were excluded from university education and from entering most professions; we have pointed to the long-term ramifications of gender inequality in our scholarship and in our professional relationships. We have also presented shocking accounts of scholars within Jewish studies harassing or assaulting colleagues and students in the field.

Yet the problems are not just the result of individual bad actors, and assuming so distracts from the underlying issues. We should not paint those who harass or assault as inhuman or the incarnation of evil. Rachel Adler told us, "Even the men I knew who were abusive, I don't want to make them into monsters. I want to put them into context. If you make them into monsters, they can't be held accountable."[1] If we imagine that someone who harasses must

1. Susannah Heschel and Sarah Imhoff, interview with Rachel Adler, July 25, 2023.

be truly evil in every way, it makes it very difficult for others to believe that someone who supports feminism could harm a female graduate student, for example.

Some scholars studying gender discrimination within the academy have arrived at pessimistic conclusions: universities and scholarship are too deeply embedded in patriarchal societal structures and ways of thinking to be easily changed. For example, one woman with two young children told us that she was offered a coveted postdoctoral fellowship at a distinguished university in a city where the cost of living—and especially the cost of day care—far exceeded the stipend of the fellowship. She would have to rely on another adult, such as a partner or family member, to provide child care or financial support.

In response to these kinds of structural issues, some scholars call for a single major overhaul, while others urge taking small but constant steps forward. Troy Vettese, concluding his review of the status of women in universities in the United States and the European Union, writes,

> The quotidian machinery of patriarchy functions as a complex of many moving parts. The same mechanisms that pull women down are the ones that push men up, compensating for the latter's initial lack of numbers in undergraduate studies until they become an overwhelming majority among the academic elite. All these various parts, some seemingly innocuous and others quite abominable, operate together, defeating attempts that remediate only a single aspect of the patriarchal machine. This explains why the results of mainstream feminist prescriptions have proved paltry. Academic patriarchy is too well entrenched and vicious to be defeated by piecemeal reform. Academic feminism needs a Cerberus-headed politics combining a social movement, activist scholarship, and new radical bureaucratic structures.[2]

2. Troy Vettese, "Sexism in the Academy: Women's Narrowing Path to Tenure," *n+1*, no. 34 (Spring 2019): 83–102, https://www.nplusonemag.com/issue-34/essays/sexism-in-the-academy/.

Many of us may feel powerless in the face of the command to create "new radical bureaucratic structures."

But even small changes can make a difference, and we can work toward greater inclusion, whether we are students or faculty, senior or new to the field, and whatever our genders. As we noted in our introduction, some of the problems are structural, some are individual, and many are cultural. Although culture can be hard to change, it is not impossible, and even individual and small group actions can make a difference in norms. Many of our suggestions, therefore, aim at what individual readers and their close colleagues can do.

In this conclusion, we offer recommendations for transforming our field through specific actions. Our recommendations include several interlocking dimensions: increasing the presence of women and nonbinary scholars; expanding in our scholarship and teaching topics and methods related to women, gender, and sexuality; and developing analytical and theoretical tools that help us ask new and more sophisticated questions in our work within Jewish studies.

Changing the culture as well as societal institutions is an enormous task. Patriarchy and sexism are ingrained in Jewish studies, academia, and our wider society. Our suggestions here make small steps in those directions, but we know that the goal will require fundamental changes in cultural expectations, assumptions, and biases about gender. The issues we raise in this book—and the suggestions we make here in its conclusion—are issues for people of all genders. Responsibility should not fall exclusively to women faculty or departments of women's and gender studies to bring about change. People of all genders should work toward inclusion, and in the end, the field will reap the benefits of a more diverse, collaborative, and interesting scholarly community.

Bystanders: Be Brave, Not Complicit

Let's interrupt sexism when we see it. Recent research has investigated what causes men to interrupt (versus do nothing) when they observe sexism at work.[3] These researchers conclude that men's individual agency plays a significant role, and they break down four components of that sense of agency: "Men more *committed* to dismantling sexism, *confident* in their ability to interrupt, *aware* of the positive benefits of interrupting, and invested in the *impact* on the common good are more likely to directly interrupt sexism."[4] In short, two major factors influence men's responses when they observe sexism: their own sense of personal agency and organizational climates that stifle them. "Interrupting" sexism means addressing words and behaviors that dismiss, ignore, or degrade based on gender. These behaviors not only display discrimination or bias but also can increase it within a work climate. Although this particular study of fifteen hundred men took place in largely corporate environments, it includes institutional factors that can help change university environments. This holds lessons for any of us who witness sexism, but particularly for men, who may be in better social and institutional locations to interrupt the culture. Making others aware that interventions are crucial is empowering: we demonstrate the impact of antisexist interventions. If we feel intimidated or if we feel that our efforts are futile and that interventions go nowhere within the institution, we become less likely to speak up. We discuss some of the institutional suggestions for interrupting sexism below.

Other researchers offer additional suggestions for interventions in the workplace, such as when you hear a sexist comment in a public setting: "To combat the paralysis that sets in mere seconds

3. Negin Sattari, Emily Shaffer, Sarah DiMuccio, Dnika J. Travis, "Interrupting Sexism at Work: What Drives Men to Respond Directly or Do Nothing?," *Catalyst*, accessed December 20, 2023, https://www.catalyst.org/reports/interrupting-sexism -workplace-men/.

4. Sattari et al.

after another man delivers a sexist comment or demeaning joke, just say something! We recommend the ouch technique: Simply say 'Ouch!' clearly and forcefully. This buys you a few extra seconds to formulate a clear statement about why the comment didn't land well with you." Then, they suggest, be sure to follow up with a direct sentence, such as "That wasn't funny," "We don't do that here," or "Did you really mean to say that?"[5] As the Jewish studies scholar Helene Meyers asks, referring to Steve M. Cohen, "Which of my male colleagues listened to an academic gatekeeper brag about 'sleeping with all of the smart Jewish women' and said or did nothing?"[6]

When we intervene, we express our own objections rather than those we think the victims might have. Instead of saying that our colleague Mary wouldn't find that joke funny, we can say that *we* think it is transphobic or sexist. We can make it clear that those statements and behaviors are unacceptable to us, not just something that shouldn't be said in front of the people whose identities are being devalued or stereotyped.

Men should speak to other men. If a man sees or hears a colleague doing something sexist, tell him you found his behavior inappropriate. These conversations are not about shaming or humiliation, and some may occur in private, though it may make sense to have others in public right away. As W. Brad Johnson and David G. Smith write, "Active confrontation of other men for sexism, bias, harassment, and all manner of inappropriate behavior may be the toughest part of male allyship. It is also utterly essential."[7] This is an excellent strategy for two reasons: first, it takes the burden off the victims of sexism, who often have to do

5. W. Brad Johnson and David G. Smith, "How Men Can Confront Other Men about Sexist Behavior," *Harvard Business Review*, October 16, 2020, https://hbr.org /2020/10/how-men-can-confront-other-men-about-sexist-behavior.

6. Helene Meyers, "When an Accused Sexual Harasser Is an Academic Superstar," *Lilith*, August 7, 2018, https://lilith.org/2018/08/when-an-accused-sexual -harasser-is-an-academic-superstar/.

7. Johnson and Smith, "How Men Can Confront Other Men about Sexist Behavior."

the vast majority of educating their peers; and second, men listen to other men about sexism in ways that are different from the ways they listen to women, whom they may interpret as having been personally upset rather than as pointing to a pattern.[8]

If we can be effective in communicating to those with whom we share an identity (like men talking to other men about sexism), we can also be particularly effective when we speak up about discrimination against people with whom we do not share an identity. Heterosexual people should interrupt homophobia; cisgender people should interrupt transphobia; white people should interrupt racism. Although it may not seem like "your issue," and you don't want to speak on behalf of others, identifying and working to stop discrimination against others can be a key mode of being an ally. Nevertheless, we should look carefully before taking on leadership in the project of stopping discrimination because there may be others already working toward that goal. Men shouldn't arrive in the conversation and start telling women how to fight sexism, for example. Instead, we should ask how to support projects or processes already underway.

In a *New York Times* op-ed, Maya Guzdar, a college student interning at the Pentagon, reported what happened when she was harassed by a senior male employee of the Department of Defense. The very next day, she encountered a "best case" scenario: men who had observed what occurred reported and corroborated the incident. She writes, "I felt supported, safe and validated." She also recognizes that because the initial report was filed by a senior male officer, it may have been taken more seriously. She also praises how the reports were handled: a female supervisor interviewed each person about the incident and the harasser was offered counseling, "a humane response that, to me, felt appropriate and even cathartic." Guzdar received empathy and compassion

8. Heather M. Rasinski and Alexander M. Czopp, "The Effect of Target Status on Witnesses' Reactions to Confrontations of Bias," *Basic and Applied Social Psychology* 32, no. 1 (2010): 8–16.

from fellow employees, and when she thanked the senior officer who had filed a report, he replied, "It's about protecting each other. . . . It's an honor and privilege to serve with you."[9] In chapter 3, we discussed why many women do not report harassment or assault by pointing to the inadequacies related to adjudicatory systems. With the kind of intervention Guzdar describes, harassment and assault can be halted on the spot. We can take Guzdar's experience at the Department of Defense as an example of how things can go differently in the immediate aftermath of such events. A bystander who takes action can be transformative both for the victim and for the community at large.

Become a Good Ally

Interrupting is only one strategy; we can also speak privately with those targeted by sexism and ask how to help. Sometimes that may simply be lending an affirmative ear so they feel heard. Sometimes it might be helping them identify institutional resources to respond to the situation.

We can also speak privately with those who have spoken or behaved inappropriately—gently or more firmly, depending on what the situation requires—and point out that their behavior is offensive and in violation of academic standards of behavior, and that it redounds to their own discredit. Here's a recent example: One of our senior, highly respected colleagues in another department attended a Jewish studies seminar and was shocked by the patronizing condescension displayed by both colleagues and community members, male and female, toward the woman scholar leading the seminar. He saw what the men within the department had failed to notice or simply had come to accept as "normal," and he offered to write a letter to the institution's provost. He recognized that

9. Maya Guzdar, "What Happened the Day after I was Sexually Harassed at the Pentagon," *New York Times*, September 5, 2021, https://www.nytimes.com/2021/09 /05/opinion/culture/sexually-harassed-pentagon.html.

patronizing attitudes undermine collegial respect and the work we do as intellectuals. People in established positions should ask colleagues how they can take affirming actions when they observe these behaviors. It may be that such offers are turned down, but by noticing and describing what we see and being willing to go on record stating that these behaviors are inappropriate, we validate the experience of those who are being patronized. If we are not in a position to write such a letter, we can still listen and validate a colleague's experience.

We may also advocate for institutional policies that aid victims or survivors. A person who has been assaulted, for example, may require an extended period for recovery. Doctoral examinations, deadlines on a dissertation, or the tenure clock should be extended. Institutions may be increasing investigations of perpetrators, but that should not be in place of supporting survivors. Harassment and discrimination against a student or faculty member deserves public rectification of institutional structures, formal apology, paid time off when needed, and, if desired, a process of restorative justice. Counseling for recovery from the trauma of assault committed by a fellow employee should be paid for by the employer. We should hold our institutions responsible not only for punishing someone who commits harassment or assault, but also for assisting the victims in their recovery.

Create Better Networks

An important way to improve our teaching and scholarship is by diversifying our exposure to new ideas. Diversity comes through our scholarly networks. We meet with colleagues in other departments and hear about new methods in their disciplines; we attend conferences in fields outside our own and discover wider frameworks in which to evaluate our own research. We need to ensure that there is interaction among scholars of different genders, races, and backgrounds, as well as junior and senior scholars, all of whom have much to learn from one another. Those who are older may offer wise guidance, while those who are younger may offer new ways of thinking. Broadening our networks enhances our work and is also a good way to disseminate awareness of our own scholarship. We improve the field by bringing Jewish studies into conversations with other fields. Those who have not attended conferences, workshops, or lectures on feminist theory should do so—and often.

Each of us should assess our own scholarly network. This is one of the key actions we can take as individual scholars, and its effects can radiate across research, publication, teaching, and even other scholars' careers. Who are our primary interlocutors? Whose work do we read when it gets published? Whom do we ask to read and give feedback on our own unpublished work? Whom do we invite to give talks at our institutions? Whom do we meet at conferences, and with whom do we sit and talk? Whose work do we read, and then do we write them a note expressing gratitude for their writing or demonstrating engagement with their ideas? Are we reading only the work of people who work at the same ten prestigious institutions? If these people all have the same background we have, we should make the effort to reach out to scholars who do not. Men in particular should make the effort to network with women and nonbinary scholars and read their scholarship; white scholars should seek out and interact with the scholars of color and their scholarship; all should reach out to those who seem marginalized in the field.[10] We should likewise consider supporting or collaborating with scholars working on gender in countries or in departments where Jewish studies is a small or marginalized field, especially if their work faces resistance and marginalization.

We need diversity in our scholarly community. Too often men's professional networks are more likely to include other men—to a significant degree. But unlike many of the enormous structural

10. Adapted from Sarah Imhoff, "404 Women Not Found Error," *Feminist Studies in Religion*, May 30, 2019, https://www.fsrinc.org/404-women-not-found-error/.

hurdles, the solution is one well within your reach. Adding to your networks can even give your own career a boost by helping you consider new ideas and perhaps even moving your research in fascinating new directions.

Inquire about the other participants when you agree to join a publication, conference panel, or workshop. We can see the effects that male-dominated networks have beyond who sits with whom at a conference. For example, although the number of women in the field has increased enormously in the past four decades, we are finding lots of new anthologies, conferences, and panels composed entirely or mostly of men. Why would a collection of articles on contemporary Jewish theology have only three of twenty-four written by women?[11] Or why would a collection of articles edited by three men seeking to advance a dialogue between Jewish studies and critical theory include out of eleven contributions only two articles by women, with no discussion of feminist theory and gender in the collection?[12] The good news is that more and more scholars do not want to participate in all-male "manthologies," "festicles," and "manels," as they perpetuate "closed networks."[13] They find them both ethically problematic and less interesting intellectually, given the potential for the similarity of the scholars' backgrounds. Sometimes when a woman refuses to be the only female contributor to a book or journal, the male editor(s) discover

11. Elliot Cosgrove, ed., *Jewish Theology in Our Time: A New Generation Explores the Foundations and Future of Jewish Belief* (Woodstock, VT: Jewish Lights, 2010).

12. Shai Ginsburg, Martin Land, and Jonathan Boyarin, eds., *Jews and the Ends of Theory* (New York: Fordham University Press, 2019).

13. Mara Benjamin popularized the term "manthology" in her essay "On the Uses of Academic Privilege"; see *Feminist Studies in Religion @TheTable*, a roundtable entitled "Manthologies," May 27, 2019, https://www.fsrinc.org/thetable-manthologies/. Eva Mroczek coined the term "festicle" to refer to a festschrift with only male contributors; see Amy Laura Hall, Twitter post, March 19, 2018, 10:52 p.m., https://twitter.com/profligategrace/status/975928072586383360. On "closed networks," see Annette Yoshiko Reed Twitter post, February 6, 2020, https://twitter.com/Annette YReed/status/1225416757369876481.

additional women to contribute; they just need a push. Asking about the diversity of other contributors can signal to editors that diversity matters. Individuals can make a difference.

Actively mentor women and nonbinary junior colleagues and graduate students. We might do so through formal mentoring structures, such as ones at our university or learned societies, as well as in informal settings. It can be hard for women and nonbinary scholars to enter a field where Jewish men are considered established authorities, so reach out and encourage others, especially if they seem to be on the periphery of the field.

Everyone, regardless of career stage, can do many of these things: introduce ourselves at a conference, send an email after reading a publication we admire, and promote good work on social media. If we are younger scholars, we can cultivate a diverse group of peer mentors. They can function as an important support system, and they may later develop into a wonderful network of diversely accomplished colleagues.

Consider Our Own Scholarship

We hope our readers will take another look at their own scholarship and that of their colleagues: Where are the women in that history book? How might we take into consideration the gender and sexual imagery laced through the texts we are analyzing? Important feminist scholarship has emerged around such questions: How has the suppression of women's voices worked in the creation of a textual canon or historical narrative? What do texts written by men about women tell us about the self-understanding of men and the gender ideology they are creating? In what ways does gender identity serve as a stand-in or metaphor for Jewish identity? If this scholarship is new to us, we should read it and consider how it might change our own scholarship.

Supreme Court justice Ruth Bader Ginsburg remarked, "When I'm sometimes asked, when will there be enough [women on the Supreme Court] and I say, 'When there are nine,' people are shocked. But there'd been nine men, and nobody's ever raised a question about that."[14] Similarly, religion scholar Blossom Stefaniw writes, "Equity is not achieved by a fraction of institutions hiring five women to a total of ten faculty positions in 2000, given that the vast majority of institutions had only male professors for 500 years. Equity would be hiring only female professors for 500 years, and only then gradually shifting to a half-and-half system."[15]

Scholars have had analogous thoughts in some academic fields. In 2021, the Political Theology Network called for papers under the heading "(How to Do) Political Theology without Men?" The organizers, aware that men's articles dominate both the publications of the journal and the submissions of manuscripts to the journal, asked contributors, "What would the field look like if there was a reversal—if it centered the ideas, insights, and scholarship of women and nonbinary people, rather than those of men?"[16] We can extend that project to consider what other spheres of knowledge long dominated by men—such as biblical studies, modern Jewish thought, and understandings of kabbalah and Hasidism—would look like if they were reversed and the ideas, insights and scholarship of women and nonbinary people became the focus of interpretation.

In writing about Jews, we should ask ourselves about the presence of women and genderqueer people in that community. They are often more present and more prominent than is first assumed or presented by the community itself. If, upon closer analysis, it still seems they do not play a prominent role, let's ask ourselves why they are submerged and what that accomplishes for the more

14. "When Will There Be Enough Women on the Supreme Court? Justice Ginsburg Answers That Question," *PBS NewsHour*, February 5, 2015, https://www.pbs.org /newshour/show/justice-ginsburg-enough-women-supreme-court.

15. Blossom Stefaniw, "Feminist Historiography and Uses of the Past," *Studies in Late Antiquity* 4, no. 3 (Fall 2020): 260–83; 267.

16. Political Theology Network, "(How to Do) Political Theology without Men?" April 21, 2021, https://politicaltheology.com/cfp-how-to-do-political-theology -without-men/.

dominant members of the group and their ideology, relationships, and reputations.

In writing about a thinker, text, or movement of thought that is entirely male, ask yourself if feminist theory might illuminate its structures, power, and relationships. Are certain terms or ideas implicitly gendered or eroticized through metaphors? How do gender and sexual arrangements function in the larger framework? Seek out scholarship by women and nonbinary authors and read and discuss it with your colleagues—you may well be inspired!

Write the Missing Footnote

Our quantitative data presented in chapter 1 demonstrated definitively that women's scholarship is not cited as often as it should be. For important scholarship to be neglected harms the entire field. Quite a few women have told us that their work has not been cited in publications dealing with the issues they have written about, even when it includes similar sources or arguments. It's not uncommon in academic studies for references to relevant published work not to appear, sometimes out of oversight, sometimes out of insecurity, and sometimes because of the pressure to meet a word limit. Lolita Buckner Inniss has used the term "plagnoring"—a portmanteau of "plagiarize" and "ignoring"—to describe this phenomenon, and she notes its gendered and racialized aspects.[17]

We need to pay attention to our citations when we write. Leading the way, #CiteBlackWomen calls academic authors' attention to how and when they (don't) cite Black women's work.[18] The

17. Elizabeth Pérez writes about Buckner Inniss's term (which had not appeared in published form) in her own excellent discussion of citation. Lolita Buckner Inniss, personal communication with Elizabeth Pérez. See Elizabeth Pérez, "Sorry Cites: The (Necro)politics of Citation in the Anthropology of Religion," *Studies in Religion*, forthcoming.

18. Christen A. Smith, Erica L. Williams, Imani A. Wadud, Whitney N. L. Pirtle, and the Cite Black Women Collective, "Cite Black Women: A Critical Praxis (a Statement)," *Feminist Anthropology* 2, no. 1 (2021): 10–17.

collective calls attention to the importance of acknowledging intellectual contributions, as well as the historical forces that have made Black women's scholarly labor seem exploitable. All scholars, including those in Jewish studies, can take a cue from their work. Are we citing women and nonbinary scholars? Are there scholars of color in our bibliographies? We not only need to cite women and nonbinary people in our scholarship, we need to look at how we cite them too: Is it only in footnotes, or do we engage their ideas substantively within the text? Fadeke Castor draws on Savannah Shange's formulation of "citations as a practice of relation" to call our attention to the ethics of citation.[19] We should "name those who come before us and on whose shoulders we stand," even—perhaps especially—when those named are junior to us or less well known, and even when they come from beyond our field.[20] If we find that our reading lists or bibliographies are overwhelmingly white and male, we can ask our colleagues, use social media, or consult websites where minoritized scholars are listed.[21]

When we peer review books or articles, we should pay attention to the citations and note them in our reviews. Are the vast majority of the citations of male scholars, and, if so, has that led to the author missing out on something intellectually important? Has the author acknowledged to whom their ideas are indebted? Are there others with whom they should be engaged? Thinking of this as part of the peer-review process can lift some of the onus from marginalized scholars to be the ones to find and fix these "missing footnotes."

19. Savannah Shange, "Citation as Ceremony: #SayHerName, #CiteBlackWomen, and the Practice of Reparative Enunciation," *Cultural Anthropology* 37, no. 2 (2002): 191–98.

20. Fadeke Castor, "Sacred Cites: Engaging the Spiritual in Ethnographic Knowledge (Re)production," *Studies in Religion*, forthcoming.

21. Among such websites are Cite Black Authors, https://citeblackauthors.com/; Women Also Know History, https://womenalsoknowhistory.com/; and Women Also Know Stuff, https://womenalsoknowstuff.com/.

Our quantitative data demonstrate in concrete terms the experiences of women. These data capture this moment; our hope is that they will become obsolete in the near future as women's status in the field improves. Data also provide an important window into a cultural atmosphere. In the not-too-distant past, a prevalent assumption was that men were more reliable, better educated, even smarter than women in the same profession. Susannah's mother used to tell her, "I would never consult a woman doctor; she can't possibly know as much as a man. After all, while he is reading the medical journals in the evenings, she's putting her children to bed. How does she keep up with her field?" Perhaps women's scholarship is not always cited prominently by male scholars out of a lingering remnant of that cultural bias: associating oneself with women's scholarship might be felt, perhaps unconsciously, by both men and women as a diminution of one's own scholarship. Even our own small acts of inclusive citation can help move the field toward greater gender inclusion.

Make Scholarly Gatherings More Inclusive

I attended a conference about five years ago at a major East Coast university, and I was really shocked—it was the most sexist environment I had experienced in years. The papers were nearly all delivered by men; the few women were mostly moderators. During discussions, very few women present raised their hands, and when they did, they were often not called on to speak, not even by the female moderators. The organizers were two men, and they strutted around, creating a very macho environment.

In addition to this scholar's experience at this conference, studies show that men are disproportionately invited to give talks on campus.[22] When we organize conferences, invite speakers to our institutions, or edit a volume, we should take gender into account.

22. Christine L. Nittrouer, Michelle R. Hebl, Leslie Ashburn-Nardo, Rachel C. E. Trump-Steele, David M. Lane, and Virginia Valian, "Gender Disparities in Colloquium

Men might consider inviting a woman or nonbinary scholar to co-organize or coedit with them, especially because research from other fields demonstrates that having women as conveners or organizers strongly influences the number of women scholars involved.[23] Keep in mind that some women, in order to survive in their sexist workplace, will mirror men and disparage other women.

This might seem obvious, but when we organize conferences or edit books, we should all be sure to invite a diverse group of scholars from the start. No woman or scholar of color wants to feel they have been invited as an afterthought, merely to provide the appearance of fixing a problem. A commitment to having a diverse group may also require extra time: underrepresented scholars often have greater service commitments, and so we may have to ask quite a few people to get the diverse lineup we want. We should give ourselves extra planning time to allow for some invitees to say "no" and still be able to invite others. One of us coedited a book with two men and ensured that six of the twelve articles were written by women, but when one of those men subsequently edited a volume by himself, only three of the twenty-three articles were by women.[24] Commitment to gender parity requires attentiveness.

At conferences or when introducing speakers, we should refer to all speakers equally. It is common for women to be referred to by their first names even when they have professional titles. A large 2018 study, inspired by one of the researchers observing the difference in how gender affected how political pundits on Israeli television were named, summarized: "Men and women were, on

Speakers at Top Universities," *PNAS* 115, no. 1 (January 2, 2018): 104–8, https://doi.org/10.1073/pnas.1708414115.

23. Arturo Casadevall and Jo Handelsman, "The Presence of Female Conveners Correlates with a Higher Proportion of Female Speakers at Scientific Symposia," *mBio* 5, no. 1 (2014): e00846–13.

24. David Biale, Michael Galchinsky, and Susannah Heschel, eds., *Insider/Outsider: American Jews and Multiculturalism* (Berkeley: University of California Press, 1998); and David Biale, ed., *Cultures of the Jews: A New History* (New York: Schocken Books, 2002).

average across studies, more than twice as likely to describe a male (vs. female) professional by surname in domains, such as science, literature, and politics. We find that this simple difference in reference affects judgments of eminence, with participants judging those professionals described by surname as more eminent and 14% more deserving of a career award."[25] The solution, albeit a small one, is easy to institute once we are aware of it.

Also at conferences, when we are the ones responsible for calling on audience members with questions, we should call on a woman or a nonbinary person first. Studies suggest that doing so makes the subsequent conversation more representative in terms of gender.[26] The Association for Jewish Studies has included some of these recommendations in its "Guidance to Chairs."[27] We have not quantified the results, but anecdotally many chairs expressed their appreciation, and we heard no complaints.

These theoretical discussions can and should also prompt us to consider our scholarly spaces. People with disabilities told us of the physical and emotional tolls that academic spaces exacted from them. They also told us of the frustration they felt at having to request accommodations again and again, many of which are already required by federal law.[28] Signing at public lectures remains uncommon, and once lectures began occurring on Zoom,

25. Stav Atir and Melissa J. Ferguson, "How Gender Determines the Way We Speak about Professionals," *Proceedings of the National Academy of Sciences* 115, no. 28 (2018): 7278–83; and Linda B. Glazer, "When Last Comes First: The Gender Bias of Names," *Cornell Chronicle*, July 2, 2018, https://news.cornell.edu/stories/2018/07 /when-last-comes-first-gender-bias-names.

26. Alecia J. Carter, Alyssa Croft, Dieter Lukas, and Gillian M. Sandstrom, "Women's Visibility in Academic Seminars: Women Ask Fewer Questions Than Men," *PloS one* 13, no. 9 (2018): e0202743.

27. Association for Jewish Studies, "Guidance to Chairs," accessed September 10, 2023, https://www.associationforjewishstudies.org/2023cfp/guidance-for-panel -chairs. For the sake of full disclosure, Sarah is a coauthor of this document because of her work on the AJS Task Force for Diversity and Inclusion.

28. Julia Watts Belser, *Loving Our Own Bones: Disability Wisdom and the Spiritual Subversiveness of Knowing Ourselves Whole* (Boston: Beacon, 2023).

simultaneous subtitles were not automatically provided. Having to repeatedly request "special provisions" is not only annoying; it is also a time burden, and it signals that the conference was not really designed for you. It can make you feel that you don't belong. In-person conferences do not always occur in buildings or rooms that are accessible—again, despite federal protections mandated at universities as well as hotel facilities. Colleagues making arrangements for informal gatherings, such as at a restaurant meal during a conference, do not always consider accommodations even when someone in the group requires them. The attitude is that the disabled person has to deal with the "problem" of finding accommodation—or not attend. What is particularly disturbing, some of our interviewees told us, is that many of the colleagues indifferent to disability accommodations are very concerned, for example, about finding a restaurant that is strictly kosher. Accommodating the dietary requirements of the participants is assumed, while disabilities do not spark a comparable sense of obligation. What we want to emphasize is that ignoring disabilities is not simply about lack of attention; it stems from bias, from an assumption that only those without disabilities are deserving of equal opportunity.

Change Departmental Culture

Recently a male scholar with a strong commitment to advancing women's status in the profession told us that he had tried over the years to convince some of the few women faculty in his large department to become chair, but all declined. Yet his own complaints about the male domination in his department suggested the reason. He told us that, often, when women faculty speak during faculty meetings, some of the men in the back of the room start chatting with each other. Perfectly understandable, then, that no woman would want to chair a department in which some of the men over whom she would have authority behave disrespectfully toward their female colleagues.

Promoting women to positions of power and authority is well intentioned, but first the culture of the department has to change. Disrespect during faculty meetings must be challenged and stopped, and a general discussion of attitudes should be aired. The department might discuss an article or book about the status of women in the academic profession, or an article depicting some of the difficulties women and nonbinary people face. Changing the culture is important for the sake of students as well, who may be afraid of complaining about sexism in the classroom.

Given that studies have clearly demonstrated that administrative responsibilities and service to the institution fall disproportionately on women and minorities, we can encourage our institutions to make certain that such responsibilities are distributed equitably. We can suggest to our institutions that service on committees and other administrative responsibilities might be compensated with additional salary or sabbatical time. We can suggest that the university handbook for departmental chairs and faculty include how to create a culture of equity, respect, and collaboration. We can grant consideration to faculty attending to children or caring for sick family members when scheduling departmental meetings or gatherings.

Supporting contingent faculty also has an important gendered component. Women are overrepresented in the ranks of contingent faculty, and they would benefit from increased salaries, benefits, and long-term contracts.[29] Faculty with tenure should feel especially responsible to advocate for those who are on the margins of their institutions both intellectually and financially.

We should also consider gender stereotyping in leadership and our relationships with colleagues. No matter our genders, we can

29. Kay Steiger, "The Pink Collar Work Force of Academia," *Nation*, July 11, 2013, https://www.thenation.com/article/archive/academias-pink-collar-workforce/. See also Melissa Fernández Arrigoitia et al., "Women's Studies and Contingency: Between Exploitation and Resistance," *Feminist Formations* 27, no. 3 (Winter 2015): 81–113.

collaborate on decision making. Modes of interaction that are often considered feminine—seeking consensus, checking in with others, listening quietly, being self-reflective before claiming credit—can lead to more harmonious processes as well as more carefully considered outcomes. Some things are worth fighting for, and a collaborative spirit does not require giving in on important issues when there is disagreement. We can ask our colleagues to correct us if they observe us saying or doing something that marginalizes others or that is condescending or patronizing. We can even institute a kind of buddy system where we agree to help each other. Although this process should also include any necessary apologies, these conversations can be held in confidence. They are about growth, not shaming.

Practice Better Public Communication

In a mixed-gender group, women do not speak up as often or speak as long as male colleagues. A now-classic study of faculty meetings showed that men at faculty meetings—without exception—spoke longer than women. In all cases but one, they also spoke more often than women.[30] In college discussion groups, male leadership translates into more male speaking and less female speaking.[31] These findings reflect larger patterns of socialization, wherein men's vocal leadership and participation comes to seem natural. Encouraging women and nonbinary students to speak can help change not only their experiences, but also the classroom environment for all.

---

30. Barbara Eakins and Gene Eakins, "Verbal Turn-Taking and Exchanges in Faculty Dialogue," in *The Sociology of the Languages of American Women*, ed. Betty DuBois, 53–62 (San Antonio, TX: Trinity University Press, 1976); and Shari Kendall and Deborah Tannen, "Gender and Language in the Workplace," *Gender and Discourse* 81 (1997): 81–105.

31. Elizabeth Aries, "Interaction Patterns and Themes of Male, Female, and Mixed Groups," *Small Group Behavior* 7, no. 1 (1976): 7–18, https://doi.org/10.1177/104649647600700102.

Do we think our classrooms, conferences, or faculty meetings don't have this problem? Beware! Our estimates can be incorrect. Numerous studies conducted over the course of the past fifty years have demonstrated that although men speak more often than women and interrupt women who are speaking, a widespread perception is that women talk far more than men at meetings, in private conversations, in person, on Zoom, and in classrooms.[32] A 1980 study by Dale Spender showed that when asked to estimate when men and women had talked "equal" amounts, men chose, on average, a scenario in which women had actually talked only 15 percent of the time. When women actually talked 30 percent of the time, men saw the conversation as dominated by women.[33] Even when Spender herself tried to give male and female students equal time, she found from audio recordings that the split was actually 58 percent to 42 percent.[34] More recent investigations of a variety of settings, including virtual as well as in-person meetings, have confirmed that men and women both overestimate what proportion of the time women speak.[35] Women speak more succinctly, perhaps to ward off interruption, a pattern repeated when meetings shift to written reports: men write longer, more verbose reports than women. The gender disparities occur in a range of contexts, from academia to the floor of the US Senate. A study by political scientists, reported in the *Washington Post*, found "that when groups of five make democratic decisions, if only one member is a woman, she speaks 40 percent less than each of the men. Even if the group has a majority of three women, they each speak 36 percent less than each of the two men. Only in groups with four

32. Adrienne B. Hancock and Benjamin A. Rubin, "Influence of Communication Partner's Gender on Language," *Journal of Language and Social Psychology* 34, no. 1 (May 11, 2014): 46–64, https://doi.org/10.1177/0261927X14533197.

33. Dale Spender, *Man Made Language* (Boston: Routledge and Kegan Paul, 1980).

34. Dale Spender, *Invisible Women: The Schooling Scandal* (London: Writers and Readers, 1982).

35. Anne Cutler and Donia R. Scott, "Speaker Sex and Perceived Apportionment of Talk," *Applied Psycholinguistics* 11, no. 3 (1990): 253–72.

women do they each finally take up as much airtime as the one man."[36] Gender (and other markers of social status) matters for our perception of who is taking air time.[37]

In the classroom, if your students have a tendency to interrupt, stop them. At first, this might not seem like a gender issue, just a matter of politeness. However, studies demonstrate that women are interrupted more often than men. One study showed that male students spoke over each other and were less likely to go quiet and yield the floor when interrupted.[38] We can talk to our students about creating a respectful classroom and inform them of the need to listen and respond respectfully. Criticism of other people's views is important, but bullying is unacceptable. Consider sharing the results of some of these research studies with students. Knowing that most of us share socialization into these gendered behaviors in communication can help students not feel personally criticized and also recruit them as allies in creating an inclusive classroom space.

These issues can be observed in faculty and committee meetings. A study published in 2014 by political scientists Christopher Karpowitz and Tali Mendelberg showed that women spoke 25 percent less than men in meetings: "Women speak far less than men, [and] they are almost never viewed as the most influential member of the discussion group; they view themselves as

36. Christopher F. Karpowitz and Tali Mendelberg, *The Silent Sex: Gender, Deliberation, and Institutions* (Princeton, NJ: Princeton University Press, 2014); and Adam Grant, "Who Won't Shut Up in Meetings? Men Say It's Women. It's Not," *Washington Post*, February 18, 2021, https://www.washingtonpost.com/outlook/2021/02/18/men-interrupt-women-tokyo-olympics/. See also Christopher F. Karpowitz, Tali Mendelberg, and Lee Shaker, "Gender Inequality in Deliberative Participation," *American Political Science Review* 106, no. 3 (August 2012): 533–47.

37. Helene Decke-Cornill, "The Issue of Gender and Interaction in the L2 Classroom," in *Gender Studies and Foreign Language Teaching*, ed. Helene Decke-Cornill and Laurenz Volkmann (Tubingen: Gunther Narr Verlag, 2007), 77–90.

38. Elizabeth Sommers and Sandra Lawrence, "Women's Ways of Talking in Teacher-Directed and Student-Directed Peer Response Groups," *Linguistics and Education* 4, no. 1 (1992): 1–35.

powerless; they very rarely introduce topics of distinctive concern to women or dwell on them; their references are rarely picked up in the conversational thread; they receive little positive reinforcement while speaking; men interrupt their speech with hostile remarks."[39] As a result of hearing less from women colleagues, we are losing their insights and perspectives. One way to change this is to announce at the start of a meeting that interruption is discouraged and that the views of everyone present should be heard, and to intervene if women are disrespected. Another is to ask women or nonbinary scholars if they might like to share their ideas, even if they do not speak up.

Karpowitz and Mendelberg demonstrate that the gender composition of a committee affects its decision-making process and outcome.[40] Gender patterns have also been found in computer mediated communication (CMC), with women using Facebook and X (formerly Twitter) more than men do, and men contributing to Wikipedia and using LinkedIn far more than women do.[41] The same study found that men and women also use different language and express different emotions in computer-posted messages. Furthermore, gender harassment is also present in CMC and is known to have been expressed in student and faculty email lists; those lists should have community guidelines for participation. Computer scientist Joy Buolamwini uncovered gender and racial biases in the

39. Karpowitz and Mendelberg, *Silent Sex*, 312. Jessica Preece and Olga Stoddard found something very similar in their study of what happens when women join teams of men in the field of accounting. Brittany Karford Rogers discusses this study in "When Women Don't Speak," *Y Magazine, a BYU Publication,* Spring 2020, https://magazine.byu.edu/article/when-women-dont-speak/?fbclid=IwAR21KoODXtbezf1TxaWeyFFWwBAAAciTunbRzxN-Uhn548m0bJNo-QoomPI.

40. Karpowitz and Mendelberg, *Silent Sex*.

41. Susan C. Herring and Sharon Stoerger, "Gender and (A)nonymity in Computer-Mediated Communication," in *The Handbook of Language and Gender,* 2nd ed., ed. Janet Holmes, Miriam Meyerhoff, and Susan Ehrlich (Hoboken, NJ: Wiley-Blackwell, 2013), 3.

algorithms used by artificial intelligence in facial recognition, which led major technology companies, including IBM and Microsoft, to change their software.[42] Technology mirrors society!

Having more women on a committee can create a more collaborative process.[43] The goal is not only to include more women in the composition of the group, but also to change the decision rules. How will the committee arrive at its decision? Should a decision be based on majority vote or is there a way to achieve consensus within the committee? Research demonstrates that consensus is more readily achieved by committees with a majority of women, as they tend to create a collaborative tone in meetings.[44] We should all be able to observe and ultimately replicate such collaborations and hopefully temper the sometimes hostile atmosphere within academia.

Teach Better

Let's consider the syllabus: Do we assign scholarly studies by people of all genders and primary sources that teach our students about varieties of sexual identities and gender expressions? Are we considering insights drawn from feminist theory when discussing questions of historiography, textual interpretation, and sociological and anthropological approaches? If not, give it a try! Theory is underused in many Jewish studies classrooms, yet it offers us new ways of thinking and new questions to pose. Many of us teach from texts, and most premodern Jewish texts were written by men and about men. Not only that, but as we showed in chapter 1, most textbooks in Jewish studies are written by men, and many of them pay scant attention to women and even less to gender. What to do?

42. Joy Buolamwini, "Gender Shades: Intersectional Accuracy Disparities in Commercial Gender Classification," *Proceedings of Machine Learning Research* 81 (2018): 1–15.

43. Karpowitz, Mendelberg, and Shaker, "Gender Inequality in Deliberative Participation."

44. Karpowitz, Mendelberg, and Shaker.

First, put women and nonbinary authors on every syllabus. If we are teaching a topic that has no primary sources by women, we can look for gender analyses and use those sources as an opportunity to raise questions with our class about why we don't have women-authored texts. We can have students pay attention to what is missing in the readings we assign and how the readings might be different if, for example, a woman had authored the text or if the author had thought about people of other genders. Ask students to think about what this exclusion accomplishes. Try to tease out of the texts some information about gender, including women, masculinity, or sexuality. Ask your students to consider how historical or cultural or intellectual developments might have affected women or gender-nonconforming Jews differently. Ask if Jewishness and gender function in similar ways and can be analyzed with the same tools. Ask students to think about other spheres of learning where a group is ignored, such as courses on medieval Europe that don't mention Jews or books on American Jewish history that don't mention Indigenous peoples. With our students, we can consider the ways antisemitism and sexism interact and exacerbate each other; consider whether outbreaks of antisemitism correlate with outbreaks of racism toward others; and consider how different minoritized groups are able to become allies with each other—and when they have not.

When teaching writings by men, we might ask students to consider the gendered factors that create the importance of a topic or a book. Why, for instance, are the Israeli novelists best known to American readers almost always men? Who selects the authors to be translated, promoted, given rave reviews, and invited to lecture in the United States? If the major Jewish newspapers and journals that review Jewish literature are edited by men, if the publishing houses are run by men, and if the major venues for lectures are run by men, is it possible that women writers are disregarded out of bias?

We should make it clear to our students that the religious lives of Jewish men and women differ. Many of the books and films about Jewish religious practice revolve around the lives of men, such as laying tefillin, praying three times a day, leading in synagogue, and studying Talmud. Our students should be taught that religious practice for Jewish women is different, and that it varies also for non-Orthodox Jews of all genders. We should encourage our students to question why Orthodox men so often become the normative figures in the study of Judaism. We should help our students understand that many women experience Orthodoxy and Haredi religious life as meaningful, despite the inegalitarian and often sexist practices, while others find them intolerable. We might have students debate whether women's religious practices constitute a rebellion against sexism or a submission to it—or the creation of an alternative practice of religiosity. We must teach texts that discuss the experiences of Jews of color. We can show our students conflicting viewpoints as a sign of Jewish vitality and debate and emphasize that there has never been a singular "Judaism."

Cultivate an atmosphere of respect and encouragement—kindness, even in critique—so that people whose voices have been marginalized or even silenced will feel included. The atmosphere in class matters enormously and affects the ability of students to gain understanding. Be careful not to foster, in any way, a culture of harassment or marginalization. Gently correct any student (or oneself) for misgendering a student. Never make sexual jokes, never comment on students' bodies or clothing, and never use gender identity or sexual orientation as an excuse to disparage. Such principles are formal rules at most colleges and universities; let Jewish studies stand at the forefront of respecting those rules.

Students who do not speak in class may have a feeling that they do not belong. Talk to them about it in private. Students need to be confident that they are part of a learning community and that they are valued by their professors and fellow students. Signals that someone does not belong can be subtle; we can speak privately to quiet students and see what they may be experiencing. Encouraging and praising a student usually improves their performance in the course. We should also keep in mind that our students have private lives that may be troubling, or that they may not want to share. A student who has accused another student of sexual assault may have to remain in the same classes with them, creating all sorts of tensions, inhibitions, and difficulties. Discussion in class of certain topics, including assault, may be particularly troubling for some students. Caution, respect, and concern can be crucial tools for education in the classroom.

Diversify Public Offerings

Many Jewish studies programs sponsor lectures that are open to the public. In the course of the academic year, do we achieve gender parity among our speakers? Do we invite younger scholars with new, fresh ideas or stick to the well-known senior figures? Do we aim to reach an audience of our faculty, colleagues, and students or the local Jewish community? If the latter, let's be sure we do not compromise the intellectual vitality of the field by presenting talks that are better suited to a synagogue than to a university. A Jewish community audience may be uncomfortable listening to a gender analysis of Zionism or a study of homoeroticism in medieval Jewish poetry, but that may be precisely what they need to hear in order to understand new directions of the field. We can make our scholarship accessible to the public without becoming pietistic or reverting to the gendered assumptions of traditions. Inviting women and nonbinary scholars will also shape the public's expectations and assumptions about what expertise looks like.

We need to speak up when we see something unfair—voices can bring change! For example, the Jewish studies program of a major university announced a conference about Israel. All the speakers were men, and quiet protests were expressed to the two senior male organizers in person and via email. Within days, the organizers announced that the conference was postponed—and they apologized in a widely disseminated statement, saying that they "take very seriously the need for equitable representation and diverse perspectives. We cannot perpetuate the problem of silencing women in academia, and we apologize for creating a panel that did not include any female scholars." We applaud their willingness to express a public apology and organize a future conference that would include women speakers, and we see this as an excellent example of an appropriate response when, as they say, "mistakes were made." We all make mistakes. It can be easy to overlook moments of exclusion or discrimination, in part because they seem so normal. But we can also normalize speaking up. In fact, speaking up is the ethical position when we observe discrimination or harassment.

If we are in fund-raising positions, we should cultivate a diversity of funders. Talk to non-Jews, secular Jews, people of all genders, and people within and beyond local communities. Economic factors mean that certain groups may be underrepresented, but that doesn't need to translate into donor homogeneity. Having one big donor might seem like a nice problem to have, but having one funder for all aspects of a single program can stifle research and create dynamics where the program must not offend a donor's politics; it can even cause faculty to defer to a donor in ways that are professionally inappropriate (whether that deference was requested or not). Having multiple donors can create more flexibility, more intellectual diversity, more openness, and more groundbreaking research because of this wider scope and flexibility.

The Professoriate

The mere presence of increasing numbers of women in the field is a good step, but it will not fix sexism at the level of the professoriate. As Kristen Renwick Monroe and William Chiu have written, "Because the percentage of women in the pool of professors has increased since the 1980s without comparable improvement in the percentage of women in the professoriate, the pipeline approach will not fix this gender inequity. More focused and systematic policies are required."[45] Most of those policies are not distinctive with respect to Jewish studies, but many will sound familiar. Support pay equity; this also means creating or supporting clear mechanisms for faculty to appeal unequal pay. When women occupy positions of power within the administration, more women become department chairs, and more women are recruited to faculty appointments. Mentoring programs can help recruit and promote faculty. Institutionalized paid parental leave, as well as medical leave to care for family members and a flexible tenure clock, have been important in recruiting women.[46] Start-up funds for research, including travel to archives and libraries, for purchase of books and journals for the college library, and for enabling regular attendance at major national conferences are all important for junior faculty on a tenure track.

Given the accounts we have presented in earlier chapters about biases in hiring, tenure, and even the treatment of women graduate students, it is clear that antibias training is crucial for Jewish studies. We can even encourage colleagues to come with us when such training or workshops are voluntary. We should also be wary when terms such as "good fit," "stature," or "prestige" are used as evaluative criteria because they can function as vehicles of implicit bias. If you are part of a hiring or organizing committee, push for explicit criteria.[47]

45. Kristen Renwick Monroe and William F. Chiu, "Gender Equality in the Academy: The Pipeline Problem," *PS: Political Science and Politics* 43, no. 2 (2010): 303–8.

46. We recognize that paid parental leave is not without its problems, not least that it seems some men use it to perform research and thereby get ahead. Nevertheless, the solution to that particular problem is not to oppose parental leave altogether. For a good discussion of the issues, see Gretal Leibnitz and Briana Keafer Morrison, "The Eldercare Crisis and Implications for Women Faculty," in *Disrupting the Culture of Silence: Confronting Gender Inequality and Making Change in Higher Education*, ed. Kristine De Welde and Andi Stepnick (New York: Routledge, 2014), 137–45.

47. This point is adapted from Susannah Heschel and Sarah Imhoff, "Where Are All the Women in Jewish Studies?," *Forward*, July 3, 2018, https://forward.com/culture/404416/where-are-all-the-women-in-jewish-studies/.

Push for institutional climates that promote open communication, collaboration, and transparency around processes for change. The earlier study of when and why men speak up to interrupt sexism at work found three major factors stifled men, even when they might have been inclined to speak up: "Organizational climates perceived by men to be more *silencing, combative,* and *futile* are associated with doing nothing in response to sexism at work."[48] Generally, our motivations to do things are much higher when we think something is important and when we think it is feasible.[49] When we occupy positions of leadership, we should help our institutions develop public accountability, review progress, and support those who come forward with concerns.

There are also ways we can nudge institutions in more inclusive directions, even when we cannot change its policies. If we serve on a tenure or promotion committee or write a letter for a colleague's tenure, we can remind colleagues of the ways in which student evaluations of teaching reinforce racism and sexism.[50] At the institutional level, advocate for tenure and promotion to "count" diverse modes of knowledge production, such as reflexive or narrative writing and public scholarship.

When we work within publishing institutions as a peer reviewer or an editor, we should take a look at each bibliography. If it is

48. Sattari et al., "Interrupting Sexism at Work."

49. Jack W. Brehm and Elizabeth A. Self, "The Intensity of Motivation," *Annual Review of Psychology* 40, no. 1 (1989): 109–31.

50. Victor Ray, "Is Gender Bias an Intended Feature of Teaching Evaluations?," *Inside Higher Ed*, February 8, 2018, https://www.insidehighered.com/advice/2018/02/09/teaching-evaluations-are-often-used-confirm-worst-stereotypes-about-women-faculty; Colleen Flaherty, "Same Course, Different Ratings," *Inside Higher Ed*, March 13, 2018, https://www.insidehighered.com/news/2018/03/14/study-says-students-rate-men-more-highly-women-even-when-theyre-teaching-identical; and Lillian MacNell, Adam Driscoll, and Andrea N. Hunt, "What's in a Name? Exposing Gender Bias in Student Ratings of Teaching," *Innovative Higher Education* 40 (2015): 291–303. For additional information on gender bias in tenure and promotion, see Katherine Weisshaar, "Publish and Perish? An Assessment of Gender Gaps in Promotion to Tenure in Academia," *Social Forces* 96, no. 2 (2017): 529–60.

overwhelmingly male, we can ask the author to consider women and nonbinary scholars. The *Journal of the American Philosophical Association* instructs authors to seek out "all the literature, relevant to their topic, that may have been published by women or other individuals from underrepresented groups."[51] Jewish studies journals can do likewise. If we serve as an editor or on an editorial board, let's consider adopting similar policies or instructions.

University presses can also create formal structures for inclusion. For example, Princeton University Press—in response to criticism of its publication of *Hasidism: A New History*, a book written by eight male authors and evaluated by two outside male reviewers—has now put into place guidelines for gender inclusivity for authors, contents, outside reviewers, and writers of blurbs. When we have a close relationship with a press, we should encourage it to follow suit.

When we are editors, judges, panelists, or organizers tasked with evaluating submissions, we should think explicitly about gender. In the sciences, research has found that editors and peer reviewers "favored manuscripts from authors of the same gender and from the same country."[52] We have no reason to think that humanities and social sciences should differ in this respect. Anonymizing submissions can be a good start, but it may not be possible in all cases (such as book prize juries or some fellowships). Keep in mind that anonymizing submissions often doesn't make them truly anonymous—not only are some topics and methods, as we've seen, more likely to be researched by women, but also many Jewish studies subfields are small, and reviewers can often guess accurately who an author is. In these cases, discuss with the jury or with the organization awarding the prize: What

51. This was reported in Isaac Wilhelm, Sherri L. Conklin, and Nicole Hassoun, "New Data on Representations of Women in Philosophy Journals: 2004–2015," *Philosophical Studies* 175, no. 6 (2018): 1441.

52. Dakota Murray, Kyle Siler, Vincent Larivière, Wei Mun Chan, Andrew M. Collings, Jennifer Raymond, and Cassidy R. Sugimoto, "Gender and International Diversity Improves Equity in Peer Review," *BioRxiv* (2019): 1–61, quote on 17.

have been the genders of recent winners? What policies do they have in place to diversify those nominated?

In other cases, anonymizing submissions may not be desirable, such as when we serve as chairs of an area for a conference. We do not want to create single-sex "manels," and we also may want other kinds of diversity because it creates a scholarly environment with multiple perspectives.

When you discover you've been invited to something that is not gender inclusive, say something. What you say and how you say it can depend on your own position. Graduate students and non-tenure-track faculty may say something like, "I learned a lot on this panel, but I do wish there were more women's voices," while a tenured professor might write to the organizers as soon as they notice the imbalance. A message like this might say, "I noticed that this conference has mostly male speakers, and I wanted to suggest that we include women. I admire the work of Dr. So-and-So and Prof. So-and-So, and they could add important perspectives on X and Y," or, if the organizers express lack of interest in adding to the lineup, "I now see that this is an all-male conference, and so I will have to withdraw." One of us, invited as the only woman to speak at a three-day conference, said she would deliver her paper from behind a screen unless additional women were invited to speak. One additional woman was immediately invited.

Professional Academic Organizations

As members of academic organizations, we can each make important changes in the status of women by making sure the institutional leadership includes women and nonbinary people and has regulations that ensure a multiplicity of voices. Some of us belong to several academic organizations, including the Association for Jewish Studies and others that pertain to our subfield and disciplines. These organizations generally offer us considerable opportunities for networking, annual national or international conferences, and smaller regional gatherings, and they often publish important journals.

We can encourage women and nonbinary scholars to hold positions of leadership at academic organizations and support the ones who do. Moreover, women in leadership positions should support those affected by sexism, as well as not perpetuate it. Some women, educated in a predominantly male environment and working in a sexist institution, may find it difficult to assume a professional role of leadership. Men and power can seem to fit together; women in positions of power often run up against suspicion and prejudice. Powerful men can still be warm toward others, whereas women in positions of power are sometimes more reserved, afraid that respect for their position may be challenged if they are too friendly. People may tolerate a gruff, imperious male, calling him "assertive" or "no-nonsense," whereas a gruff, imperious female is derided as "bitchy." When we hear any such language, we should point out its sexist assumptions.

We also want to be sure that issues related to gender are raised and discussed—and not only by women. Gender is not a topic simply to be relegated to a women's caucus or a diversity, equity, and inclusion committee. Policies of academic organizations can ensure equity at annual meetings, making sure that women are invited to present plenary papers and that our conference panels are inclusive. We should encourage presidents, boards, and other leadership to look at gender representation across the elements of the organization, such as in its publications, during its conferences, and in its highest positions.

Gender intersects with other embodied experiences. Sometimes it does so in explicit ways: for example, all conference presenters should speak into microphones both because many attendees are hard of hearing (about 15 percent of American adults report difficulties with hearing) and because the average vocal pitch range for women is higher and thus does not carry as far as the average vocal pitch range for men.[53] Where our organizations

---

53. "Quick Statistics about Hearing," National Institute of Health, accessed January 8, 2024, https://www.nidcd.nih.gov/health/statistics/quick-statistics-hearing.

hold their conferences is also important. The facilities at a hotel, convention center, or university have to adhere to federal disability laws, but that does not mean they always do, nor does it mean that they make any nonrequired accommodations. The location chosen for a meeting should consider whether the local police may pose a danger to people of color and whether the state endangers lives by permitting unregulated, unlicensed, and concealed weapons. The organization should provide child care free of charge, with costs shared by all members; child-care costs should not devolve solely on parents whose contributions benefit all participants. Lectures held via video conferencing should include captions, and lectures held in person should provide accommodations for those who are Deaf or hard of hearing. Handouts should be projected in a large size, made available in large print, or both. Conference registration forms should have a place to indicate whether attendees would benefit from accommodations, including American Sign Language (ASL) interpretation and braille handouts. Creating an inclusive conference often requires resources, so organizations should budget money for accommodations from the earliest planning stages.

Academic organizations should institute policies about discrimination, harassment, and assault. The policies themselves are important, but the organizational process of discussing these matters also brings them out of the shadows. Some Jewish studies organizations address professional belonging and conduct in their bylaws, some have separate documents addressing harassment or assault, some have documents outlining best practices for inclusion at conferences, and some have no public statement at all. To give a sense of the range, here are selections from four of the largest organizations' public documents and statements:

- The Association for Jewish Studies has a stated goal of "eliminating barriers to full participation based on sex, sexual orientation, gender identity, religion, race, ethnicity, ability, and employment status. Diversity encourages innovation and creativity and strengthens community by harnessing a variety of skills, perspectives, talents, and resources to meet new challenges."[54] It also has official guidance for conference session chairs that aims for greater gender equity and inclusion of people with disabilities, as well as an office on sexual misconduct.[55]

- The Society of Biblical Literature's constitution lists "inclusivity," "equity," and "diversity" among their "core values."[56] It also has a professional conduct policy that defines and prohibits discrimination, sexual harassment, and sexual assault, as well as outlines the investigation procedures in the instance of a report.[57]

- The Association for Israel Studies bylaws guarantee that there will be no membership or participation "restrictions based on gender, race, ethnicity or age," but they have no public statement on harassment, assault, or discrimination.[58]

- The American Society of Overseas Research (ASOR) has neither a mission statement nor programs geared toward women, and none of their standing committees is dedicated to gender-based inclusion.

54. "Core Values, Policies, and Resolutions," AJS, accessed January 8, 2024, https://www.associationforjewishstudies.org/about-ajs/resolutions-policies.

55. "AJS Conference Guidance for Session Chairs, Moderators, and Attendees," AJS, accessed January 8, 2024, https://associationforjewishstudies.org/2023cfp/guidance-for-panel-chairs; "AJS Office on Sexual Misconduct," AJS, accessed January 8, 2024, https://www.associationforjewishstudies.org/about-ajs/resolutions-policies/the-ajs-office-on-sexual-misconduct.

56. "Mission," Society of Biblical Literature, accessed January 8, 2024, https://www.sbl-site.org/aboutus/mission.aspx.

57. "Professional Conduct Policy," Society of Biblical Literature, accessed January 8, 2024, https://www.sbl-site.org/assets/pdfs/Meetings/Professional_Conduct_Policy.pdf.

58. "By-Laws of the Association for Israel Studies (AIS)," accessed December 21, 2023, https://events.eventact.com/AIS/32125/WebSitePage/uploads/AIS_Bylaws_Updated_June_2021.docx?webid=18177937192.

There is no magic formula, and we are skeptical about how much change a written statement or policy can enact. Nevertheless, we should push our academic organizations to have discussions about what their behavioral norms are and then make those behavioral norms public. We recognize that statements or codes of conduct are often the result of such discussions. Thus, while making rules will not suddenly create perfect environments, communal discussion of such rules helps move the culture toward recognizing gendered issues when they arise. We are heartened to note that several of these professional organizations added policies while we were in the process of writing, which we take as a strong sign that these issues are being discussed.

Confronting sexism directly is difficult. And many of us feel that it's better to win allies than create enemies, so we often tread gently. Moreover, it can be exhausting to feel a responsibility to identify sexist behavior and systems, push against them, and educate people. When we can, let's be active and courageous as bystanders when we observe behavior that is discriminatory and harassing. When we see that others do not have the energy or the power to do so, let's step up and use our own.

Working to overcome sexism means listening to women, nonbinary people, and trans people. It means scrutinizing our own scholarly practices, welcoming moments for self-critique in the field, interrupting sexism when we see it, and moving to dismantle discriminatory cultures and structures. It also means welcoming scholars of all genders, working together to build inclusive structures and to include new scholarship on gender and sexuality as a central topic in Jewish studies. It would be thrilling to know how the field will look a hundred years from now!

INDEX

AAAS (American Academy of Arts and Sciences), 26

AAJR (American Academy for Jewish Research), 36–37

ableism, 130n

abusers: challenges to research of, 120–22; defense of, 116–19, 120, 126–27, 129–33, 231; inclusion of, in scholarly works, 118–19; media coverage of, 114–16, 118, 129–31, 134–35; rehabilitation of, 116–19; sanctions against, 117–19, 125–26; sympathy for, 117–18, 129–30, 134

adjunct faculty, 25, 211, 262

Adler, Rachel, 160, 168, 187, 244

AHA (American Historical Association), 79, 80

Ahmed, Shabab, 173–74

AJS (Association for Jewish Studies): bible studies, 196; founding of, 208, 211–12; harassment at meetings of, 77–78, 114–15; policies of, 82, 277–78; public prayer at, 211; surveys of, 29, 35; women in, 12, 27, 77–78, 82, 105, 188–89, 211, 275; Women's Caucus, 117n, 118, 211

AJS Review, 54, 56t, 57

Ali, Kecia, 41, 46

American Council of Learned Societies, 212

American Philosophical Association, 53

antisemitism, 17, 88–89, 148, 199, 209, 214, 217, 218

apologies, 116, 134, 270–71

Arab scholars, 239

Aramaic, 171, 173, 184, 185

archeology, 175–80, 201, 217

archival research, 146–47, 218

army service, in Israel, 107, 109, 237

Asian scholars, in Jewish studies, 14, 85–86, 164, 235

Asian women, 85, 159, 198

ASOR (American Society of Overseas Research), 278

assault: acceptance of, 113; apologies for, 115–16, 134, 270–71; investigations of, 79, 114–16, 117, 120, 231; recovery from, 108–9, 109n, 251; and trauma, 70–71, 73–75, 78, 99–100, 115, 119, 124–25; visibility of, 109–10, 126–27

Association for Israel Studies, 278

authority, perceptions of, 35, 89, 98–99, 102, 142, 163–65, 173–74, 184–86, 210

Baeck, Leo, 150

Baker, Cynthia, 187

Banet-Wiser, Sarah, 134

Baskin, Judith, 225, 229, 242

Batnitzky, Leora, 59, 62

Beit-Halachmi, Rachel Sabath, 231

Belser, Julia Watts, 168, 187

Benaroya, Becky, 233

Benjamin, Mara, 175

Benya, Frazier, 72, 73

Berkowitz, Beth, 191

Berman, Lila Corwin, 230, 232

feminist scholarship, 160–61, 167–68, 195–96, 201–2, 209, 218
fertility, 120–23, 155, 223
Fingerhut, Eric, 231
Fonrobert, Charlotte, 168, 187
Ford, Christine Blasey, 134
Frankel Center Institute for Advanced Jewish Studies at the University of Michigan, 37–38, 39, 40
Freedman, Jonathan, 213
Freidersdorf, Conor, 130
Frenkel-Brunswik, Else, 156
Fuerst, Ilyse Morgenstein, 172

Gardner, Catherine, 8–9
Geiger, Abraham, 145, 146
Geiger, Roger L., 241
gender: and attributions of authorship, 46–47; and author citations, 42–43, 45, 46–47, 47f, 48–51, 49f, 52–53, 52f, 53, 56–57, 255–59; and authority, 35, 89, 98–99, 102, 142, 163–65, 173–74, 184–86; in Christian institutional environments, 193–94; and computer-mediated communication, 266–67; and conference environments, 258–60, 264–66, 270–71, 275; in course materials, 12, 13, 58–65, 188, 267–69; and editorial boards, 55–56, 56t; and eroticized denigration, 65, 146–50, 152; and family responsibilities, 4, 33–34, 80, 122–23, 178, 262, 271–72; in fields of scholarship, 37–38, 56t, 62, 85–86, 188, 195, 198, 219, 237–39; in hiring practices, 24, 27, 33–38, 157, 172–73, 188, 207–8, 212; in Islam, 173–74, 178; in Israeli academic environment, 235–37; in Jewish religious life, 88–94, 185, 226, 268–69; LGBTQ+ people, 78, 102; and membership in organizations, 36–37, 195–96, 211, 226; and networking, 37, 40–41, 46, 218–20; and segregated educational spaces, 107,

108, 185, 238n; in surveys, 26–27, 29; the third gender, 154–55; in university publications, 44–45, 274; and Wissenschaft des Judentums, 152–54
Genderize (gender-prediction software), 45
genderqueer people, 9, 17, 45, 50, 255–56
Gerber, Jane, 160, 211
German feminism, 154–55
German Protestantism, 198–99
German universities, 145, 148, 155–56, 217–18
Gilman, Sander, 160
Gilmore, Leigh, 116, 125
Ginsburg, Ruth Bader, 254–55
Ginzburg, Louis, 153n
Gordon, Lewis, 86–87
gossip, 104–7, 116, 125, 126
graduate students: dissertation topics of, 97–98; domestic roles of, 33, 157; and hevruta study, 97, 170–71; and relationships with professors, 110–11; sexual harassment of, 69, 73, 76–79, 190; Talmud study, 184–85, 188–89
Gray, Hanna Holborn, 156–57
Greek texts, 200
grooming, 75–76
Guzdar, Maya, 249–50

Hahn, Barbara, 152
Hahn Tapper, Aaron, 63
Halperin, Liora, 233–34
Hamlin, Kimberly, 33
harassment: on archeological expeditions, 177–80, 201; counseling for recovery from, 109n, 251; institutional policies regarding, 128–29, 247–51; language of, 127–33; legal sanctions against, 73–74; media coverage of, 114–16, 118, 129–31, 134–35; as normative, 10, 79; personal accounts of, 71, 76–78, 128–29, 249–50; reporting of, 1, 6–9, 6–10, 16, 69, 71,

A NOTE ON THE TYPE

This book has been composed in Arno, an Old-style serif typeface in the classic Venetian tradition, designed by Robert Slimbach at Adobe.